The National Income
of
Communist China

the national income

of

COMMUNIST CHINA

By *ALEXANDER ECKSTEIN*

with the assistance of Y. C. Yin
and Helen Yin

The Free Press of Glencoe, Inc.

A DIVISION OF CROWELL-COLLIER PUBLISHING COMPANY

For information, address:
THE FREE PRESS OF GLENCOE
A DIVISION OF THE CROWELL-COLLIER PUBLISHING COMPANY
60 Fifth Avenue, New York 11

DESIGNED BY SIDNEY SOLOMON

Library of Congress Catalog Card No. 61-9164

To My Parents

This study is a product of research conducted at the East Asian and the Russian Research Centers of Harvard University, and its publication is sponsored jointly by the East Asian Research Center and by the Research Center in Economic Development and Cultural Change of the University of Chicago.

PREFACE

IN A VERY REAL SENSE, this monograph is an outgrowth of my earlier work on "Conditions and Prospects for Economic Growth in Communist China."[1] Working on that study made me acutely conscious of the difficulties one inevitably faces in attempting an aggregative analysis of economic trends and prospects based on partial and highly fragmentary information. It is my hope that this study will at least go part of the way toward meeting this difficulty.

National income accounting provides a broad avenue for systematically surveying the state of a country's statistical development, for identifying the most serious statistical gaps and for appraising the reliability of the data. This function may be particularly important in areas where statistics are not regularly published, but are presented in scattered and unsystematic fashion. While this statistical mobilization and survey function is methodologically quite important from the standpoint of further studies of China's Mainland

[1] *Prospects for Communist China,* by W. W. Rostow in collaboration with Richard Hatch, J. R. Kierman and Alexander Eckstein, (New York, 1954), Part 5: "Communist Power and the Chinese Economy"; and "Conditions and Prospects for Economic Growth in Communist China," *World Politics,* VII (Oct., 1954; Feb., 1955, April, 1955), 1-37, 255-283, 434-447.

economy, it is a subsidiary rather than the primary purpose of this monograph. Thus, the major focus is upon an analysis of the structure and flows in the economy, upon composition rather than just size of the national product.

Research on the Chinese Communist economy, its performance, and capacity for growth, the relative importance of different sectors, the rate of saving and investment, and the sources of saving has been greatly handicapped by the absence of national income estimates for some recent period. Official estimates have been unsatisfactory from several points of view:[2] (1) The national income concept used is based on the Marxist definition of production and therefore, as in the Soviet Union, it excludes passenger transport, government and all other types of services; (2) Detailed income and expenditure accounts are not presented; (3) The estimates are usually confined to net national product by industrial origin or highly aggregated figures for national product by use; (4) Definitions of investment in fixed and working capital and of personal and government consumption are greatly at variance from those used in non-Communist countries; (5) They are not buttressed by a detailed exposition of sources and methods used, which makes it difficult to appraise their statistical reliability and conceptual validity.

In recent years, particularly since 1955, we have begun to obtain much more information on various aspects of the Chinese economy, e.g., agricultural and industrial production, government budget, agricultural taxation and marketing, profits of state enterprises, and levels of investment expenditure. However, it has been very difficult to interpret and appraise these data since they could not be fitted into a broader framework and could not be assessed against the background of performance and intersectoral flows in the economy as a whole. Thus, the proliferation of these new data of varying quality has on the one hand made it possible to attempt the compilation of national income estimates, while on the other hand, it has rendered this task the more necessary as a means of obtaining an analytically meaningful yardstick for measuring economic growth and appraising plan performance.

In the United States three different approaches to national income estimation for China have been undertaken. The first by Hollister is based

---

2 See Speech by Po I-po, Chairman of the National Economic Commission, at the CCP Eighth National Congress on Sept. 18, 1956, text reprinted in *HHPYK*, (1956), No. 20, 72-76; Yu Tien, "A Preliminary Discussion on Proportion between Consumption and Accumulation in our National Income," *TKP* (Peking), March 24, 1957, translated text in *SCMP*, No. 1510:18-26; *Wo-kuo kuo-min shou-ju ti chi-lei ho hsiao-fei* (Accumulation and Consumption in the National Income of China), by Niu Chung-huang, (Peking, 1957). Translated in *CB*, No. 511, (June 26, 1958).

on the final expenditures method, the second by RAND (under the direction of T. C. Liu) relies on the value-added method, and our own which combines the value-added approach for agriculture with the factor shares method for all other sectors. There is also a difference in the time periods covered. Hollister deals with the period 1950-57, both in constant and current prices. RAND's estimate is for 1933 and 1950-59, while our own is only for one year, i.e. 1952.

As of this writing, (summer of 1960), only Hollister's study has been published.[3] His estimate is very ingenious, but artificial. Adoption, without qualification, of the final expenditures account framework of the United States Department of Commerce requires a much wider range and variety of data than an underdeveloped Soviet-type economy, such as that of China, is capable of generating at the present time. Faced with this problem, Hollister resorts to a number of questionable expedients. Frequently he closes gaps in the data by assuming stable input-output relationships from year to year, or even using data of one year for another on the assumption that there has been no change in that component, without indicating the biases or possible margins of error resulting from this procedure.

These shortcomings are compounded when he turns to estimates of economic growth. Before reliable and soundly based growth estimates can be made for China, a great deal of additional spadework is necessary. Studies of economic growth over time require (1) estimates of production trends in agriculture and industry, carefully adjusted for statistical biases and incomparabilities in the major production series and (2) studies of price trends, relationships and changes in the price structure. Only with such data, can more or less reliable sectoral deflators be constructed and adequate measures of economic growth be obtained. Instead of following this path, Hollister uses official Chinese price and wage indices, the construction and biases of which are obscure and in any case, not examined by him. As a result, not too surprisingly, his rates of growth are quite close to those officially reported by the Chinese Communists. In sum, Hollister is to be admired for the ambitiousness of his attempt, but is open to criticism for not analyzing the statistical reliability of his estimates and for failing to point up the economic and national accounting implications of his findings.

As compared to Hollister and Liu we have set ourselves a much more modest task, namely that of constructing as detailed and methodologically and analytically as soundly based accounts for one year as presently available data permit. Starting with this estimate for 1952—the last pre-plan year—it is our hope to subsequently derive a series of national

---

[3] W. W. Hollister: *China's Gross National Product and Social Accounts, 1950-1957.* (Glencoe: The Free Press, 1958).

income estimates for the last year of each of the successive Five-Year Plans, i.e. 1957 and 1962. To begin with, all of these estimates will have to be valued in current established prices. Only when we have at our disposal reliable studies of industrial and agricultural production, of wholesale and retail prices, and of wages for a number of years, will we be in a position to measure economic growth on the one hand and pricing distortions on the other. In the meantime, all we can attempt to do is to test for the presence of pricing distortions and indicate the direction rather than the extent of the pricing bias.

In essence, this monograph should be viewed as an attempt to explore a new field of inquiry rather than to furnish definitive estimates. One of the purposes here is to apply the national accounting framework to an underdeveloped, Soviet-type economy and to work out a method of approach to the available data which can then also be used for future estimates. There is no doubt that as the work on Chinese national income now under way in several institutions proceeds, and as new information becomes available, these methods will be improved.

The first two chapters of this study are introductory. They are designed to place the estimates in Chapters III in their institutional context on the one hand and their conceptual context on the other. Chapter IV attempts to explore the meaningfulness of the estimates in terms of established prices, and the analytical implications which can be derived therefrom.

A preliminary version of the national income accounts developed in this study was published in the May 1958 issue of the *Review of Economics and Statistics*. Since that time a great deal of additional information was released which both permitted and necessitated an almost complete revision of the estimates. Given the inevitable lag between completion of a manuscript on the one hand and its processing and publication on the other, we could not take account of data published after mid-1959.

In making these revisions, I profited immensely from the knowledge and insights of Shigeru Ishikawa of Hitotsubashi University. He read both the first and second drafts with great care, pointing up pitfalls and obscurities in the data and making many suggestions which contributed greatly to resolving a number of thorny problems. Especially helpful were the discerning and constructive comments of Simon Kuznets and Gregory Grossman to whom I wish to express my profound appreciation. At the same time, I have benefited greatly from the criticisms of Abram Bergson, Everett Hagen, and Li Choh-ming. I am particularly grateful to Mr. and Mrs. Y. C. Yin for their most competent, careful, diligent and invaluable research assistance. It goes without saying, however, that these creditors are not responsible for the use to which their intellectual property was put.

In addition to those who read the manuscript, there are many others

I should like to thank. I owe an exceptional debt of gratitude to Alexander Gerschenkron and the late Clyde Kluckhohn for bringing me to the Russian Research Center at Harvard, and for enabling me to embark on this study. I am also deeply thankful to William L. Langer and Marshall D. Shulman for their constant encouragement and support. In my years of association with the Russian Research Center I have learned a great deal from my colleagues Joseph Berliner, Alexander Erlich, Gregory Grossman, David Granick, Frank Holzman, Alex Inkeles, Barrington Moore and Benjamin Schwartz to all of whom I wish to express my sincere thanks.

During the second half of my stay at Harvard, this study was sponsored by the East Asian Research Center. To John K. Fairbank, Chairman of its Research Committee, I owe a great deal not only for his continuous support, but for helping me immeasurably in broadening my understanding of China.

I would also wish to acknowledge the support of M.I.T.'s Center for International Studies in the early stages of this investigation. Walt Rostow, Everett Hagen and Max Millikan gave generously of their time in discussing sticky and difficult substantive problems whenever they arose. This list of acknowledgements would not be complete without John M. H. Lindbeck and Bert F. Hoselitz who have done so much to facilitate and speed the publication arrangements for this study.

The marked improvements in the language and style of the manuscript can be credited to Hilda A. Coates to whom many thanks are due for her editing. The helpfulness of my wife covered an astonishingly wide range: checking the edited manuscript, typing parts of it, proofreading, and, last but not least, putting up with the birthpains and irritations of bringing this study to completion.

A. E.

August, 1960
Rochester, N. Y.

LIST OF ABBREVIATIONS

CB	*Current Background* (Key speeches and documents translated by the American Consulate General in Hong Kong).
CCCP	*Ching-chi chou-pao* (The Economic Weekly; Shanghai).
CCJP	*Ch'ang-chiang jih-pao* (Ch'ang-chiang Daily; Wuhan).
CCP	*Chung-kuo kung-ch'an-tang* (Chinese Communist Party).
CCYC	*Ching-chi yen-chiu* (Economic Research; Peking), bi-monthly.
CFJP	*Chieh-fang jih-pao* (Chieh-fang Daily; Shanghai).
CHCC	*Chi-hua ching-chi* (Planned Economy; Peking), monthly.
CPJP	*Chin-pu jih pao* (Chin-pu Daily; Tientsin).
CPR	Chung-hua jen-min kung-ho-kuo (Chinese People's Republic).
CYTC	*Chung-yang ts'ai-ching cheng-ts'e fa-ling hui-pien* (Compendium of Laws and Regulations regarding Financial and Economic Policies of the Central (People's) Government, compiled by the Financial and Economic Committee, GAC, Peking). First series (Aug., 1950), 824 pp.; second series (June, 1951), 1149 pp.; third series (March, 1952), 1096 pp.
Ch'un- chung JP	*Ch'un-chung jih-pao* (Ch'un-chung Daily; Sian).
ECMM	*Extracts from China Mainland Magazines* (Articles appearing in Chinese Communist periodicals translated by the American Consulate General in Hong Kong).
FKJP	*Fukien jih-pao* (Fukien Daily; Foochow).
GAC	Cheng Wu Yuan (Government Administrative Council).
ha	Hectare.
HHJP	*Hsin-hua jih-pao* (Hsin-hua Daily; Chungking).

HHPYK	*Hsin-hua pan-yueh-k'an* (New China Semi-Monthly; Peking), successor to HHYP since Jan. 1956.
HHYP	*Hsin-hua yueh-pao* (New China Monthly; Peking), predecessor of HHPYK.
HWJP	*Hsin-wen jih-pao* (Hsin-wen Daily; Shanghai).
ILO	International Labor Office.
JMJP	*Jen-min jih-pao* (People's Daily, Peking).
JMP	*Jen-min pi* (People's Currency).
JMST	*Jen-min shou-ts'e* (People's Handbook). Published annually in Shanghai and Tientsin-Peking by Ta-kung pao.
NCNA	*Hsin-hua-she* (New China News Agency).
NFJP	*Nan-fang jih-pao* (Nan-fang Daily; Canton).
NIC	Government of India, Ministry of Finance, Department of Economic Affairs, *Final Report of the National Income Committee,* New Delhi, 1954.
NPC	Ch'uan-kuo jen-min tai-piao ta-hui (National People's Congress).
MT	Metric ton.
SCMP	*Survey of the China Mainland Press* (News translated by the American Consulate General in Hong Kong).
SPJP	*Su-pei jih-pao* (Su-pei Daily; Yang-chow).
SSB	State Statistical Bureau.
TCFK	Ministry of Finance of the Chinese People's Republic, *I-chiu-wu-wu chung-yang ts'ai-cheng fa-kuei hui-pien.* (Compendium of Central Financial Rules and Regulations for 1955), Peking, 1957, 572 pp.
TCKT	*T'ung-chi kung-tso* (Statistical Work; Peking), semi-monthly; successor to TCKTTH.
TCKTTH	*T'ung-chi kung-tso t'ung-hsin* (Statistical Bulletin; Peking), semi-monthly.
TCYC	*Ts'ai-ching yen-chiu* (Finance and Economic Research; Shanghai), bi-monthly.
TKP	*Ta-kung pao* (Impartial Daily; Shanghai and Tientsin-Peking).
TTJP	*Tientsin jih-pao* (Tientsin Daily; Tientsin).
TPJP	*Tung-pei jih-pao* (Tung-pei Daily; Mukden).
USAS	United States Department of Agriculture, Agricultural Statistics.

CONTENTS

TABLES IN THE APPENDIXES

TABLES IN THE TEXT

The National Income
of
Communist China

c h a p t e r   i

THE SETTING

THE ADVENT of Communism in China brought with it a far-reaching social, political and economic transformation bearing all the earmarks of a forced draft industrial revolution. This study attempts to illuminate an early phase of the process. It is in the nature of a cross section view of one year, 1952, which served as the point of departure for comprehensive economic planning.

This approach is predicated on the assumption that economic growth and structural transformation of an economy may be surveyed best through a series of periodic national income estimates. These serve in effect as flash photographs of the economy at different points in time. The present study then represents the first of a series of exercises in comparative statics to be followed by estimates for 1957, the last year of the First Five Year Plan, and possibly for some other years. In this context, the specific purpose of this chapter is (a) to provide a brief bird's eye view of the pattern of economic evolution in Mainland China between 1949 and 1958, in order to give a better understanding of where and how the year 1952 fits into this continuum, and (b) to give the reader a general idea of the character and quality of statistics in Communist China.

1. THE PATTERN OF ECONOMIC DEVELOPMENT IN MAINLAND CHINA

Since the advent of the Communist regime, economic development in China may be divided into five distinct phases: (1) the period of recovery and rehabilitation extending from 1949 to 1952; (2) the period of preparation for long-range planning, 1953 to mid-1955; (3) the big push, mid-1955 to the end of 1956; (4) the year of retrenchment, 1957; and (5) the "leap forward," 1958 to the present.

A. Recovery and Rehabilitation[1]

The Communists, upon gaining control over the Chinese mainland in 1949, inherited an economy in which productive capacity was appreciably curtailed, first by the Sino-Japanese War, and later by the Soviet occupation and civil war. Manufacturing capacity was particularly impaired in Manchuria, where over half of the capital stock in industry was dismantled and carried off by the Soviets in 1945. In China proper, industrial capacity was also shrinking, though to a much lesser extent, owing to depreciation and obsolescence, and to the flight of some of the movable facilities to Hong Kong and Taiwan. The situation was aggravated by the constant shortage of raw materials throughout 1949. At the same time, because of the disruption of internal trade and transport, domestic supply difficulties were aggravated. Industrial output was further curtailed by gradual demoralization of labor under the impact of hyper-inflation and a breakdown of plant discipline following the Communist conquest of large cities.

On the whole, the rural sector of the economy was much less affected by the vicissitudes of the civil conflict. Actually, civil war brought to the countryside more disorganization and disruption than devastation. Owing to the great importance of the subsistence, non-monetized sector of the rural economy, agriculture could much more easily fall back on its own resources than industry. Unfavorable weather, particularly floods, rather than civil war was the most important factor accounting for the drop in production, but undoubtedly under more peaceful conditions the same weather would have created less havoc.

This was the situation in which the regime undertook the task of restoring by 1952 industrial and farm production to pre-1949 peak levels. In broad terms, the objective seems to have been attained.

Pari passu with restoring production, the new regime was determined to capture "the commanding heights" in the economy and to bring an increasing share of output under government control. These objectives required a restructuring of the institutional framework, a task in which nationalization, land, fiscal, monetary, and distribution policies were fused into an instrument for resource mobilization and allocation.

The Chinese Communists inherited from the Nationalist government a sizable state enterprise segment which they have consistently enlarged, partly at the expense of the private sector, though there has been little outright nationalization of private trade and industry. Instead, Chinese Communist tactics have consisted of squeezing out private enterprise through tax pressures, credit rationing, capital levies, state competition, and union demands. Furthermore, government control over the economy was reinforced through allocations of raw materials and credits, through introduction of "cash and currency control," and through monopoly of trade in key agricultural and industrial commodities.

The same general pattern was evident in Chinese Communist land policy which aimed at gradual, step by step expropriation of the Chinese peasants' land. The first stage, land reform, was completed by the end of 1952. It was designed to harness land hunger and agrarian unrest into a potent weapon in order to break the political and economic power of the landlords. In the strategy and tactics of Chinese Communism, land reform performed a triple function: it helped to pave the road to power, it helped to extend and consolidate that power at the village level, and it served to transfer the wealth-accumulating function from the landlord to the state. In effect, it provided a vehicle by which the land rent could be appropriated by the state for its own use. Inasmuch as land rent in China was mostly dissipated in consumption, conspicuous and otherwise, in hoarding, and after 1936 also in capital flight, expropriation of this rent furnished a means for raising the level of investment in the economy.

As the regime consolidated its control over the Mainland, it felt ready to launch a comprehensive attack upon the problem of inflation, the part of the inheritance from the past which posed the first major challenge in economic policy. The attack was multipronged; it involved: (1) restoring budgetary balance by broadening the revenue base on the one hand and curtailing expenditures on the other hand, (2) establishing confidence in the monetary medium through tying a whole range of transactions in the economy to real commodity basket units, (3) controlling money and credit, and (4) reactivating exchange and distribution. The success of the whole stabilization experiment depended upon the government's ability to guarantee the supply of consumer necessities and the faith of the public in such a guarantee. However, the state trading mechanism could perform the function assigned to it only if the volume of goods entering distributive channels could be greatly expanded. In turn, this required not only a recovery in agricultural and industrial production, but also restoration of the badly disrupted transport network. For this reason, rehabilitation and expansion of transport became one of the regime's high priority targets.

During the recovery period, the government placed great reliance upon indirect controls and market forces as instruments for stabilization, resource mobilization, and resource allocation. On the whole, these policies proved to be rather effective in arresting inflation and in gradually instituting price stability. The inflationary spiral was broken in March 1950, but under the impact of the drastic deflationary policies, a temporary crisis ensued. However, with the outbreak of the Korean War in June, wholesale prices rose rapidly once more, so that by the end of 1950, they approached the March peak. During 1951, the regime gained greater control over price formation, as illustrated by the fact that the average price level rose only about 20 per cent. However, prices of producers' goods increased much more rapidly under the competing pressures of Korean War requirements and domestic reconstruction. By 1952 virtual price stability was attained. Actually, the first half of the year, particularly the first quarter, was characterized by deflation under the impact of the "Three Anti's" and "Five Anti's" campaigns.[2]

B. The Period of Plan Preparation

There is considerable indirect evidence to suggest that the first Five-Year Plan was really inaugurated not in January 1953 but in mid-1955. It is possible that for political and psychological reasons the Chinese Communists found it necessary to announce the start of a Five-Year Plan in 1953, before they were really fully prepared to engage in a process of comprehensive and long-range planning. Thus in 1953 preliminary and quite fragmentary targets were announced for the first Five-Year Plan, while full details were published only in mid-1955. Many of the elements of long-range planning were still missing in Communist China in late 1952 or early 1953. Even a national statistical bureau, for example, was not established until the autumn of 1952.[3] This was probably the first time in Chinese history that a statistical bureau was ready to function on a national basis. This is not intended to suggest, of course, that there had not been various statistical services established by pre-Communist regimes. However, since the Nationalist government at no time effectively controlled and administered all of the Chinese Mainland, its statistical coverage was partial. Moreover, very little was done in the way of systematic collection of industrial statistics on a national scale, and statistics for a wide variety of other fields were lacking. It is therefore not surprising that the Chinese Communists found themselves compelled to assign a fairly high priority to the development of statistical services as a prerequisite for planning.

Although the National Statistical Bureau was established only in late 1952, data were being collected in Communist China from the very advent of the regime. The procedures however, were *ad hoc,*—not standardized, lacking in uniformity, and generally inferior in quality to those of later years. As techniques improved a great deal of effort was expended to gather retroactively data for the earlier years as well. This was particularly true for 1952, the year on which the Five-Year Plan was based.

Closely related to the problem of national statistical services was that of standardized accounting procedures for enterprises. A modern system of business accounting was limited to the comparatively small number of large-scale establishments, chiefly those operating on a corporate basis. This, of course, represented a serious drawback to planning control.

The period of preparation for long-range planning included extended negotiations with the Soviet Union concerning deliveries of Russian equipment and capital goods for China's industrialization under the first Five-Year Plan. It would have been very difficult to define production and investment goals without clear commitments from the Soviet Union as to these deliveries.

During these two and a half years from January 1953 to mid-1955, Mainland China was operating presumably on the basis of annual plans within the framework of some long-range targets which were, however, projections rather than specific Five-Year Plan stipulations. This must have been a period of testing and experimentation in long-range planning, for the Chinese Communists lacked a trained corps of planners, administrators, economists, accountants, statisticians, etc. Therefore when in mid-1955 the Chinese Communists published detailed targets for their Five-Year Plan, they were in effect postulating goals for a two-and-a-half year plan which they were fairly confident of fulfilling in the light of experience gained in the first two and· a half years and the expectation of a very good harvest for that year.

This whole period of plan preparation was at the same time one of change in several other respects. This was the time during which a gradual transition to collectivization was made just short of the final step. As soon as land reform was completed at the end of 1952, new measures were introduced designed to push the newly created small farm units into various forms of cooperation which were expected to lead them in the end to collectivization. Concurrently, the non-agricultural branches of the economy were being progressively nationalized, although the process of socialization was as yet proceeding rather cautiously. At the same time, considerable inflationary pressures began to be generated under the impact of rising investments amidst the quite inferior harvests of 1953 and 1954. In order to cope with these, and also facilitate a rise in the involuntary rate of saving, the government, in the fall of 1953, introduced rationing and compulsory farm collection of principal grains, oil seeds, cotton and some other products.

C. The Big Push

With the publication of the first Five-Year Plan in mid-1955 and following the excellent harvest of that year, the regime apparently decided to push ahead rapidly and simultaneously on all fronts. Thus, seemingly after considerable hesitation and debate within the party, and upon Mao's personal intervention, the signal was given for an intensified drive for collectivization. As a result, within a year, that is, between the end of 1955 and the end of 1956, farm households encompassed in collectives (officially termed "producers' cooperatives of the advanced type") grew from 4 percent to 87 percent of the total.[4] A parallel drive was inaugurated to mop up the remnants of all private enterprise in industry and trade, but instead of outright nationalization, the device of joint private-public enterprises was used as the principal vehicle for socialization. Thus, private business was compelled through a combination of carrot-and-stick techniques to part with some of its stock to public bodies; or, if it was a partnership or other form of business organization, similarly to co-opt public organs as co-owners or co-sharers. Consequently, by the end of 1956, there were practically no purely private enterprises left on the Chinese Mainland.[5] Great strides were also being made in organizing small traders, peddlers, and handicraftsmen into various types of cooperatives.

With this big push in the field of nationalization, there came a very marked increase in the level of investment. Thus, public investment in 1956 was raised to 62 percent above the 1955 level.[6] This, in combination with a mediocre harvest in 1956, caused China to experience its most acute strains and inflationary pressures since the height of the Korean War, i.e., 1951. In effect, China went through the throes of what in retrospect may be considered an economic crisis in the form of acute shortages, forced and unforeseen liquidation of state reserves and enterprise inventories, and marked supply bottlenecks throughout industry and transport. As might be expected, shortages were most pronounced in consumer goods. This, along with the technical bottlenecks, forced the regime in 1957 to make concessions to the consumer and generally cut back and retrench.

D. The Period of Retrenchment

1957 was a year of reaction to the acute strain of 1956. It was marked by cutbacks in investment levels, by reduction in production targets, and by certain reallocations in the structure of investment in favor of argiculture and the consumer goods industries.[7] In part, this was a reflection of the changed organizational pattern of Chinese agriculture. The intensified drive for collectivization in 1956 coupled with a mediocre harvest, curtailed collections from farms in 1956 to the point where they fell considerably short of marketing targets. This, along with the growing recognition by planners and policy-makers that agricultural backwardness constitutes a serious hindrance to further industrialization, may account for the considerable overfulfillment in the agricultural investment plan in 1956 and particularly in 1957.[8]

E. The New Forward Leap

Following the period of retrenchment and consolidation in 1957, the Chinese Communists proclaimed a "New Forward Leap" in 1958. This was made official in Po I-po's Report on the 1958 Plan presented to the fifth session of the National People's Congress in February, 1958.

Originally, the New Forward Leap postulated investment and output objectives which were considerably above 1957 levels, but only slightly above those of 1956. However, as the year advanced both the goals and the output claims rose progressively to the point where officially released data showed more than a doubling in agricultural and steel production within one year.

There is no question that with 1958 there began another era of cataclysmic experimentation, innovation, and transformation in economic and social forms. The two dominant *leitmotifs* of the new era were mass labor mobilization on a scale heretofore not attempted in modern times and the closely related introduction of communes in agriculture. These moves represented a dramatic and radical attempt for release from the vicious circle of backwardness by utilizing the only abundant resource, i.e. labor. On farms, mass labor methods were applied to the extension of irrigated areas, the close planting of crops, and a painstakingly careful, garden-type, tending of crops. In industry, a phenomenal effort was directed toward expansion of iron and steel production in small blast furnaces operated by primitive handicraft techniques. In effect, the Communists tried to apply in its purest and most extreme form Nurkse's prescription for capital formation in underdeveloped areas. In this context the function of communization was three-fold: to augment the supply of mobilizable labor, to step up the actual rate of mobilization, and to assure controls over consumption sufficient to prevent any leakages which would spoil the purity of Nurkse's model.

To what extent these measures have actually succeeded in raising agricultural and industrial output is very difficult to assess at this juncture. The scaling down of the original 1958 output claims for agriculture and industry does not resolve the problem. The revised figures still show such unusually high rates of growth, particularly in agriculture, that, pending the construction of independent estimates, one must reserve judgment. Construction of such estimates would be well beyond the scope of this study.

2. THE CHOICE OF 1952 AS A BASE YEAR

As indicated in the Preface, this study of Mainland China's national product should be viewed only as a point of departure, as a first step designed (1) to help us in our understanding of the structure of the economy and (2) to lay the foundations for future studies of other years. The question naturally arises as to which year should be selected as the point of departure and why.

In these terms, the year 1952 commends itself for a number of reasons. It is the first year under Communist rule for which a detailed structural analysis can be attempted, not only because of the greater abundance of data, but more importantly because it was the first normal year since the advent of the Chinese Communist regime. It was normal in the sense that physical plant was more or less restored and channels of distribution re-established. This year therefore, provides a convenient vantage point for both a backward and a forward glance. Precisely because farm and industrial production was more or less restored to average pre-Communist levels, comparisons with former years are facilitated. Moreover, since this was the last pre-Plan year, it can serve as a yardstick for measuring rates of economic growth and changes in structure, and performance under planning.

In making intertemporal comparisons however, the available data and estimates have to be used with very great caution. Pre-war and generally pre-Communist data are not comparable with those for the period since 1949. Similarly, pre-Five Year Plan data, i.e., prior to 1953, are not fully comparable with later statistics and estimates. Even within each period, year-to-year comparisons require great care. All such comparisons are complicated by constantly expanding coverage, better reporting, improved methods, and changing concepts and statistical definitions.[9] This does not, however, mean that all such comparisons need to be rejected, but only that estimates need to be adjusted for conceptual consistency and, as far as possible, for differences in coverage.

There are other considerations which prompted the choice of 1952 as a base year. It was the year which marked the end of a long cycle of open inflation dating from 1937, the beginning of the Sino-Japanese War. In 1950 the economy was still characterized by very sharp price fluctuations which would greatly complicate national income analysis for that year. Moreover, the political hold of the regime over the whole country was not yet fully consolidated. Even in 1951, while the rate of price increase was considerably slowed down it was far from negligible. In this period, too, the tensions of the Korean War produced marked economic stresses which assumed close to critical proportions in 1951.

In contrast, 1952 seems to have been a year of relative economic normalcy in several senses. A favorable harvest and rapid increases in industrial production, on the one hand, and a lull in the Korean War, on the other hand, led to supply-demand relationships conducive to a measure of price stability. As compared to earlier years, a larger share of the total output could be channeled to the civilian sector of the economy with *direct* price control still playing a minor role.

In one respect, however, 1952 was very abnormal. The far-reaching and relentless "Five-Anti's" and "Three-Anti's" campaign led to a decline in prices and a severe disruption in private industry and trade, particularly pronounced in the first quarter of the year.

As indicated earlier, by the end of 1952, land reform—i.e., the process of land redistribution—was completed in most regions of the Chinese Mainland, while the process of collectivization had not yet started. This meant that private peasant farming still dominated Mainland agriculture. Farmers had to pay a land tax in kind, levied as a share of "standard" or "normal" yield, the latter calculated from the average yield of several years. No compulsory deliveries were required above the tax in kind. Yet, state trading companies were already very active in the countryside, handling about 70 per cent of all the grain marketed in 1952. Actually, were one to include grain deliveries on tax account, this share would rise to about 80 per cent.[10] State trading companies also played a major role in the marketing of cotton, and of soybean and its products, but as yet assumed an appreciably smaller role in the sale of livestock products, fruits and vegetables. Thus, of all farm commodities marketed, apparently about one third still moved through private trading channels in 1952.[11]

At the same time, according to official sources, 63 percent of wholesale and 42 percent of retail trade was within the purview of the State trading sector, while foreign trade was a virtual State monopoly.[12] Moreover, by 1952 nationalization of industry, transport, and banking was fairly far advanced, as is shown by the data in Table E-1.

Yet the government still relied primarily upon indirect controls over resource allocation. There was no rationing of foodstuffs and other consumers' goods, and direct material allocations were confined to narrow channels. Price control was limited largely to price leadership by public enterprises and State trading companies based on their market power, which, as the figures cited above show, was far from unlimited.

There was some allocation by administrative fiat in the labor market, but the practice was not yet as widespread as in later years. In effect, while many high school and college graduates and workers possessed of scarce skills would be assigned to jobs, there was still considerable freedom of movement and choice in occupation. Similarly, wage regulation and planning of the wage structure was in its beginning stages. For all of these reasons, 1952 price relationships represented perhaps less of a departure from true scarcity relationships than was the case in later years. An attempt will be made to test the validity of this tentative view in Chapter IV.

By 1952, the government budget served as one of the most important instruments for economic control and resource allocation. At the same time, while budget and accounting practice followed more and more the Soviet model, there were some notable differences on the revenue side. In contrast with the Soviet Union, there was an agricultural tax in kind, while the yield from government enterprises constituted a relatively more important source of Chinese budgetary income than did indirect taxes. The indirect tax took two principal forms, one levied on the total business turnover of each enterprise and the other specifically applied to commodities, with a varying rate for different products. In addition, there was a variety of other minor indirect taxes such as customs duties, salt tax, etc.

Soviet practice was to dominate government enterprise accounting, but in 1952 *khozraschët,* or the system of "economic accounting," was still in its infancy in China. No sharp line was as yet drawn between government enterprises and organizations encompassed by or falling outside the purview of this system. Economic accounting really was standardized only in 1955, but it should be pointed out that since the budget figures used in this study were published after 1955, they are presumably defined in terms of post-1955 practice. According to this practice, enterprises under the accounting system pay their net revenues and depreciation allowances into the budget, except for certain funds retained for special purposes. On the other hand, government organizations outside the system carry all of their receipts (i.e., not just profits) through the government budget. Unfortunately, the published figures combine these two items without providing any basis for separating them out.[13]

On the other side of the ledger, practically all of the fixed capital investments of governmental enterprises and organizations were financed out of the budget. Therefore, this is not a government budget in the usual or narrow sense, but rather an approximation of a consolidated account for the public sector as a whole. Under such a system there are also close links between the budget and the operations of the banking system. Government receipts are deposited in banks and many government payments are made through banks. Banks also serve as an important source of extra budgetary financing of working capital requirements. Conversely, budgetary surpluses are transferred to the banking system where they serve as a counterpart for loanable funds. In all of these latter respects then, 1952 Mainland practice for the most part followed the Soviet example.

On balance, the choice of 1952 as compared to other years presents both certain advantages and disadvantages. In terms of availability and adequacy of data, it is better than earlier years, but poorer than 1955-57. At the same time, 1952 prices and value aggregates based on them are probably less distorted and relatively more representative of scarcity relationships than those for recent or perhaps for any other Communist year. Ultimately, however, the choice of 1952 is imposed by the fact that, as the last pre-plan year, it cannot be ignored if we want to measure growth and structural changes in China's Mainland economy.

3. THE NATURE AND QUALITY OF THE DATA

The state of our knowledge concerning the Chinese economy and the factors and forces that have shaped its development (or lack thereof) lags considerably behind that for most of the other underdeveloped areas and behind that for Russia as well. In the case of China, both past and present, the task of the economic analyst is greatly complicated by the wide proliferation of fragmentary and highly unreliable quantitative information, on the one hand, and the almost complete absence of even approximately reliable and comprehensive statistical series on the other. The very nature of the available information therefore forces the student to resort to methods of analysis that could be characterized as economic archeology, involving reconstruction and piecing together of fragments. Yet, before one can overcome these obstacles, one must first jump the additional hurdles presented by linguistic and cultural barriers. In view of this situation, it is not to be wondered at that so few competent and well trained economists have directed their attention to China. Moreover, owing to the paucity of data and the character of the sources, the application of sophisticated techniques of analysis has been narrowly circumscribed.

Both *a priori* and on the basis of empirical observation, one can conclude that the quality and scope of statistical services in any country are correlated with the level of economic development, the efficiency of the state apparatus, and the degree of government participation and intervention in the economy. Of course, these variables themselves, particularly the first and the second, are in turn mutually interdependent. This generalization is certainly borne out by the Chinese experience. In China the problem of statistical reporting has been greatly complicated by the fact that since the collapse of the Manchu dynasty in 1911, and up to the arrival of the Chinese Communist regime in 1949, no central authority was capable of exercising full and effective control over all provinces of Mainland China. As a result, pre-Communist Chinese statistics were particularly inadequate.

Actually, the quality of these statistics varies widely among economic sectors or regions. Data on foreign trade can be considered as more or less satisfactory and usable over an extended period. On the other hand, production statistics were very poor, especially in industry, owing to incomplete coverage and low degree of reliability. In agriculture, area planted and farm production were consistently underestimated. There had never been a complete census of population, agriculture, or manufacturing prior to 1953, so that in most fields exclusive reliance had to be placed upon sampling studies. Many of these were so restricted in scope that no valid generalizations could be drawn from them.[14] This inadequacy has not, unfortunately, inhibited generalization at any time, and accounts for the sharp controversies and the radical differences in the assessment of a number of economic problems. The contradictory estimates of population, degree of tenancy and a number of other variables, are based on the reading of partial and highly conflicting evidence.

As a general rule, the coverage and reliability of statistics in the thirties and early forties is much better for Manchuria than for China proper. As a matter of fact, Manchurian data are much closer to Japanese than to Chinese statistical standards. This does not mean that even they can be used uncritically, since there are frequently wide discrepancies in the series compiled by the South Manchurian Railway Administration and by the Manchukuo Government. For the most part, these divergences are a function of differing coverage and definition, which, unfortunately, are not always specified.

There is no question that with the coming of Communism to China, the efficiency of statistical organization and data collection was considerably improved. It would, indeed, be surprising if it were not so in view of the centralized administration, the increasing scope of the nationalized economic sector, and the ever-widening spheres of economic activity encompassed by central planning. Of course, the building of a statistical organization and of a data-collecting network cannot be accomplished overnight and there are many indications that Chinese Communist statistics were at first confused and grossly inconsistent. Lacking time systematically to collect information anew, they continued to use prewar data. This, for instance, was the case with population and acreage figures in food crops. However, the situation changed perceptibly with the establishment of a national bureau of statistics late in 1952. Improvement was further accelerated by the preparations for the first Five-Year Plan, by the population count taken in mid-1953, and by the gradual, nationwide standardization of accounting procedures in state enterprises, in government organs, and in fiscal administration. Paradoxically, many of the inconsistencies in Chinese Communist statistics are a by-product of this change in the quality of data; but, as a rule, statistics published since 1953 are based on a broader coverage and are at the same time methodologically more consistent and sounder.

Yet, there is no question that in spite of these improvements, many areas of economic activity remain inadequately covered to the present day. In general, data for the high priority sectors tend to be much better than for the segments considered unimportant. Similarly, activities falling within the purview of the state plan are more adequately accounted for than those outside the scope of the plan, so that data for the public sector are more reliable than those for the private sector, and within the private sector there is more and better information on large-scale modern undertakings than on the so-called "individual economies" like peasant farms and small handicraft establishments. Moreover, whatever the sector, aggregative value data tend to be less trustworthy and more difficult to check than highly disaggregated physical output series.

It would, however, be erroneous to conclude that physical output series can be automatically accepted at face value. For instance, there seems to be some evidence that crop production figures contain a strong upward bias, since they were incomplete for the early years, and may in part reflect progressively more adequate statistical coverage, rather than an increase in yields and/or in areas harvested.[15] Similarly, the coal figures appear to be somewhat questionable, particularly as compared to prewar data. It is possible that currently reported production figures refer to unwashed coal while those for the prewar period were in terms of washed coal. Comparisons of pre- and post-Communist figures are manifestly of dubious validity with respect not only to coal, but to cotton yarn and a number of other products because of the methodological and definitional changes noted above.

In Chinese Communist statistical reporting one may detect an inverse correlation between quality of data and degree of statistical camouflage. It would seem that the more confidence the compilers have in their data the more clearly and unequivocally are they presented. On the other hand, marked inconsistency and conceptual obscurantism are frequently associated with statistical groping by the planning and statistical organs themselves. There are, of course, no regular statistical yearbooks, and no systematic statistical reports of the type we are generally accustomed to for most of the non-bloc areas. However, since 1953, there are two reports published each year: the annual budget report which gives revenue and expenditure totals and breakdowns in value terms, and the annual communique of the State Statistical Bureau on plan fulfillment, very much patterned on the Soviet model of statistical reporting. Up to mid-1955, when the first Five-Year Plan was submitted to the National People's Congress,[16] most of the data released were in percentage or index number form with the physical quantities or values for the base year unknown or highly conjectural. However, in connection with the publication of the Five-Year Plan, a vast array of production data as well as hitherto unpublished value categories were released, not only for the period covered by the Five-Year Plan (1953-1957), but for the preceding years as well, and particularly for 1952 as the last pre-plan year.

In effect, one could characterize the pre-Communist period as one during which the preconditions for adequate data collection were absent, but during which statistics were being published more freely than now. Yet, even then, basic economic information was occasionally suppressed.[17] On the other hand, the technical improvement in statistical organization and reporting under Communism is accompanied by greater statistical secrecy combined with systematic attempts at statistical camouflage. In this respect, the situation facing the investigator analyzing economic developments in Communist China is more complex and difficult than that confronting the Soviet specialist. Not only were pre-World War I Russian statistics more extensive and more reliable, but there were great advances in quality and proliferation in the reporting and publication of data during the first two decades of Soviet rule. The flow slackened in the later thirties and continued to do so during and after World War II. It was these restrictive and secretive post-World War II Russian statistical standards which were adopted from the outset by Communist China. However, beginning in 1955, there were, as indicated above, definite signs of relaxation in the severity of Chinese Communist publication policy, but this relatively liberal course was reversed in late 1959.

All of this still leaves the question unanswered as to whether Chinese Communist statistics are credible. Could not the published data be outright falsifications or fictions presented for propaganda purposes? Do not the Chinese Communists, keep in effect, two sets of books, one for economic planning and administration, and another for public consumption? While one cannot categorically rule out this possibility, there is certainly no evidence to support this hypothesis, and there are a number of indications to the contrary.[18]

The economic information and statistics published by the regime is presented not for its own sake, nor for the advancement of knowledge, but for certain very definite objectives. Apart from their propaganda aspects, which are the ones usually emphasized, all pronouncements and publications in a Communist system serve a certain didactic function. Most frequently they serve as guides to policy, and directives for implementation to the party cadres and to the people at large. Statistics are very rarely offered disinterestedly, but most often are cited in support of specific arguments. Hence the context within which data are presented provides significant clues to understanding. Nevertheless, it is very difficult to envisage how a huge bureaucratic apparatus in vast countries such as China or Russia could function in a system of double bookkeeping. Two sets of economic plans and targets, or two sets of reports about plan-fulfillment, would certainly tend to create or aggravate administrative confusion throughout the state and party structure.

Besides, the process of statistical collection and reporting constitutes an integral part of the operating economic mechanism. Accounting data are needed to assess the performance of individual plants, enterprises, and industries; at the same time, they are an essential pre-requisite for allocation of resources and for planning. In effect, these are needed by the economic and social engine to keep functioning. In order to keep two sets of books, and maintain their functional distinction, a special government agency would have to be organized, charged with the task of deliberately falsifying statistics and then presenting them to the world in a manner which would be mutually self-consistent.

This is not to suggest that all Chinese Communist statistics published are in fact internally consistent or that they can be necessarily taken at face value. What statistical discrepancies there are do not seem, generally, to be the products of outright falsification, but rather of conceptual obscurantism, methodological vagueness, and shifting definitions and coverage. The statistical sins of Communist regimes are more frequently those of omission rather than commission. Poor performance, unfavorable developments, and outright failures tend to be camouflaged or not reported at all, while accomplishments may be presented in a misleading context to create the most favorable impression possible. In such a situation, the task of the investigator is to penetrate behind the maze of statistical concealment and methodological bias; if he is willing and able to employ in the task patience, ingenuity, and skill, he should be in a position to dissipate the mirage.

It should be noted, however, that these observations concerning Chinese Mainland statistics are intended to apply only to data concerning the 1949 to 1957 period. The statistical practices of the Chinese Communist authorities during the past two years raise a host of new problems, the solution of which may require methods quite different from those used in this study.

THE PROBLEMS OF
NATIONAL INCOME ACCOUNTING IN AN
UNDERDEVELOPED SOVIET-TYPE ECONOMY

1. INTRODUCTION

NATIONAL INCOME ACCOUNTING is usually regarded as the end of a statistical chain, a culmination of a long process of accumulation in the stock of data, the product of a rich and gushing flow of wide-ranging, comprehensively based, and reliable economic statistics of all sorts. To what extent does this counsel of perfection emanate from the statistical experience of highly developed industrialized countries where this was indeed the pattern of statistical evolution, and where it is therefore possible to construct highly detailed and disaggregated sets of social accounts?[1] Furthermore, is this experience fully applicable to the underdeveloped areas of today? Is it possible for these areas to telescope statistical history and to benefit by a statistical leap akin to the technological leap which is responsible for much of their industrialization? Perhaps there is a strong case for reversing the order of statistical evolution in areas of more or less inadequate data: that is, under these conditions, national income analysis, instead of being the product of a long chain of statistical improvement and growth, may become one of the principal sources of stimuli for such growth. Thus, national income accounting could be seen as contributing to the statistical development of an under-developed area in several ways. It forces the mobilization of a vast array of economic data, at the same time providing a convenient framework within which the scattered statistical fragments can be assembled.

An appraisal of the meaningfulness, usability and reliability of our own estimates can perhaps be more appropriately treated in the next chapters and in the appendices. It may, however, be worthwhile to note even at this stage that the social accounting approach "permits the effective utilization of every scrap of economic information by providing a number of cross-checks. It thereby reduces the area of unconfirmed estimate to the smallest possible range and presents in a single account the sum of the available data and of the deductions that can be drawn from the material."[2] Moreover, if certain statistical gaps bar one approach, frequently another approach, within the context of another account, may yield what we are after. Of course, the larger the number of gaps, the lower will be the reliability of the data, and the skimpier the accounts. Inevitably this means that "the smallest possible range of unconfirmed estimate" will be much greater in a country such as China than in industrially and statistically highly developed regions of the world. But one cannot necessarily conclude from this that the absence of what is frequently considered as the most elementary type of information invalidates or renders inapplicable the whole national income approach. What is elementary in one setting may not be elementary in another. For example, the fact that one country has comparatively reliable population records going back quite far, while China had no adequate population registration until 1953, does not in and of itself mean very much. In a vast country, such as China, it may be feasible to collect fairly accurate foreign trade, industrial, government budget, and financial statistics and yet not possible to keep good population records. The problem of counting a population of five to six hundred million is monumental compared with that faced in a population of two million or even two hundred million.

In such a situation, data for the urban population and for the urban labor force may be much better than for the rural. This, of course, may limit calculations of per capita national product and may also inhibit certain rural-urban breakdowns without barring the process of national income accounting *per se*. At the same time, such limitations and others, naturally narrow the number of possible approaches and the analytical uses to which the results can be put. This is not intended to minimize the obstacles encountered in the process of social accounting in underdeveloped Soviet-type economies, but only to point up that these obstacles need not spell defeat if accounts are (a) defined in terms which are institutionally relevant, (b) adapted to the data limitations, and (c) interpreted with all the necessary caution.

2. THE PROBLEMS OF NATIONAL INCOME ACCOUNTING IN AN UNDERDEVELOPED SOVIET-TYPE ECONOMY

An investigator attempting to construct a set of national accounts for an economy such as that of Communist China, North Korea, or North

Vietnam is immediately confronted by a host of conceptual difficulties in many ways more intractable than those encountered by students of social accounting in preponderantly market-oriented and industrialized economies. Complications, arising from the fact that these economies are underdeveloped and at the same time of the Soviet type, may be categorized under the following three headings: (1) definition of final *vs.* intermediate products, (2) problems of pricing and valuation, and (3) imputation of values to goods and services produced and consumed within the household and thus not entering marketing channels.

A. Final and Intermediate Product

In a sense the whole process of national product estimation is based on a "means-ends" or "input-output" dichotomy. This, of course, necessitates a definition of "ends" and of "output" that is operationally and institutionally relevant for the particular economy. Needless to say this is a question that has plagued national income theory for a long time and has been the subject of extended and heated discussions.[3] How does one define "gross" as compared to "net," and where should one draw the line between "intermediate" and "final products?" The U. S. Department of Commerce concept of final product as "products purchased not for resale" may serve as a first approximation and as a working definition. This is a rather broad and comprehensive concept and therein lies perhaps one of its principal advantages, inasmuch as it can encompass alternative and narrower definitions. Given the accounting framework, the accounts can be rearranged in such a way as to provide the same information about structure, flows, and transactions, but from the point of view of alternative approaches to "ends" and to the problem of "net" *vs.* "gross."

This issue assumes particular importance because of the significant differences in the character and ends of economic activity as between Soviet-type and consumer-oriented economies. To some extent these are differences in degree, representing a continuum on a scale, but they are so marked that in effect they represent differences in kind.

As Professor Kuznets puts it, estimates of peacetime national product in the United States should be based on the assumption that "economic activity is to produce goods to satisfy ultimate consumers; that production is for man, not man for production."[4] At the same time he concedes that this view may need to be modified in wartime when the relative priority of objectives shifts. However, a fully mobilized wartime type of state tends to be the normal rather than the exceptional condition in Soviet-type economies. As a matter of fact, these tend to be economies which are oriented preponderantly towards production rather than consumption, and to which one might indeed apply the dictum that "man is for production." In such a context, personal consumption may in effect be viewed as one of the "means" rather than "ends" of economic activity. From this point of view consumption becomes an input, a cost of maintaining and augmenting a factor of production. Wage goods are produced as a means of provisioning an expanding labor force and of raising its productivity.[5]

Definition of ends, real or alleged, ultimate or intermediate, is an extremely difficult task for any society, particularly since in most cases these tend to be implicit rather than explicit, nebulous, multiple, and mutually conflicting. Granting all the necessary qualifications, power objectives unquestionably loom very large in the preference scales of Soviet and Chinese Communist planners. Economic activity is in many ways viewed as a handmaiden for the expansion of state power or world Communist power. This necessarily means that military production and expansion of industrial capacity for military production are accorded a central place in the planning process. In an extreme statement of the case, one could say that the central task of a Soviet-type economy is to allocate resources in such a way as to maximize the rate of growth in military production. In these terms, the appropriate definition of final product might be military consumption and capital formation, while household consumption could be considered an intermediate product.

Thus, if final product is not defined in terms of "purchases not for resale," but from the viewpoint of "ends," one could conclude that the appropriate definitions should be quite different for the two types of economies. Proceeding from the highest level of generality, it could be said that in both cases the ultimate purpose of economic activity is the flow of goods to present and future consumers. However, in one case these consumers are individuals while in the other case they are the state, or, more specifically, the military establishment.

Having reached these conclusions, it must be noted that the emerging concepts of final product are more applicable to the models of these systems than to their realities. That is, if these ends were consistently pursued in the two types of economies respectively, the concepts outlined above would be relevant without qualifications. This, however, is hardly the case. In all living systems the means-ends dichotomy is blurred, and a precise ranking of ends is most difficult if not impossible. In the post-World-War-II economy of the United States, it would be very hard to distinguish between military and defense expenditure as an input, as a cost of maintaining the social system, and as a final product produced for the satisfaction of certain ends which in our society today may be accorded nearly equal rank with the objective of consumer satisfaction. At any rate, it would be well-nigh impossible to determine what part of our defense establishment is absolutely necessary for the maintenance of our social system and what part is designed to serve other ends, ends which may be considered ultimate in every sense of the word. Similarly, while the objective of consumer satisfaction is undoubtedly subordinated to the pursuit of power in Soviet-type societies, this does not necessarily mean that it can be viewed just as an input rather than as a low-priority end.

On the basis of all these considerations combined, it would seem that in measuring the comparative performance of different types of economies, much can be said for using three alternative concepts of final product, each directed towards a different aspect of comparison. These could be designated as the welfare, the power, and the comprehensive definitions respectively: the first referring to household consumption and capital formation that may contribute to it, the second focusing on government expenditure and capital formation associated with it, and the third encompassing both.

For the purposes of this study, the third concept is most relevant since our primary interest is in the structure of China's Mainland economy, in the prevailing pattern of resource allocation, and in the magnitude and interrelationships of the broad financial flows. However, should these estimates be used by investigators in the future for, let us say, comparisons of economic growth in India and China, a rounded assessment would need to take account of the first two product definitions as well.

B. Problems of Valuation

In market-oriented economies prices serve as allocators of scarce resources among alternative uses or ends. Under conditions of the competitive model, optimum resource use is assured, and the market for goods and factors is cleared. In this situation, prices and costs reflect the underlying scarcity relationships, these being a function of consumer scale of preferences on the one hand and resource availabilities on the other hand.

Theoretically, at any rate, an optimum and equilibrium solution could also be attained in centrally planned economies based on the planners' scale of preferences; that is, in this system too, prices, expressing scarcity relationships on the basis of a different set of ends, could serve as allocators. This, however, need not be the case, since inputs may be distributed on the basis of technical coefficients through a process of physical allocations regardless of price and cost considerations.

In such circumstances, prices in a Soviet-type economy do not primarily serve as allocators, but as administrative devices designed to accomplish certain specific purposes. In effect, prices in such an economy may perhaps be said to perform three types of functions: clearing the market for consumer goods, control of plan-performance within the context of cost-accounting at the enterprise level, and micro-allocation within narrow ranges. That is, in the absence of rationing, consumer choice prevails without the exercise of consumer autonomy, while prices of consumer goods are fixed through the trial and error method in such a way that the market is cleared.[6] To put the same thing in another way, consumers cannot directly affect allocative decisions, but have to take these as given. Similarly, the individual enterprise, whatever its size, cannot affect allocative decisions directly, so that the purpose of cost accounting is to check on plan performance without cost valuations necessarily reflecting scarcity relationships. Finally, in a number of specific instances, the actual implementation of the allocative decisions made by the Planning Board is attained through price manipulation.

In effect, partly because of reliance on physical allocation, Soviet-type economies do not necessarily attempt to equate prices with opportunity cost in terms of planners' preferences and such consumers' preferences as may be permitted to express themselves. Hence, aggregates based on such prices yield "distorted" results, in the sense that the values in terms of which they are expressed are divorced from opportunity cost.[7] At the same time, this need not mean that the pattern of resource allocation itself is "distorted" in the same sense.

Several alternative approaches to this problem have been attempted, at least for the Soviet Union. In their pioneering studies of Soviet national income, Professor Bergson and his associates used an "adjusted factor cost" standard for correcting these distortions.[8] In spite of the data and conceptual difficulties that these investigators faced, much can be said for this type of an adjustment as compared to valuation procedures based on foreign prices. Wyler and Colin Clark attempt to cut the Gordian knot by valuing Soviet national income in dollar prices.[9] This procedure, however, yields distortions of its own that may be more serious than those arising from valuations of unadjusted Soviet prices. U. S. prices which are based on entirely different preference patterns and factor endowments, may reflect Soviet scarcity relationships more inadequately than would domestic prices, however irrational the latter may be. In any case, for measurements of allocative efficiency, adjustments in valuation based on criteria that are internal to the system itself are likely to prove more useful than foreign price weights.

There is no question that this problem of pricing and valuation is still one of the major unresolved issues in Soviet economies. Bergson's work and the theoretical controversies concerning the rationality of ruble prices have served to clarify many of the issues and pinpoint the difficulties.[10] One of the complicating factors in this whole context is that the pricing distortions are not of a random character, but rather tend to introduce a systematic bias in the direction of more or less consistent undervaluation of some sectors and overvaluation of others. Thus, as Bergson's studies show, investment tends to be undervalued; the same applies to agriculture, but industry, and particularly trade, are overvalued. Similarly, the boundaries of profits as an economically meaningful category are very hard to delineate and measure in this system. Possibly one way out of this dilemma might be to adopt a labor standard of valuation using the sectoral wage bills as weights. Actually, Bergson's method comes quite close to this, but it raises problems of its own. First of all, it makes sense only if it can be shown that the wage structure is fairly rational, or at least more rational than other factor prices in these Soviet-type economies. All of the available evidence for both the Soviet Union and China would suggest that this seems to be the case. However, there are more fundamental problems to be faced. If valuation is based only on the input of labor, this would tend to overstate the weight of the labor intensive industries as compared to the capital and land intensive ones. Furthermore, it may be very difficult to measure the opportunity cost of capital or land.

What is the relevance of all this to Communist China? As we will try to show later on, these problems appear in 1952 in an incipient form. As compared to the Soviet Union, resource allocation via the market and the price mechanism played, at that time, a larger role in China. However, this is becoming less and less true in recent years; yet even in 1952 the state economic organizations already had such an important part in agricultural procurement, transport, mining, manufacturing, and trade, that price distortions in the sense discussed above were by no means negligible.

C. Problems of Imputation

The conceptual and measurement problems associated with national income accounting in Soviet-type economies are greatly complicated in the case of Communist China by virtue of its being an underdeveloped area in which a large, if not preponderant share of transactions take place within, rather than between, households. This, of course, means that the values of the goods and services produced and consumed within the same household must be imputed. The problem is twofold: (1) what is productive activity, i.e., how should production be defined and where should its boundaries be drawn? (2) once the categories to be encompassed have been defined, how should the intra-household transactions be valued?

The first question is conceptually troublesome for all economies.[11] It is most doubtful that a theoretically fool-proof definition of productive *versus* non-productive or economic *versus* non-economic activity can be advanced. To some extent, at least, the precise dividing line will have to be determined by convention and expediency. The only rule one may perhaps state in abstract terms is that the delimitation of the concept will depend partly upon the economic and social structure of the particular country under study and the social ends pursued.

In spite of all of its shortcomings, from the point of view of a working definition, Pigou's classical prescription is probably still of most general applicability even for underdeveloped areas; that is, to take into consideration all those activities that "can be brought directly or indirectly into relation with the measuring rod of money"[12] and to interpret the "indirectly" as applicable to all those activities for which a market analogue can be found within the particular economy under consideration. To go beyond this and attempt to extend the boundaries of production to the point of introducing market analogues from other countries and periods may yield an extremely artificial concept of national product. In a sense it may represent an approximation of what the economy under study may look like if it were structured and organized like some other economy, rather than following its actual contours and production possibilities.

Actually, one may question the feasibility of constructing national income and product estimates which are empirically and conceptually valid measures of structure, resource flows, and production possibilities in one economy, and at the same time satisfy the requirements of interspatial and intertemporal comparison. Comparison with different economies and different periods would demand different types of adjustments. Thus, analogues would have to be added (or possibly subtracted), depending upon whether the Chinese national product was, for instance, compared with that of India, Japan, or the United States. Similarly, whatever the countries or periods being compared, the character of the adjustment will also have to be geared to the criteria—welfare, power, or some other —in terms of which the comparisons are to be made.

As indicated above, this study focuses primarily upon an analysis of the structure of Mainland China's economy, upon the pattern of resource allocation and income flows. This focus will necessarily govern the character of the imputations. In investigating this problem, a distinction should be drawn between the treatment of self-consumed commodity production and imputed service flows.

In the case of commodity production there is very little doubt that it should be included within the boundaries of economic activity.[13] But at what price should self-consumed farm output be weighted? Should these be farm prices, i.e., the prices which the farmer receives for the marketed portion of his produce, or should they be urban retail prices? The first procedure has been most frequently used, but for purposes of international welfare comparisons, primary reliance needs to be placed upon the second.[14] From the standpoint of resource use and factor inputs, the first method actually understates while the second overstates value added; the first in effect ignores all food processing costs, while the second includes costs of transport and distribution even though none were incurred.

For purposes of this study, an intermediate road was pursued. In estimating agricultural product, farm output was valued at producers' prices, while value added in farm processing was calculated and entered as part of farm household income and expenditure. Conceptually, this is supposed to include all of agricultural processing performed on the farm, e.g., not only conversion of wheat into flour, but also of flour into bread or its equivalent. Owing to some obscurities in the data, one cannot, however, be certain that this is actually the case. At the same time that processing is included in the household account, it is carried, on the product side, as a part of manufacturing and processing. The same general procedure is used for self-consumed farm handicraft output.

The problem is much more complex with respect to services. In some cases the question is primarily one of valuation, while in others it is a question as to whether they should be considered as falling within the purview of economic activity. As an example of the first category one might cite housing services, which should unquestionably be included; however, imputation of rentals for owner-occupied dwellings in rural areas, where very few houses are actually rented, presents some very difficult empirical problems. One is confronted with a somewhat similar situation in accounting for unpaid domestic work, except that the case for inclusion is not as unequivocal, at least in terms of prevailing national accounting practices. Our inclination would be to estimate this item if an adequate basis could be found for valuing these services in Mainland China today. There is no question that their omission represents an underestimate of national product.

Yet whether this exclusion necessarily leads to a more serious underestimate of national product in underdeveloped as compared to highly industrialized economies is far from certain. As Rao has correctly pointed out, the services of consumer durables and the services provided by the highly mechanized kitchen are unaccounted for in the product estimates of the developed areas.[15] It should be noted that this high degree of mechanization raises the productivity of housework, and also increases the range of alternative employment opportunities for a housewife in developed economies; thus, both productivity and the opportunity cost is higher. In one important respect, omission of unpaid domestic service may be a more serious problem for underdeveloped economies, i.e., it reduces intertemporal comparability. As the process of industrialization and commercialization proceeds in its early stages, and particularly amidst conditions of rapid growth, a vast range of activities previously within the purview of unpaid housework may be encompassed by the market, and be automatically included in the national accounts. This means that if an upward bias in the growth rates is to be averted, great care must be taken to identify these activities and to adjust for the incomparabilities involved.

Finally, there is a whole range of service activities which is *par excellence* culturally and socially conditioned. This constitutes what Professor Kuznets calls culture-myth services.[16] They are performed in some form in all societies, but while they tend to become professionalized, and thus subject to monetary reward in urbanized societies, in traditional societies, they are typically within the province of the family system rather than the economic system. This category comprises religious services, including burials, and the various forms of insurance, life, old age, social security, which in the past were carried on as an integral part of family and clan organization in China. Therefore, within the context of the prevailing value system and the structure of institutions in such societies, the treatment of these activities as economic is most doubtful. In a sense, the same applies to educational and recreational activities carried on within the family system, although here the problem is minimized by the inability of the traditional peasant family to provide much formal education. Therefore, in our accounts only those educational, welfare, and recreational services are included which are conducted outside the family, i.e., which are professionalized. In Mainland China of today these are almost exclusively the function of government.

The difficulties of imputation, however, are not confined to the self-consumed output of goods and services. Equally troublesome, if not more so, is the problem of non-monetized capital formation, i.e., capital formation based on farm family labor using largely local materials, materials not purchased, but locally produced. This is primarily a problem of data and valuation, rather than a conceptual one. As a rule, it is possible to obtain data on changes in livestock numbers and in farm equipment inventory, or, in the absence of the latter, to estimate farm equipment purchases in varying ways. However, to ascertain the value of farm construction and farm improvements becomes extremely difficult.

THE ESTIMATES

1. THE CHARACTER OF THE NATIONAL INCOME ACCOUNTS

GROSS NATIONAL PRODUCT at market prices, rather than national income at factor cost, is the fulcrum of this study. Ideally, of course, it would be best to have estimates based on both concepts, but with available data there is no reliable way by which different use categories can be estimated on a factor cost basis. Similarly, it would be very difficult to determine capital consumption for each economic sector.

In terms of general form and structure, the accounts in Tables 3, 4, and 5 are patterned after those found in the Soviet national income studies of Bergson and his associates.[1] These necessarily reflect the changing property relations in the Soviet Union, particularly between 1928 and 1937. As indicated in Chapter I, Mainland China's economy in 1952 was far from fully collectivized or nationalized, so that in this respect it bore many points of resemblance to the Soviet economy on the eve of its first Five Year Plan. Consequently, for our purposes Hoeffding's accounts were most relevant, although naturally there are some differences in individual items, reflecting differences in particular institutional arrangements or stages of development in the two countries. Ultimately all of these accounts represent modifications and adaptations of forms evolved by the U. S. Department of Commerce, by Richard Stone and others in the United Kingdom, and by the United Nations.

Originally, it was our intent to develop two independent estimates, one from the income and the other from the expenditure side. This would have provided something of a cross check on the validity of the estimates and could have served as a partial measure of the margins of error.[2] Unfortunately, in the end, this objective had to be abandoned, since it was not possible to estimate inventory changes. This meant that we could derive a complete estimate only from the income side while leaving an unexplained residual in the expenditure account. This unexplained residual then appears as a large statistical discrepancy, which in effect, includes inventory investment.

The income account rests mainly on four items: agricultural product, the non-farm wage bill including incomes of self-employed, net earnings of private and government enterprises, and indirect taxes. Government enterprise earnings and indirect taxes could be derived from officially published data. But the other major income categories had to be estimated, so to speak, "from the bottom up." The data, methods, and sources from which these estimates were derived are presented in Appendices A, B, C and D.

In general terms, the "value added" approach was used to derive agricultural product, on the basis of (a) officially published production data, (b) price data collected by us, and (c) inputs as estimated in Appendix A. Published labor force and employment data in combination with average wage rates obtained from wage quotations, were used in calculating the wage bill. Private enterprise earnings were estimated from the data given in Appendix C. In effect, then, the income accounts represent a combination of the "value-added" approach for agriculture and the "distributive shares" approach for the non-farm sector. On the expenditure side, data for retail sales to households, government investment in fixed capital, and government consumption were culled from published sources, with considerable adjustments to avoid double counting and to insure conceptual consistency. Private investment and a miscellany of smaller items, on the other hand, had to be estimated.

There are, of course, a number of alternative ways in which national income and product may be computed and/or presented. In choosing our particular approach we were in part guided by the type of data available, and in part by the fact that others have published or are in the process of compiling estimates based on different methods.[3] Whichever approach is employed, if the basic statistics are trustworthy, aggregates may be used with perhaps just minor adjustments. In countries where data are poor and methods of compilation are misleading, undue reliance on aggregates may yield some spurious results. Hence, whether one attempts to estimate Mainland China's national product by the value added, by the factor shares, or by the final expenditures approach, considerable disaggregation and reconstruction of data "from the bottom up" is required.

Given the nature of the data, it seemed to us much more difficult and hazardous to place primary reliance either on "the value added" or the "final expenditures" method. The first requires detailed data on production quantities and prices of an infinite array of products or detailed estimates of outputs and inputs for each economic branch and sector. The second, by its very nature, must almost exclusively depend on value rather than on physical categories. To trace final expenditure flows through the economic system when there are large gaps in the data, requires assumptions at almost every step, only some of which can be validated. Indubitably, all national income estimates involve the use of assumptions; but in statistically advanced countries these need to be used only sparingly. For statistically underdeveloped countries, the problem is how to mobilize the available data in such a way as to reduce to a minimum the dependence on assumption.

Against this background, the basic accounts are presented in Tables 3, 4, and 5, while Table 6 attempts a reconciliation of the public sector account and the government budget for 1952. Finally, estimated distributive shares by industrial origin are given in Table 9. The data in this table do not add up to an independent estimate of gross national product; they represent rather a rearrangement of the different items from the income side of the accounts in Tables 3 and 4. The primary purpose of this reclassification is to obtain an estimate of value added by industrial origin.

The definition and meaning of the different items in the accounts are spelled out below, with computation details, methods and basic data given in the appendices. However, whenever major methodological issues are involved in the estimate of a particular item, these are discussed in the body of the Chapter.

2. THE HOUSEHOLD AND
PRIVATE SECTOR ACCOUNT (TABLE 3)

As its title implies, this really combines what are usually two separate accounts, one for household and the other for business transactions, so that household consumption and private enterprise investment appear together on the expenditure side, while wage and business income are ranged together on the income side.

One of the advantages, as well as one of the justifications, for this type of mixed account is that in an under-developed and only partially commercialized area such as Mainland China, the bulk of economic activity is carried on by family enterprises. As a result, the line becomes very blurred between the household as a supplier of labor, a consumer of final goods, and as an entrepreneur. This is the case not only for agriculture, but also for most of handicraft, local trading, and native transport. Owing to this fact, it becomes very difficult to separate the incomes of wage earners from those of the self-employed. Similar considerations bar the way to any real distinction between money rents for housing and imputed rent for owner-occupied dwellings.

A. Incomes

(i) Incomes of Farm Households

Farm households in a country such as China derive their income from four principal sources: agricultural production, including crop and livestock production; local processing of agricultural products; farm handicrafts; and dwelling services. Given the predominantly subsistence character of this type of peasant agriculture, the bulk of farm income accrues in kind rather than in monetary form.

It was not possible, however, to calculate money income and net income in kind for all of these categories separately. A different procedure had to be followed. First, value added in agriculture, fishing, farm processing, and farm handicrafts was estimated separately. In this connection, a conscious attempt was made to distinguish the latter two categories from the former. In many national income accounts all these are lumped together as agricultural product.[4] Such an approach obviously exaggerates the importance of agriculture and underestimates the contribution of processing and manufacturing activity in the economy. Thus it aggravates the problem of interspatial and intertemporal comparability of national products and incomes. With these considerations in mind, farm processing and handicrafts are placed under mining and manufacturing in Table 9. Next, net farm money income from all sources was estimated, with farm income in kind then derived as a residual from total farm product. The steps involved in this calculation are spelled out below.

(1) Agricultural Product

As a first step in this process, gross agricultural output was arrived at by applying 1952 farm price weights (P) to 1952 physical production quantities (Q). The value of raw material inputs consumed in the process of production was then deducted from gross product value (PQ). No allowance was made for capital consumption. Agricultural production as defined here includes food and oil-bearing crops, plant and animal fibers, sugar, tea, tobacco, fruits and vegetables, other miscellaneous crops, and the products of livestock husbandry.

(a) *Production.* The crop production figures used are for the most part based on official Chinese Communist releases as is shown in greater detail in Appendix A. A crucial problem in this context is the reliability of Chinese Communist crop statistics, reliability not in terms of possible ambiguities in the published data, but in terms of the underlying accuracy of the data as collected by the administrative authorities and the statistical organs.

Actually, Chinese farm production figures are probably subject to two opposite types of biases. On the one hand, since agricultural taxes were levied as a certain percentage of output, there was a strong incentive for under-reporting by the peasantry. This may perhaps have been counteracted by a system of local crop inspection prior to actual harvesting. However, the effectiveness of the latter depends very much upon the attitude of the local officials and Communist Party cadres.[5] On the other hand, these statistics may be subject to an upward bias generated by the desire of the reporting authorities to point up achievements and constant improvements.

Completely apart from possible biases, the system of reporting was, and in many respects still is, quite inadequate. Within this system, however, coverage has been improving from year to year. The weight of available evidence definitely indicates that coverage was still incomplete for 1952 and that for this, if for no other reason, 1952 crop output figures are understated.[6]

This under-reporting greatly complicates the comparability of annual farm output data. Agricultural production data seem to be less comprehensive for the early fifties than for recent years. Similarly, they are probably more complete for 1952 than for the pre-Communist years, which casts doubt on Chinese Communist claims that 1952 farm production exceeded previous peak levels. In this connection, it is interesting to note that the figure for the 1952 food crop area, which the Chinese Communists began to use after the completion of the 1953 census,[7] closely approximates unofficial prewar estimates based on Buck's land use survey.[8]

Although the crop data may be subject to the reporting biases referred to above, the administrative and statistical organs have compiled and published production figures for all of the more important crops. This, however, does not apply to livestock products. As shown in Appendix A, only livestock numbers are regularly published, so that production of meat and other animal produce must be estimated on the basis of slaughter rates, meat, hide and skin, wool, leather, casings, bristles, eggs and fat yield per head, as given in a detailed technical study of animal husbandry in China published in Shanghai in 1953.[9] It is nowhere explicitly stated whether these rates are computed from actual data for any one year or whether they represent averages for several years taken from sampling observations by the author, but the latter would seem to be the case. Moreover, the published livestock statistics do not include poultry; for these only scattered references, more in the nature of guesses, can be found. Therefore, we adopted the poultry figures cited in this study of animal husbandry with the full recognition that they represent no more than an informed guess.

(b) *Prices*. As compared to production statistics, price information presented a much more difficult problem. In principle, physical outputs were valued at the farm procurement prices paid by the state trading companies or their agents. How valid is the use of such prices for valuing agricultural product? This question needs to be posed in two ways: first, how adequately do these prices reflect the actual value of farm sales, and, second, do these prices provide an appropriate basis for valuing farm income? The first question can perhaps be answered in the affirmative in the sense that by 1952 the bulk of the farm output entering marketing channels went through the state trading system. This was certainly the case with grain, oilseeds, cotton, and other industrial crops. On the other hand, probably a much larger share of fruits, vegetables, and livestock products were sold by the farmers either to private traders or directly to the final consumers. This latter group of commodities constituted about one third of total agricultural product.

However, even if the larger share of the marketed product is sold at state procurement prices, how justifiable is their use for valuing farm product as a whole? Should not the self-consumed part be valued at different prices, i.e., prices that more adequately reflect scarcity relationships? The method adopted is based partly on expediency, i.e., lack of adequate data on which alternative methods of valuation could be based. Moreover, even if one could compile a representative sample of prices obtaining in private trade, it is truly doubtful whether this would provide a more adequate basis for valuation, given, (1) the comparative thinness of private trade, (2) the formidable market imperfections, and (3) the effect of state purchase prices upon the bids made by private traders.

(c) *Inputs*. The source of input data and their derivation is given in Appendix A. From these it is apparent that the estimates for every one of the cost items, with the possible exception of fertilizer applications, is uncertain. Thus, the margin of error for each input category may be quite considerable, yet the input estimate as a whole can be regarded as fairly reasonable. Tables 1 and A-1 indicate that inputs absorbed a little over 15 per cent of gross production value. In India, this percentage is around 20 per cent, including depreciation, while official Chinese Communist national income estimates give an input ratio of 25 per cent. However, in both of these cases intermediate products entirely produced by and consumed within agriculture are included on both sides of the account. The effect of this may be illustrated by the following numerical example, which roughly corresponds to the actual Mainland situation in 1952. Supposing that gross production value excluding intermediate products (our method) is Y35 billion, while inputs. are Y5 billion. If one adds the intermediate products to both sides of the account, the corresponding values rise to Y40 and Y10 billion respectively. Accordingly, the input ratio in the first case is close to 15 per cent, while in the second it is 25. As far as India is concerned, by use of our method the ratio would drop below 15 per cent. Agricultural product data for a number of other underdeveloped countries in Asia yield relationships within this same general range.

(2) Forestry

Owing to lack of data no estimate for net afforestation, i.e., for net growth of forest inventory, could be made. On the other hand, the timber cut in the forests is accounted for in the non-agricultural wage bill on the one hand, and in the industrial product on the other hand.

(3) Fisheries

Gross output value was estimated on the basis of an official figure for the annual catch of 1,666,300 metric tons and a government purchase price for fish of Y220 per metric ton.[10] In the absence of input data we applied a 10 per cent cost deduction to gross output value.

(4) Farm Income from Processing and Handicrafts

Chinese Mainland statistics distinguish between gross agricultural output which comprises crop production and livestock husbandry, and so-called farmers' "subsidiary production." To this we must add "farm handicrafts for sale."

All of these official estimates for "subsidiary production" and for "farm part-time handicrafts" must be considered as informed guesses rather than as detailed and reliable estimates. This type of economic activity, with its highly scattered character in numerous small households is very difficult to encompass statistically in any underdeveloped country.

The different elements of the farm product account are summarized in Table 1 with the more detailed calculations and documentation provided in Appendix A. The value of farm output sold represents, in effect, the gross money income of the farm population from all sources. The overwhelming bulk of this is derived from the sale of agricultural products, to which must be added, however, the net money income from "farm handi-crafts for sale."

The value of farm output sold, given in Table 1, is based on what, in official sources, is termed "total purchases of farm products by the society." It is not entirely certain whether this is inclusive or exclusive of the agri-cultural tax, which is preponderantly collected in kind and therefore does not yield money income to the farmer. On the other hand, the state trading organs sell the farm products collected as tax, so that they do represent "purchases by the society." The original sources themselves are ambiguous and inconsistent on this point. Thus, in some contexts, purchases are defined in such a way that they include the tax, while at other times the tax is ex-cluded. Upon reviewing the available evidence, we concluded that the figure of Y15.61 billion given in the sources probably includes the tax, which ought to be deducted to obtain gross farm money income.[11] To derive net farm money income, cash purchases of production requisites consumed in the process of production, such as seeds, insecticides, and chemical fertilizer, must be deducted from the value of farm output sold.

Table 1

Mainland China's Farm Product in 1952
(Millions of New Yuan)

1.	Value added in agricultural production		30,100
	(a) Gross crop production value	28,610	
	(b) Gross silk production value	130	
	(c) Gross livestock production value	6,720	
	Total gross production value	35,460	
	Less: Inputs	−5,360	
2.	Value added in fishing		330
	Gross production value	367	
	Less: Inputs	−37	
3.	Value added in subsidiary production		6,200
4.	Value added in farm handicrafts for sale		875
	Gross production value	2,500	
	Less: Inputs	−1,625	
5.	Total farm product		37,505
	(a) Net farm money income		11,190
	Value of farm output sold	12,310	
	Less: Production requisites purchased	−1,120	
	(b) Net farm income in kind		26,315

Sources: Appendix A.

(ii) Imputed Rent on Farm Dwellings

In an exclusively peasant-type agriculture such as prevailed in Mainland China until recently, there is characteristically very little rental housing. This was even more true following the completion of land reform in 1952 (and prior to the introduction of communes in 1958), when practically all dwellings became owner-occupied. Precisely for this reason there was very little information on money rents or the value of the rural housing stock. In the absence of market analogues, the process of imputation became particularly difficult, so that we were forced to resort to some rather unsatisfactory expedients in dealing with this item. Thus we relied on the results of Buck's prewar surveys to estimate imputed rent on farm dwellings. These indicated that five per cent of total farm income was spent for this purpose; we applied this percentage to our farm income figure.

(iii) Non-farm Wages and Salaries, Including Incomes of Self-employed

This estimate is based on the employment and wage data in Table 2, with notes on sources and methods in Appendix B. For a few sectors, i.e., construction, privately operated modern transport, and miscellaneous services, different methods of estimation were used due to the unavailability of employment and/or wage data. Several sectors include large numbers of self-employed which could not be separated from wage labor because of the absence of more detailed labor force statistics. This is the case in non-farm handicrafts, native transport, hauling, porterage, etc., trade, and miscellaneous services.

In appraising the reliability of these data, it must be borne in mind that at no time in its history did Mainland China have a full-fledged population or occupational census. Even the so-called census of 1953 was really only a population registration, with no detailed occupational questions in the registration forms. Therefore, in the past, labor force information had to be based on sample surveys of varying reliability, and on more or less vague estimates. Since the advent of the Chinese Communist regime, the quality of this information has markedly improved; however there is still very considerable scope for further improvement. Actually, labor force data for the public sector can probably be used with a fair degree of confidence. This is much less true for the private sector, although even here one detects an improvement in the data as a result of more frequent and methodologically more reliable surveys.

In contrast with employment statistics, wage information is much scantier and much less trustworthy. Just as with price statistics, there are

Table 2

Non-Farm Civilian Wage Bill Including Incomes of Self-Employed in 1952

ECONOMIC SECTORS	Private			Public			Total	
	EMPLOYMENT (1000)	AVERAGE WAGE (Y/Yr.)	WAGE BILL (Million Y)	EMPLOYMENT (1000)	AVERAGE WAGE (Y/Yr.)	WAGE BILL (Million Y)	EMPLOYMENT (1000)	WAGE BILL (Million Y)
1. Mining & Manufacturing								
Industry	2,057	560	1,151.92	3,140	560	1,758.40	5,197	2,910.32
Handicraft (Non-Farm)	7,013	210	1,472.73	218	210	45.78	7,231	1,518.51
Total	9,070	—	2,624.65	3,358	—	1,804.18	12,428	4,428.51
2. Construction	n.a.	n.a.	n.a.	(1,021)	n.a.	n.a.	n.a.	1,300.00
3. Transport								
Modern	414	550	227.70	596	550	327.80	1,010	555.50
Native	3,370	210	707.70	—	—	—	3,370	707.70
Hauling, etc.	800	380	304.00	—	—	—	800	304.00
Total	4,584	—	1,239.40	596	550	327.80	5,180	1,567.20
4. Post & Tele-Communication	—	—	—	120	550	66.00	120	66.00
5. Trade								
Resident Trade ("Tso" Trade)	4,012	400	1,604.80	n.a.	n.a.	n.a.	n.a.	n.a.
Itinerant Trade ("Hsing" Trade)	329	550	180.95	n.a.	n.a.	n.a.	n.a.	n.a.
Stalls and Small Merchants	2,427	250	606.75	n.a.	n.a.	n.a.	n.a.	n.a.
Catering Trade (Food and Drink)	1,450	195	282.75	n.a.	n.a.	n.a.	n.a.	n.a.
Total	8,218	—	2,675.25	1,247	450	561.15	9,465	3,236.40
6. Banking and Insurance	—	—	—	305	720	219.60	305	219.60
7. Government Services								
Government Administration	—	—	—	1,573	n.a.	n.a.	n.a.	n.a.
Culture, Education, and Health	—	—	—	2,282	n.a.	n.a.	n.a.	n.a.
Urban Public Utilities	—	—	—	41	n.a.	n.a.	n.a.	n.a.
Total	—	—	—	3,896	430	1,675.28	3,896	1,675.28
8. Miscellaneous Occupations	n.a.	n.a.	2,400.00	—	—	—	n.a.	2,400.00
Grand Total	21,872	—	8,939.30	10,543	—	4,654.01	32,415	14,893.31

no systematic reports or complications of wage rates available for Mainland China. For some economic and industrial branches, wage information is comparatively full, sufficiently so that one may be able to estimate average wage rates with a certain degree of confidence. This, for instance, is the case for the public sector of mining and manufacturing, on the one hand, and for the iron, steel, engineering, and textile industries, as a whole, on the other hand. In other cases, however, as in railroad transport, only a few scattered quotations could be found. The situation is further complicated by the fact that (1) piece rates began to come into increasing use by 1952, and (2) in some cases workers received free housing or other perquisites with wages adjusted downward accordingly. On the other hand, we used only those quotations which clearly refer to monthly wage income in all its forms, in money or in kind.

Ideally, we should have at our disposal wage information based on level of skill and responsibility, industry by industry, and corresponding breakdowns for the labor force. However, this type of information is not readily available even in economically and statistically more developed areas, much less in China. Therefore, except for mining and manufacturing, the wage rates used by us do not represent averages in any rigorous sense of the word. They were drawn from a wide number of scattered fragments from which we estimated an average wage, taking into account such factors as the comparative importance of the plant or locality for which the information was given, and the context in which the quotation appeared.

Yet, despite these shortcomings, the margin of error in our aggregate non-farm wage bill need not be too great. There is actually a way of testing, to some extent, the plausibility of our wage bill estimates. The Chinese statistical authorities have published figures for the public sector wage bill as well as for the average wage of workers and employees in the economy as a whole. These are quite close to those that emerge from our calculations in Table 2, our average wage being five to seven per cent above the official figure.[12] The reliability of at least 45 per cent of our wage bill estimate can be cross-checked in this way. Unfortunately, the average wage data for the workers and self-employed in the small private enterprises cannot be similarly tested.

Over and above the data problems, one might legitimately raise the question of how meaningful the wage rates are. Are they subject to the same kinds of manipulation and distortion as commodity prices? As indicated in Chapter I, direct and compulsory allocation of labor to different tasks, localities, and economic branches was of comparatively minor importance in 1952.[13] Therefore, despite a certain amount of wage fixing and

Table 3

Household and Private Sector Account in 1952

(Millions of New Yuan)

A. Incomes

1.	Incomes of Farm Households		38,910
	(a) Net Money Income from Agricultural and Handicraft Products	11,190	
	(b) Net Income in Kind from Agricultural and Handicraft Products	26,315	
	(c) Imputed Net Rent on Farm Dwellings	1,405	
2.	Non-Farm Wages and Salaries Including Incomes of Self-Employed		15,015
	(a) Direct Wages, Salaries and Incomes	14,890	
	(b) Supplementary Incomes in Kind	125	
3.	Private Business Earnings		1,490
4.	Rental Income (Imputed and Monetary) from Private Non-Farm Dwellings		1,395
5.	Pay and Subsistence of Armed Forces		1,500
6.	Total Income Currently Earned		58,310
7.	Transfer Receipts		900
	(a) Rural Relief	145	
	(b) State Unemployment Relief	40	
	(c) Veterans' Benefits	210	
	(d) Stipends of Students	320	
	(e) Pensions, Allowances, and Other Benefits	50	
	(f) Amortization of Bonds and Interest on Bonds and Savings Deposits	135	
8.	Total Income		59,210

B. Expenditures

1.	Retail Sales to Households		20,995
2.	Farm Consumption in Kind		21,600
3.	Expenditure on Housing Services		3,425
	(a) Farm	1,875	
	(b) Non-Farm	1,550	
4.	Consumption of Subsistence by Armed Forces		1,000
5.	Trade Union and Other Dues		65
6.	Expenditure on Miscellaneous Services		2,900
7.	Total Household Expenditures for Goods and Services Consumed		49,985
8.	Gross Investment		3,765
	(a) In Fixed Capital	2,345	
	(b) In Inventories	(1,420)[a]	
9.	Total Current Expenditure on Consumption and Investment		53,750
10.	Transfer Outlays		4,185
	(a) Increase in Bank Deposits of Households	320	
	(b) Direct Taxes	3,775	
	(c) Gifts	55	
	(d) Private Enterprise Contributions to Social Insurance	35	
11.	Other Transfers and Statistical Discrepancy		1,275
12.	Total Expenditure		59,210

[a] Questionable basis for estimate.

regulation already practiced in 1952, the burden of labor resource allocation was primarily borne by the wage mechanism.

(iv) Supplementary Wage Payments in Kind

In effect, these represent sickness, death, and similar benefits extended in kind to workers covered by labor insurance. Such expenditures were over and above the contribution made regularly by the enterprises to the social insurance and trade union funds; in effect, they were *ad hoc* outlays representing benefits in kind paid by the enterprises directly to the workers, whenever the need arose. For the basis of this and all subsequent estimates in the household account see Appendix C.

(v) Private Business Earnings

These earnings are gross of depreciation and before payment of direct taxes. They include profits of private industry, of large-scale private trading enterprises—both wholesale and retail—private construction, modern transport, and a share for an imputed profit item "earned" in small-scale and self-employed enterprises such as pawnshops, native trade, and banks, etc.

(vi) Cash and Imputed Net Rent on Non-Farm Dwellings

Generally speaking the urban population resides in three types of housing: owner occupied dwellings, government dormitories or public housing projects, and privately owned apartment houses or residences of varying kinds. On the first, no cash rent is paid so this is an imputed item; the second may involve cash rent or may in effect be a form of wage payment in kind, while the third unquestionably requires cash payments to private owners. Strictly speaking, only incomes derived from the first and the third should be treated as part of the Household and Private Sector Account, with incomes from the second assigned to the Public Sector. Unfortunately, in the absence of data on rents paid for different types of housing or on government receipts from rental property, there is no way of distinguishing between these different categories. Since the drive for nationalization of housing came only in later years, in 1952 the preponderant proportion of urban residences was still privately owned. It is therefore fair to say that the magnitude of error in this procedure can not be very large; nevertheless it yields something of an overstatement of private sector incomes, and a corresponding understatement of public sector revenues.

Much more serious than this error is the dubious quality of the basic rental estimate. In the absence of aggregate data or of reliable and representative sample household budgets for different parts of the country, our estimate of net urban rental incomes had to be necessarily very crude. In fact, it was derived as a multiple of rural expenditure on dwellings.

(vii) Pay and Subsistence of Armed Forces

The method of computation was in this case the same as for the non-farm wage bill, i.e., data concerning the size of the armed forces were related to average per capita income in money and kind combined.

(viii) Transfer Receipts

These could be estimated with a fair degree of reliability, as shown in Appendix C. Rural relief and veterans' benefit payments are specifically indicated in published sources; for the other items most of the material needed for the estimates is fairly readily available. A large share of these receipts was financed through government appropriations. This applies to disaster relief, largely for rural areas stricken by floods and famines, and to veterans' benefits and student stipends as well. Interest on bonds and their amortization also represent a charge on the budget. These were bonds sold in 1950, to be amortized over five years, paying an annual interest of five per cent.

In contrast, urban unemployment relief is drawn from three sources: (1) contributions of one percent of the monthly wage bill both by enterprises and workers in those cities in which unemployment funds have been established, (2) voluntary gifts, and (3) government budget. Pensions, old age benefits, etc., are financed exclusively by the labor insurance fund.

B. Expenditures

(i) Retail Sales to Households for Consumption

The official retail sales figures refer to sales of consumer goods to individuals and to "groups" and to sales of production requisites to farmers. For this purpose, "groups" are defined as government organs, mass organizations, the military establishment, and enterprises. Thus, sales of food-stuffs, clothing, and other consumer goods to the army and of office supplies to all these "groups" are considered as retail sales. Therefore, to estimate household purchases for consumption, these items must be deducted from the official figure.

(ii) Farm Consumption in Kind

The farm household has to meet varying claims out of its income in kind before it can use it for its own current consumption. Foremost of these is the tax in kind to be paid both to the central and village government. To this must be added the annual increment in livestock holdings and in inventories. Farm consumption in kind was therefore estimated by deducting these items from farm income in kind.

(iii) Expenditure on Housing Services

This represents total gross rental expenditure, farm and non-farm, with the bases of estimation given on the income side. The difference between this expenditure item and total net rental income represents an allowance for maintenance and repair.

(iv) Consumption of Subsistence by Armed Forces

According to scattered reports, the annual pay of Chinese Communist armed forces ranged in 1952 from about Y80 to Y100 for enlisted men up to much higher figures for officers. The monetary wage bill of the armed forces may then be estimated as Y500 million. This may be somewhat high, since the figure of five million given in Appendix C includes militia and local district troops, which may receive a much lower remuneration. On the other hand, this may be counterbalanced by the fact that officers' salaries are much higher. The figure for cost of subsistence is thus derived by subtracting the money payments from the total pay and allowances of armed forces estimated in the income account.

(v) Trade Union and Other Dues

In addition to trade union dues, this category includes membership fees for the Communist Party and a number of so-called mass organizations, such as The Peasants Association, The New Democratic Youth League, and The All China Federation of Democratic Women. As indicated in Appendix C, only trade union dues could be reliably estimated from the available information. The figures derived for the other organizations had to be based on a number of more or less arbitrary assumptions and may therefore be subject to a considerable margin of error.

(vi) Miscellaneous Service Expenditures by Households

Under this category are ranged household expenditures on public utilities, recreation, travel, health care, education, worship, and a variety of other personal services such as laundering, outlays on public baths, haircuts, domestic servants, etc. The best information concerning these types of expenditures may be obtained from household budget surveys conducted on the Chinese Mainland in recent years.

Our figure for miscellaneous service outlays is based on the 1955 survey, which provides the most detailed household budget data. We estimated that 5 percent of total farmer expenditures and 8 percent of the urban wage bill was devoted to this purpose, on the assumption that the structure of household outlays did not change appreciably between 1952 and 1955. Since the rise in real wages was quite modest in these three years, this may not be an unreasonable assumption.

(vii) Gross Investment in the Private Sector

Available data permit only an indirect estimate of private investment. Aggregate investment was estimated first, then public sector investment was deducted from it, so that private investment was derived as a residual.

Aggregate investment, in turn, was built up from data on the total value of construction costs, value of domestic manufacture of equipment, and equipment imports. Official sources give the gross value of construction as Y4,560 million in 1952.[14] This includes all types of construction (residential, industrial, administrative, monumental, etc.) in various stages of completion, and is not a figure for "completed assets" only.[15]

The official output figure for the engineering industry of Y1.4 billion raises two problems, the importance of which is difficult to assess.[16] One is whether all of the Y1.4 billion can be interpreted as the final product of the engineering industry, and the other is whether engineering production and repair in military establishments is included in this figure.

To domestic engineering output must be added equipment imports. Unfortunately, Chinese sources do not give a detailed commodity composition of imports. Official sources state that in 1952, fifty per cent of the machines and equipment needed were imported,[17] so that equipment imports may be estimated at Y1.4 billion.

Total investment in fixed capital may therefore be approximated at Y7,360 million (4,560 + 1,400 + 1,400). While there is no direct way of checking this aggregate, the construction equipment ratio of 62:38 which emerges from it seems eminently reasonable if compared with the investment data of other underdeveloped countries.

Public investment in fixed capital is given below as Y5,015 million, which would leave Y2,345 million for private investment, financed out of household and business saving and creation of new bank credit. Gross business saving cannot, unfortunately, be ascertained. However, on the basis of total business earnings, with allowances for payment of direct taxes, some dividend payments, and owner-operator withdrawals in small enterprises, one can deduce that there must have been some gross business saving, possibly around Y500 to Y1,000 million. Adding the net increment in bank loans to the rural sector and the private business sector, aggregate sources of financing seem to have been roughly commensurate with the private fixed capital investment figure derived above.

It was not possible to estimate investment in inventory accumulation with any degree of reliability, and for this reason it is bracketed in Table 3.

(viii) Transfer Outlays

Altogether five different kinds of claims on private sector income are included in transfer outlays. All of these, except household savings, represent expenditures by the private business sector. The household savings refer to bank deposit formation both in the urban and rural sector. On the other hand, owing to lack of data, changes in private cash balances had to be ignored.

Official sources supply figures for the net increment in saving deposits and for agricultural taxes. However, the latter had to be adjusted since it is quoted on a crop, rather than a budget (calendar) year basis. The estimate for private sector contributions to social insurance shown in Table 3 could be derived from official data detailed in Appendix C.

Additional claims upon the private sector were the business income taxes, cash donations to support the Korean war, and fines and capital levies paid during the "Five-Anti's" campaign. These last two items are treated as "other revenue," while the first is entered under "commercial and industrial taxes" in the budget. There were practically no individual income taxes paid in 1952; the estimate of business income taxes is discussed below under public sector incomes and in Appendix D. Fines and capital levies could not be ascertained for lack of data. Therefore, both of these items had to be combined with "Statistical Discrepancy" into a residual category. On the other hand, cash gifts could be derived from published sources.

3. THE PUBLIC SECTOR ACCOUNT (TABLE 4)

This account is closely interrelated with the government budget but far from identical with it, since there are certain categories of transactions which take place outside the budget. Thus, government enterprises retain some earnings which then go into financing major repairs, special awards, plant welfare measures, etc. Cooperative organizations are considered as part of the public sector and are treated as such by us, but they are not included in the budget. Similarly, on the expenditure side, major repairs and inventory accumulation are partially financed by extra-budgetary sources: retained enterprise earnings and bank credit respectively.

Of the Mainland statistics available, budget data may be considered to be among the most reliable, but also among the most difficult to use. This is primarily due to the constant changes in budgetary definitions and practices. Frequently these changes are not defined explicitly, and if so, only after a considerable delay. Thus, at times, total revenues are given including budget carry-overs from previous years and foreign loan proceeds; sometimes the carry-overs are dropped but foreign loan proceeds retained; often both are omitted. More recently, revenues are occasionally quoted exclusive of depreciation allowances. It is, of course, natural and legitimate that for different purposes, different concepts may seem most appropriate, but there should be no ambiguity as to how terms are being used, or what practice is followed. The definition of many other budget categories is often unclear as well, and this, as will be shown later, becomes a particularly troublesome problem in investment.

A. Incomes

Several of the revenue items in the public sector can be obtained directly from published government budget data. This applies to receipts from government establishments; in contrast, retained earnings of state enterprises, profits of cooperative organizations, incomes of social insurance funds, and subsidies had to be estimated by methods outlined in greater detail in Appendix D.

(i) Earnings of Government Enterprises and Organizations

This is an official budget figure which includes profits of government enterprises gross of depreciation, as well as so-called "operating receipts" of different types of government establishments and facilities. Thus hospital fees, receipts of educational and cultural institutions, etc., are treated as "operating revenues," and are combined with the profits and depreciation allowances paid into the budget by enterprises functioning within the frame-

Table 4

Public Sector Account in 1952

(Millions of New Yuan)

A. Income

1. Earnings of Government Enterprises and Organizations		5,980
(a) Paid into the Budget	5,450	
(b) Retained Earnings	530	
2. Profits of Cooperative Organizations		200
3. Receipts of Social Insurance Funds (incl. Trade Union Funds)		125
4. Indirect Taxes		6,640
Less: Subsidies		n.a.
5. Total Charges Against Current Product		12,945
6. Transfer Receipts		6,055
(a) Private Enterprise Contributions to Social Insurance	35	
(b) Gifts	55	
(c) Money Savings by Households	320	
(d) Direct Taxes by Private Sector		
1. Agricultural Taxes	3,300	
2. Business Income Tax	475	
(e) Other Transfers	1,870	
7. Total Income		19,000

B. Expenditures

1. Government Administration (incl. local)		2,110
2. Defense		4,370
3. Community Services (Health, Welfare and Education)		1,195
4. Gross Public Investment		4,085
(a) In Fixed Capital	5,015	
(b) Inventory Change	n.a.	
(c) Net Foreign Investment	-930	
5. Total Outlays Net of Transfers		11,760
6. Transfer Outlays		990
(a) Unemployment Benefits	40	
(b) Pensions, Allowances, and Other Benefits	50	
(c) Veterans' Benefits	210	
(d) Stipends to Students	320	
(e) Interest and Amortization on Bonds & Interest on Savings Deposits	135	
(f) Disaster Relief	145	
(g) Public Contributions to Social Insurance Funds	90	
7. Statistical Discrepancy		6,250
8. Total Expenditures		19,000

work of the accounting or accountability system, i.e., the equivalent of the Soviet *khozraschet*. This system was not fully delineated and defined until

1955; as a result, enterprise, business, and economic accounting was far from standardized. However, budgetary data and other relevant economic statistics published since mid-1955, regardless of whether they refer to recent or earlier years, are based on the new procedures and definitions. According to these, net earnings and depreciation allowances of all *khozraschet* organizations must be paid into the budget, except for certain funds set aside for special purposes.

To the extent that the "operating receipts" are included in this budget item, they overstate the income side of the public sector account. Unfortunately, there is no published information on these receipts, but one could, perhaps, approximate them on the basis of 1952 government revenues originating from "other sources."[18]

It is not entirely clear whether profits, depreciation allowances, operating receipts, and unspent liquid balances are gross or net of losses. Since all enterprises reporting earnings must pay these into the budget, they are probably aggregated without making allowances for enterprises operating at a loss. If these losses are financed out of budget appropriations, and if the amounts set aside for this purpose are known, this accounting procedure need not result in an overstatement of the public sector's contribution to national product. But, if the extent of these subsidies is not known and/or the subsidies are financed out of bank credit rather than the budget, then the income side of the government account will undoubtedly be exaggerated.[19] For all of these reasons, the figure for enterprise earnings given in Table 4 unquestionably represents an overstatement by possibly as much as ten per cent (see Section 6 of this chapter).

(ii) Retained Earnings

Government enterprises are permitted to channel a small part of their earnings into two special funds over which they retain control, subject to government regulations. These are the so-called "enterprise reward" and "major repair" funds.

Enterprise reward funds have to be maintained by all public enterprises in mining and manufacturing, in transport, and in telecommunication, but not in commerce, banking, and agriculture. The "enterprise reward fund" represents a claim upon total earnings in enterprises that fulfill or overfulfill the profit plan; enterprises operating on a basis of planned losses approved by government economic organs were permitted to accumulate such a fund if actual losses did not exceed the plan. As its name implies, the fund is used to finance: (a) rewards for model workers, (b) other incentive measures, (c) temporary emergency relief to needy employees, (d) employee welfare expenditures, and (e) expenditures on safety and sanitation equipment.[20]

There are no published data on the size of this fund, and there is not enough information to furnish any real clues. According to the regulations, this fund should not exceed 15 percent of the total basic wage of the industries in which it is established. Since only enterprises that have fulfilled or overfulfilled the plan are eligible, the actual size of the fund must necessarily be less than the maximum. Our estimate, consequently, is based on the assumption that the enterprise earnings retained for this purpose correspond to 10 percent of the wage bill in the public sector of mining and manufacturing, transport, and telecommunication, i.e., Y220 million.

Major repairs in Mainland China are financed out of two sources: "major repair" funds retained by the enterprise and the "operating expenditures" item of the budget. In the absence of published data, this item was computed from major repair requirements budgeted for in the Five Year Plan. (For details of the estimate see Appendix D).

(iii) Profits of Cooperative Organizations

Cooperatives were of considerable importance in retail trade as early as 1952. This was much less true of wholesale trade, industry, and even handicrafts. The large-scale integration of handicraft establishments into cooperative organizations came only several years later. Profits of cooperatives is another one of those small items which cannot be reliably estimated. It was derived from a statement in official sources indicating that, in general, a 3 percent profit rate may be considered as reasonable. Furthermore, the same sources give actual profits earned on a total turnover of Y47.5 million, i.e., on close to one per cent of the total cooperative trade volume. For cooperative industry, the private sector rate of 3.5 percent was applied on the assumption that, given the small-scale nature of cooperative establishments, private sector relationships would be more pertinent than those encountered in the government sector.

(iv) Income of Social Insurance Funds

These consist of the so-called "labor insurance" and "trade union" funds. Contributions to these funds by private and public enterprises and organs can be estimated with a fair degree of reliability from data given in official sources.

(v) Indirect Taxes

Prior to the advent of the Communist regime, the Chinese tax system was extremely complex and chaotic, consisting of a wide variety of miscellaneous taxes. Soon after assuming power, in early 1950, the new government introduced a series of reforms designed to simplify the tax structure and improve the efficiency of collection and administration.[21] However, the essential character of the old system with its dependence on indirect rather than direct taxes remained virtually unchanged.

The budget distinguishes four categories of taxes: industrial and commercial taxes, salt, agricultural, and customs duties. The largest category, industrial and commercial taxes, is a conglomeration of many different kinds of levies. In general terms, these were of three types in 1952: income, commodity, and business taxes. The figure for indirect taxes was arrived at by deducting income taxes from the industrial and commercial tax aggregate and adding the indirect village taxes.

Unfortunately, there are no data on income taxes, which are almost exclusively levied on business earnings. There was and is practically no individual income tax.

Mainland sources indicate that 35.8 percent of total private industrial profits were paid out in income taxes for the 1950-1955 period as a whole. It is interesting to note that this average rate is above the maximum rate of 30 per cent provided in the regulations. Given the special conditions of 1952, the average rate must have been even higher, possibly 50 percent. Assuming this to be the case, and applying it to business earnings as a whole, income taxes may be placed at Y475 million.

(vi) Subsidies

According to prevailing regulations and practices, subsidies were paid to state enterprises apparently out of the budget for three general purposes: (a) to cover enterprise losses, (b) for industrial manpower training, and (c) for "promotion of new techniques."

Neither the budget nor any other source available to us supplies information on the size of these highly disaggregated expenditure categories. We were, therefore, forced to omit "subsidies" from our account. This means that the public sector incomes are overstated.

(vii) Transfer Receipts

These are all transfer payments by the private sector and were discussed above, except for a new item "other transfers."

The budget includes a category labeled "other revenue," which embraces the following elements: revenues from fees, from penalty and confiscation, from public property, from people's donation, from the "Three Anti's" and "Five Anti's" movements, from warehouse clearance, from the production of "labor reform," unspent balances of government departments, and other miscellaneous revenues.[22] Each of these items, except for production in forced labor camps, represents a transfer receipt. Some of these are intra-sector transfers such as take place through the turning back of unspent balances, rental payments made by public enterprises or organs occupying public property, the sale of merchandise to public enterprises during warehouse clearance. Nearly all of the other types of revenue in this category represent transfer payments by the private and household sector, with revenues from the *wu-fan* and *san-fan* undoubtedly occupying a leading place.

Since it is not possible to determine the output of forced labor camps, we could not separate it out from the other receipts. To this extent the transfer receipts are exaggerated. The question may be raised as to why this item was not also entered in the private and household sector account. It may be recalled that in Table 3, we combined "Other Transfers" and "Statistical Discrepancy." This procedure had to be resorted to since it was not possible to ascertain what proportion of "Other Revenue" in the budget represents payments by households or private business establishments.

B. Expenditures

(i) Government Administration

This is a budget figure which covers the costs of administration of both central and local government organs exclusive of certain village government outlays. Since the agricultural surtax, village slaughter taxes, and some other locally levied indirect taxes are reserved for village administration, these enable us to estimate local outlays excluded from the budget. As is indicated in Appendix C, these amount to Y380 million, which must be added to the Y1,727 million given in the budget. Actually, total village government outlays may exceed this amount, but the excess would be financed out of the budget. At the same time, not necessarily all of the Y380 million is devoted to administrative expenditure only, some may also go into economic or cultural and social "construction." To the extent that this is the case our procedure leads to an overstatement of administrative outlays.

Administrative expenditure probably also includes the operating and administrative expenses of the state security organs, although there is very little firm evidence on how these organs are financed.

(ii) Defense

The figure in Table 4 is taken from the budget. Whether it includes all military outlays is difficult to determine. It is perfectly possible, or even probable, that some current defense costs may be defrayed through the "economic construction" or "other expenditures" items. This is particularly likely since a number of plants engaged in military production are under the jurisdiction of one of the "machine-building" ministries.

(iii) Community Services

These refer to expenditures on health, education, and culture, net of transfers and of investment outlays in these fields. The standard term for the government budget category out of which these outlays are financed is "social, cultural, and educational construction." "Social" comprises welfare and health, while education includes cultural outlays and student stipends. The latter, together with all of the welfare expenditures, represent transfer payments to the household sector.

Separation of current outlays (net of transfers) from investment is rather difficult. Although use breakdowns are published only for investments "comparable from year to year," we had to resort to them in the full recognition that they do not include all investments in community services.

(iv) Gross Public Investment

In Mainland China's planning and budgetary practice, four terms are used which, unless understood properly, can cause a great deal of confusion. The first is so-called "accumulation," which corresponds closely to our concept of net investment in fixed and working capital combined. Mainland Chinese sources give the ratio between accumulation of fixed and liquid assets for different years. This, however, cannot be used for our purposes because (a) our interest is in gross rather than net investment, (b) they define liquid asset accumulation more broadly than just inventory change, and (c) fixed capital accumulation is viewed in this context as net change in capital inventory rather than as the current stream of expenditures on investment.

The second term in need of clarification is "economic construction." This, in effect, represents total government budget allocations to economic departments and organs. A large part of this goes into financing of fixed capital investment and working capital requirements of public enterprises. In addition, "economic construction" finances enterprise losses, trial manufacture of new products, technical and operational improvements in production, industrial research and training, purchases of miscellaneous fixed assets, and the operating expenses of economic departments. It is not clear to what the last refers, possibly administrative outlays for economic departments.

"Social, cultural, and educational" construction is another confusing concept. It parallels economic construction and thus represents total budgetary allotments to these departments, including investment in the expansion of old and the construction of new social welfare, health, educational, and cultural facilities. Such investments were estimated by us above at Y320 million.

Finally, and most relevant from our point of view is "basic" or "capital construction," which refers to investment in fixed capital. This concept cuts across several of the aforementioned outlay categories, i.e., the two kinds of "construction," as well as defense, and administration. However, in studying fixed capital investment in Mainland China one is confronted by the fact that there are several different and apparently inconsistent "basic" or "capital construction" series. The first presents budgetary expenditures on "capital construction," while the others refer to "capital construction actually completed."

The meaning of the term "actually completed" is somewhat ambiguous. According to Mainland Chinese accounting practice, a distinction is made between "completed project," "uncompleted project," and "uncompleted work." "Completed project," as the term implies, is an investment project that is ready to be put to use. When part of such a project is completed, it is treated as "completed work" in an "uncompleted project." Both of these are considered as "capital construction actually completed," while "uncompleted work" is viewed as work in process and is thus considered as a liquid asset.[23]

However, as shown by the data below there are two or three different series for investment "actually completed." The first distinction that needs to be made is between "within plan" and "total" investment, with the latter encompassing investment financed by extra-budgetary sources as well as certain kinds of investment not included in the Five Year Plan or in the annual plans. But, between 1955 and 1956, the definition of "within plan" investments seems to have changed. As a result, two different figures were published for 1955, one with a coverage that is comparable with earlier years and another which is comparable only with later years.[24]

The following data will serve to illustrate the discrepancies in the different series arising from the different definitions discussed above:[25]

YEAR	EXPENDITURE ON CAPITAL CONSTRUCTION	"WITHIN PLAN" INVESTMENT		TOTAL INVESTMENT ACTUALLY COMPLETED
		COMPARABLE	NON-COMPARABLE	
		(In Millions of New Yuan)		
1952	5,013.45	3,711	––	4,550
1953	8,145.40	6,506	––	7,550
1954	9,592.38	7,498	––	8,686
1955	9,517.38	8,212	8,630	––
1956	14,874.29	––	13,986	––

Our estimates are based on the last series since they are closest to the standard definitions of investment. The divergence between these figures and the budget data are due to the inevitable time lag between a current stream of investment expenditure and its embodiment in operational fixed assets. Moreover, while the budget figures exclude the balance of reserve materials, equipment, other assets, and funds from the previous year, they include these items for next year's capital construction. Inasmuch as capital investment has been increasing every year, next year's reserve may be expected to be larger than last year's balance, so that this factor alone would tend to overstate fixed capital investment based on budget appropriations. This overstatement may be partially offset by the fact that some capital investments are financed by extra-budgetary sources (e.g., retained earnings, trade union, and workers' welfare funds).

On this basis, total investment may be placed at Y5,015 million, of which Y4,550 million, constitutes "investment actually completed," while Y465 million represents major repairs.

(v) Inventory Accumulation

Infinitely more vexing data problems arise in any attempt to throw light on inventory changes in Mainland China's economy. Inventory data are very difficult to collect and to audit satisfactorily. There is considerable danger of double counting unless very meticulous accounting is practiced. Since these preconditions were absent from China in 1952, the inventory estimates at the disposal of the statistical organs must have been of dubious validity. The problem is further compounded by the dearth of published data on inventory accumulation. For all of these reasons, no inventory investment estimate was made. As a result, it appears, in effect, under "Statistical Discrepancy."

(vi) Net Foreign Investment

During 1950 and 1955, Mainland China had a balance of payment deficit, the principal source of which has been the import surplus. This clearly was the case in 1952, as is demonstrated by the following data:

Total trade	Y6,490 million
Exports	Y2,725 million
Imports	Y3,765 million
Trade Balance	—Y1,040 million

There is no information whatever on diplomatic, tourist, and other similar expenditures in China, and corresponding outlays by Mainland Chinese abroad. In any case, these were probably small and the net balance on this account was almost certainly negligible, especially for the earlier years.

This leaves two other items of some importance to be dealt with, namely foreign debt service and remittances from abroad, i.e., one on the debit and one on the credit side of the account. In order to estimate foreign debt service, the foreign credit situation of Mainland China needs to be reviewed briefly. We know that "since the founding of the Peoples Republic of China, the Soviet government has extended to China loans amounting to Y5,294 million. Of this sum Y2,174 million was used before 1953."[26] What proportion of this latter total was drawn in 1952? Presently available evidence strongly suggests that foreign loan proceeds in 1952 were only Y167 million, and that therefore credits drawn upon prior to that year must have amounted to Y2,007 million. The 1950 Sino-Soviet loan agreement provided for a one per cent rate of interest on these credits.[27] Foreign debt service may be put then at Y20 million.

Remittances of overseas Chinese to the Mainland cannot be estimated with certainty. The bulk of these flow through Hongkong exchange banks which are in a position to make reasonably well-informed guesses concerning the total volume of such transactions. On the strength of these, C. M. Li postulates 1952 remittances to be HK$300 million.[28] According to an unpublished study by Professor Wang Po-shang, they may be estimated at US $40 million, which converted into Hongkong currency, would be somewhat less than HK$300 million.[29] Assuming that the latter figure approximates reality and converting it into yuan at the official rate of exchange prevailing in 1952 (0.427 yuan per HK$1), remittances may be placed at Y128 million.

Thus a skeleton balance of payments for 1952 shows an aggregate deficit of Y930 million, derived as follows (in millions of new yuan):

Inpayments		
Exports	2,725	
Remittances	130	
Total	2,855	
Outpayments		
Imports	3,765	
Foreign Debt Service	20	
Total	3,785	
Balance		−930

As indicated earlier, Soviet credits were around Y170 million, so that the rest of the deficit was probably financed by gold exports and drawing down of foreign exchange reserves. In the course of the *wu fan* and *san fan* movement, the regime gained access to considerable gold, foreign currency, and hidden accounts held abroad (except in the United States where they were frozen). According to one report, this campaign "netted the Peking regime considerable exchange and treasure estimated at over US $200 million."[30]

As a matter of fact, one may hypothesize that a major purpose of the movement was to augment the foreign exchange resources of the regime, and thus make it less dependent upon Soviet credit which was being rapidly depleted. From recently published evidence, it is clear that the 1950 Soviet credit of US $300 million was carried on the Soviet side as a loan of 1,200 million rubles.[31] This loan agreement was made prior to the Korean War. As a result of the war, the Chinese apparently had to draw much more rapidly upon these credits than anticipated. This very fact, combined with the determination to begin rapid expansion of industrial capacity in 1953, may have forced the regime to use Soviet credits sparingly in 1952 and to count more heavily on mobilizing foreign exchange reserves. Whatever the reasons, foreign investment was clearly negative in China in 1952.

(vii) Statistical Discrepancy

The large statistical discrepancy in the public sector account is due on the one hand, to an overstatement of incomes and, on the other, to our inability to take account of certain sizeable outlays.

The overstatement in the income account results primarily from our failure to ascertain subsidies and then to deduct them from indirect taxes. However, the bulk of the statistical discrepancy arises from the impossibility of estimating inventory accumulation.

Scientific research financed out of operating costs is another expenditure item which could not be determined. Depending, in part, upon the nature of the research, this should be viewed either as investment or as a government service. In effect, then, one may venture the guess that if the omitted items were to be included on the expenditure side and subsidies deducted on the income side, the statistical discrepancy would become negligible.

4. THE GROSS NATIONAL PRODUCT ACCOUNT (TABLE 5)

This account is derived by consolidating the private and public sector accounts in Tables 3 and 4, with transfer payments and receipts cancelling each other out. It should, however, be noted that owing to gaps in the data, the transfer items are not completely symmetrical. Thus, the counterpart of transfer receipts in the private and household sector may be found in the

Table 5

Gross National Product Account in 1952

(Millions of New Yuan)

A. **Incomes**

1.	Incomes of Farm Households	37,505
2.	Compensation of Employees and Self-Employed	16,515
3.	Rental Incomes	2,800
4.	Enterprise Earnings	
	(a) Private	1,525
	(b) Public	6,270
5.	Indirect Taxes	6,640
6.	Gross National Product at Market Prices	71,255

B. **Expenditures**

1.	Household Consumption	49,985
2.	Community Services	1,195
3.	Government Administration	2,110
4.	Defense	4,370
5.	Gross Investment	
	(a) In fixed capital	7,360
	(b) In inventories	n.a.
	(c) Net foreign investment	−930
6.	Statistical Discrepancy	7,165
7.	Gross National Expenditure at Market Prices	71,255

transfer outlays of the public sector, with one exception: public contributions to social insurance funds represent transfers within the public sector from the expenditure to the income side. At the same time, "other" public sector transfer receipts are not fully offset by the corresponding item on the expenditure side of the private sector account, since they, too, reflect in part intrasector transfers, the value of which cannot be separately estimated.

Many of the other items in this consolidated account are self-explanatory. "Compensation of employees and self-employed" includes supplementary wages and remuneration in cash and kind for the armed forces. "Private and public enterprise earnings" include contributions to the social insurance funds.

5. THE GOVERNMENT BUDGET AND THE PUBLIC SECTOR ACCOUNT

Given the broad scope of government activities in Soviet-type economies, government accounts necessarily extend beyond the boundaries of standard budgets. Thus, they serve not only as one of the principal means for plan implementation in the public sector, but also in the economy as a whole. This, in turn, is made possible by the fact that (a) large segments of the economy are nationalized, (b) principal reliance is placed upon involuntary methods of saving, (c) the budget serves as the principal vehicle for mobilizing these savings, and (d) investment is financed largely out of the budget.

In principle, Chinese Communist budgets are comprehensive, in the sense that they encompass all levels of government: central, regional, provincial, county and municipal. Apparently prior to 1953, village government fiscal operations were left outside the purview of the central government budgets. In 1953, even those were partly integrated, with the proviso that village governments could carry on some limited fiscal operations autonomously, if receipts or expenditures did not exceed 7 percent of the agricultural tax.[32]

Table 6 which presents the official budget statistics is designed to show the interrelationships and differences between these statistics and our public sector estimates. On the revenue side, non-agricultural tax figures in the public sector account are identical with those appearing in the budget, except that the former include some local slaughter and other indirect taxes which are not entered in the national budget. Also, in order to derive total indirect taxes, we estimated the business income tax portion of the industrial and commercial tax aggregate.

Our figure for earnings of enterprises is also based on the budget, except that we deducted "operating receipts" and added earnings retained by the enterprises. Moreover, we incorporated insurance revenues, which in the budget are included in foreign loans, into enterprise earnings. Foreign loan proceeds on the other hand figured in our estimate of net foreign investment. Other revenues were treated by us as public sector transfer receipts.

The economic construction budget has proved to be one of the most troublesome items. It finances fixed capital investment by the economic organs and public enterprises, contributes to the financing of inventory accumulation (with the rest financed largely by bank credit), and finances subsidies and scientific and industrial research. Unfortunately, only the capital investment component of this aggregate can be computed, while all the rest is treated in official sources as operating expenditure.

Public sector investment in fixed capital is actually financed out of three sources: the economic construction budget, the social and cultural construc-

Table 6

The 1952 Government Budget

(Millions of New Yuan)

Revenues		Expenditures	
Taxes	9,769	Economic Construction	7,626
Industrial and Commercial Taxes	6,147	Social, Cultural, and Educational Services	2,280
Salt Tax	405		
Customs Duties	481	National Defense	4,371
Agricultural Tax	2,704		
Other	32	Administration	1,727
		Servicing of Foreign and Domestic Debt	392
		Aid to Foreign Countries	
Enterprise & Operating Receipts	5,728	Other Outlays	391
Insurance and Foreign Loan Proceeds	193	Total Expenditures	16,787
Other Revenues	1,870	Surplus	773
Total	17,560	Total	17,560

Source: "Statistics on State Receipts and Expenditures During the First Five Year Plan Period," *Tsai Cheng* No. 8, (August 5, 1957).

tion budget, and the major repair fund which lies outside the scope of the budget. As shown earlier, the cost of rural and urban relief, pensions, veterans benefits, student stipends, etc., are taken care of by social and cultural construction appropriations.

National defense and administrative outlays shown in the public sector account were adopted unaltered from the budget, except that village government expenditures not encompassed in the budget were added to the latter. The national defense item as shown in the budget is probably incomplete, since both fixed capital investment and the operating expenditure portion of economic construction contain some military items.

The budget figure for foreign and domestic debt service is very puzzling. It was shown earlier that domestic and foreign debt service combined may be placed at around Y60 million. Therefore, on the basis of the available data about Y330 million of this budget item cannot be accounted for. For 1952 the joint item of "aid to other countries" and "other outlays" is, in effect, confined to the latter, since in 1952 China had not yet entered the foreign aid field.

It is evident from Table 6 that revenues exceeded expenditures, leaving a budgetary surplus. In keeping with Chinese Communist fiscal and financial practice, which was adopted from Soviet experience, these surpluses are channeled to the banking system where they become the counterpart of credit creation.[33]

6. THE STATISTICAL RELIABILITY OF THE ESTIMATES

There are two general observations which can be made about the statistical reliability of our findings: (1) as might be expected, the margin of error is undoubtedly smaller for the aggregate than for the individual items, and (2) the estimate as it stands probably errs on the side of understatement rather than overstatement. The reasons for this will be brought out below.

Before proceeding with an analysis of statistical reliability, we shall com-

	OFFICIAL MAINLAND ESTIMATES[34] (In Billions of Yuan)	OUR ESTIMATES (In Billions of Yuan)
Agriculture	36.19	30.43
Industry	11.00	14.74
Construction	1.83	1.85
Transport and Communications	2.44	3.02
Trade	9.66	5.38

pare our results with official Mainland Chinese estimates, though given the character of the latter, this can only be done for national income composition by industrial origin.

In analyzing these two series the differences in concept and sector definitions must be borne in mind. Thus, the official figures are for NNP at market prices, while ours are for GNP, at factor cost. Officially estimated depreciation allowances are probably not large so that is not likely to affect the comparison very much. On the other hand, indirect taxes are a very sizeable item.

Agricultural output, however, is valued at farm procurement prices and is, in this respect, comparable with our estimate. The difference, therefore, between the official and our figure is due to our subsuming "subsidiary occupations" under industry, while in official sources they are considered part of agricultural product. Our agricultural product thus estimated would be Y36.63 billion,[35] which even allowing for depreciation, still is quite close to the official figure. As was indicated in Section 2, owing to incomplete statistical coverage, farm production figures were undoubtedly under-reported in official sources, although the extent of understatement cannot be determined. According to official sources, gross agricultural output value increased almost by 15 per cent between 1952 and 1955.[36] Unquestionably part of this increase was statistical. On the extreme assumption that farm output in 1952 and 1955 was the same, with the 1955 statistics more reliable, total agricultural product including "subsidiary occupations" could be roughly estimated as Y42 billion (instead of Y36.6 billion) in 1952. This would mean a 7 to 8 per cent underestimate in GNP, which may be considered as the upper limit of the margin of error on this account.

If we deduct the "subsidiary" product from our industry figure it would be only Y8.54 billion as compared to Y11 billion in the official sources. Similarly, our trade estimate is significantly smaller, the difference in these two sectors combined being Y6.74 billion. Indirect taxes, the bulk of which are concentrated in industry and trade, were estimated by us at Y6.64 billion. Therefore, on a comparable basis the two sets of estimates are quite close for these sectors as well. Nevertheless, the official figure may be rather high, given the fact that it is net while ours is gross.

The transport and communications estimates may be considered as quite close, too, if we allow for the fact that (a) the official estimates exclude passenger transport and possibly all communications by "non-productive" organs, and (b) they are net of depreciation. For construction the identity of the two estimates is inevitable, since ours is based on the official figure.

In making this comparison, one must sound another note of caution: our estimates are valued at average 1952 prices while the official figures, for industry at least, are based on third quarter prices. How much this may affect the size of this component is difficult to say.

Besides the probable error in the agricultural statistics referred to above, there are many shortcomings in the other data as previously noted. Their effect upon the estimates will be examined now.

Employment and wage bill figures may be considered fairly dependable for the public sector on the one hand, and all of the modern sector on the other hand. In contrast, the data for handicraft and native small-scale trade are less reliable, while for native transport they are, at best, rough approximations. Given the difficulties of collecting data for these occupations, it is likely that employment in them is understated. This is at least partially corrected by the allowance for miscellaneous occupations in the total wage bill. What the margin of error is after the adjustment cannot be determined, but it is likely to be no more than 20 per cent, which would mean about a 4 percent error in GNP as a whole.

As shown in this chapter and Appendix C, our estimates of private business earnings and imputed rental incomes, rural and urban, are very weakly based. Except for private industry, the information for business enterprises is so scant and untrustworthy that to assess the magnitude and even the direction of the error is very difficult. With the disruptions of the *wu-fan* campaign and the uncertainties of collecting profit data from private enterprises under these conditions, the margin of error in this category must necessarily be large. However, since the size of this item is relatively small, even a 50 percent error would affect total GNP only by about 1 percent.

Rental estimates had to be approximate though the problems in this case are not purely statistical. Since all of rural rent and part of urban rent would in any case have to be imputed, the question arises of a suitable yardstick for these imputations. Urban rents actually paid were very low because of rent controls on the one hand, and serious overcrowding on the other. These rents departed more from actual scarcity relationships than perhaps any other category of prices in the economy. Our urban rent estimate is undoubtedly higher than the aggregate of actual rental money payments and imputed equivalents based on these low payments. As a matter of fact, our estimate is probably closer to something like "true" market value, as evidenced by the fact that it constitutes about the same proportion of GNP as in India and Burma.[37]

With respect to public sector incomes, the important items are, of course, government enterprise earnings and indirect taxes. The elements of uncertainty in the enterprise earnings figure arise from three sources: (a) the value of operating receipts which are included in the earnings paid into the budget, (b) the size of the "enterprise reward fund," and (c) the size of the "major repair fund." However, none of these is likely to affect the earnings figure appreciably. Our estimate of operating receipts is probably quite close to the mark, but the same cannot be said for retained earnings. Yet, this item is so small that even a 50 percent margin of error would involve only a 4 percent change in the figure for total public enterprise earnings, with negligible effect upon GNP as a whole.

As far as indirect taxes are concerned, the problematical element arises from the difficulty of determining business income taxes which must be deducted from the industrial and commercial tax total. To estimate these income taxes an uncertain percentage must be applied to an uncertain base. Assuming that the percentage was at least 35 (the average five year share for 1950-1955) and at most 75, and that the margin of error in private business earnings for the modern sector upon which income taxes were levied might be placed around 50 percent, income taxes would range from Y166 million to Y1,070 million. Indirect taxes would then range from Y6,045 million to Y6,950 million, with a margin of error between -9 and + 4 percent, and a less than one percent effect upon GNP.

As indicated earlier, one of the most serious flaws in our public sector account arises from our inability to calculate subsidies. A number of public enterprises operated at a loss, but these losses are not reflected in our accounts. These subsidies are paid out of the economic construction item of the budget, which also finances fixed capital investment, part of working capital requirements, part of major repair fund requirements, and scientific and industrial research. With fixed capital investments in economic departments estimated by us at about Y4,700 million, all other economic "construction" outlays must have been around Y2,900 million. If it is assumed that at least half of this must have gone into working capital, research, and major repairs, Y1,400-Y1,500 million would remain for subsidies, this figure probably representing an over-estimate. If subsidies were indeed, this high, public sector incomes would be overstated by about 11 percent and GNP by about 2 percent.

Totaling all of these hypothetical errors yields a margin of error in GNP ranging from about -6 to + 13 percent, with the corresponding estimates at least around Y67 billion, and at most around Y80 billion.

A measure of uncertainty also surrounds the expenditure items, the most important to be considered being retail sales, farm consumption in kind, miscellaneous services, and investment. Total retail sales are given in official sources as Y27,665 million of which Y21,027 is attributed, probably with a greater degree of accuracy, to commercial establishments. The more comprehensive figure supposedly includes farmers' trade as well, but this was probably under-reported. From both of these, group consumption and purchases of producers' goods by farm households must be deducted. These deductions can be estimated with reasonable precision, confining the error to uncertainties in the value of "non-commercial" retail sales. The extent of undervaluation resulting therefrom cannot, unfortunately, be assessed. If one assumes that non-commercial sales were understated by as much as 50 percent, the total retail sales figure in Table 3 would have to be raised by about 15 percent.

It may be recalled that farm consumption in kind was derived by deducting net farm money income from total farm product. Net farm money income was derived, in turn, from published figures for the value of farm marketings. It was not entirely clear whether the latter included agricultural taxes paid in kind. We concluded that they probably did, and that in calculating net farm money income this tax would have to be deducted. However, if the tax is not included then the net farm money figure would have to be increased by Y3.3 billion and farm consumption in kind correspondingly reduced. This would entail a 6 percent reduction in total private sector expenditure.

Our estimate of miscellaneous service expenditure must be considered as quite rough, with very little basis for assessing the probable margin of error. In this case, international comparisons are not particularly helpful since the definition of this category varies markedly from country to country.

The quality of the investment estimate may best be evaluated by considering private and public investment together. Probably a fair degree of confidence can be attached to our figure of total fixed capital investment. Of the three elements on which it is based, domestic equipment manufacture and equipment imports can be looked upon as more reliable than construction. At the same time, it should be pointed out that, since we had to treat all of the engineering industry output as final product, the equipment component of our fixed capital investment estimate is likely to be overstated. On the other hand, the construction component is more difficult to estimate, even for the statistical authorities, and particularly in agriculture. Because of the omission of mass construction projects from the published figures, construction as well as total fixed capital investment is almost certainly underestimated in our accounts.

The division between private and public investment in fixed capital is less reliable than the aggregate. Private investment cannot be estimated directly, and is derived as a residual after estimating public investment. However, as shown above, there are several series for public investment with varying definitions. The one adopted by us for reasons given there may represent an underestimate, and the budget figure, probably an overestimate, the difference between the two being about Y460 million. Moreover, the major repair estimate which we consider as part of gross investment is of a low order of reliability. If the margin of error is as much as 50 percent in the latter, and depending upon which of the aforementioned investment series are used, public investment may range between a low of Y4,780 million and a high of Y5,710 million. Private investment would then be between Y1,650 and Y2,580 million, with a margin of error ranging from -5 to +10 percent for the former, and of -30 to +10 percent for the latter.

For inventory accumulation only a partial estimate could be made. It lies probably somewhere between Y4 and Y6 billion, perhaps closer to the upper than the lower limit. This would mean a total gross investment of at least Y11.4 billion and at most Y13.4 billion, with nearly 30 percent accounted for by private investment.

Current government outlays can be computed with a comparative degree of reliability, although a small margin of error may be involved in each item. For government administration an error arises from our estimate of that part of local village expenditure which is excluded from the national budget. Our figure of Y380 million may be the upper limit of such outlays, but the margin of error on this account is likely to be small. The defense figure based on official sources is probably understated, since some defense expenditures may be hidden in other items. This would have no effect on total outlays of the public sector but would undoubtedly affect its structure. The element of uncertainty in community services arises principally from the difficulty of separating investment and current expenditures in this sphere. Our estimate of investment in community service facilities is probably too low, i.e., Y320 million. As indicated earlier, the maximum figure may have been Y430 million in which case current outlays in this field would have been 9 percent less.

On balance, apart from the problem of inventory investment, our accounts probably also minimize rather than exaggerate, aggregate national expenditure in Mainland China, with possible understatements in retail sales and fixed capital investment more than outweighing small overstatements in administration and community services.

c h a p t e r   i v

ECONOMIC IMPLICATIONS

WITH THE ACCOUNTS laid out and the GNP estimates presented in Chapter III, the problem before us now is to examine what the findings show. Specifically what do they tell us about the structure of Mainland China's economy, the pattern of its resource use, the degree of socialization, and the effect of price policies upon all of these? To what extent are our domestic price estimates internationally comparable? What methods might be most appropriate for attaining interspatial comparability? Are the currently used dollar estimates of per capita product for China and India valid? Comparisons with the situation in India and in the Soviet Union on the eve of their respective Five Year Plans, with occasional references to the United States will serve to bring these analytical implications into bolder perspective.

1. TOTAL AND PER CAPITA PRODUCT

A wide range of per capita United States dollar estimates has gained currency in recent years. Among these, the figures most generally quoted are $12 in terms of prewar prices and $27 in postwar prices as compared to about $60 in India.[1] To what extent do our results accord with these figures?

Ignoring the spuriousness of the population figures used, let us consider the validity of the national income aggregates and the methods of currency conversion on which these per capita estimates are based. The national income estimates seem to be those of Ou Pao-san, which must be considered as gross underestimates.[2] They make India's per capita product appear to be more than twice as high as that of China, a ratio that is hardly borne out by comparisons of the per capita outputs for any of the more important agricultural and industrial products in the two countries.

These dollar figures were obtained by converting the national currency estimates at official rates of exchange. How appropriate are these rates for these purposes? Economic literature is replete with protestations against the use of exchange rates, and yet until very recently this was practically the only method of conversion used, presumably on the assumption that the margin of error thus introduced is small. However, as Gilbert and Kravis have amply demonstrated,[3] and as our findings in Appendix F show, this is hardly the case.

First of all, an exchange rate, even when adjusted in terms of purchasing power equivalents, reflects price and scarcity relationships of only those goods that enter international trade. These relationships are not an adequate and faithful reflection of the domestic expenditure and product structure. *A priori* one would expect that the less important foreign trade is in relation to the national product of a given country, the more inadequate would the exchange rate be for real product comparisons. Moreover, within a general class of products, and also among general classes of products, each country tends to produce in greater quantity items which it can produce relatively more efficiently. When its output is valued at the prices of a more developed country, its high-price products are diminished in relative aggregate value, while the value of its low-priced goods is correspondingly enhanced. Since the latter loom large the effect is great. Thus, valuation of the output of country A in the prices of a more highly developed country B, indicates a larger output for country A relative to country B than does valuation in the prices of country A.

To what extent are these generalizations borne out by our estimates for China and by the official Indian national income data? To answer this question fully and rigorously would require ascertaining the exchange ratios in each economic branch for China, India and the United States on the basis of the Gilbert-Kravis method. This would constitute a task of such vast proportions that it must be deferred and made the subject of a separate study. Meanwhile, it is possible to test some of these generalizations—at least in a tentative way—by confining comparison to the agricultural sector for which detailed output and price data are more readily available than for other sectors.

One principal finding that emerges in this context is that the Indian and Chinese aggregate and per capita farm and national product figures usually quoted in United States dollar terms are grossly misleading. They yield a marked downward bias, exaggerating the product differentials between China and India on the one hand, and the United States on the other hand. For example, the gross output values of Chinese and Indian farm production apeared to be at about 43 and 30 per cent of the United States level when expressed in dollars converted at the official rates of exchange but comparisons based on Chinese, Indian and United States price weights show rather different results, as indicated by the data in Table 7. A comparison in terms of Chinese price weights shows China's agricultural output to be over 70 percent of the United States level, while with United States price weights it rises to 101 percent. A similar comparison for India shows an analagous tendency, with farm product raised to 37 percent of the United States level when weighted by Indian prices, and to 47 percent in terms of United States prices.

When the farm products of India and China are compared in terms of each other's prices, however, the relative magnitudes do not seem to be significantly altered by the system of price weights used. Thus, Indian farm product was 51 percent of the Chinese level in terms of Indian prices, and 55 percent in terms of Chinese prices. At the same time, comparisons based on official exchange rate conversions yield quite different results, with India's farm product appearing at about two-thirds of the Chinese.

Table 7

Comparison of Agricultural Production in China (1952), India, (1949/50-1951/52), and the United States, (1952)

Gross Agricultural Output Value Indices

Kind of Conversion Rate	AGGREGATE			PER CAPITA		
	Crops	Livestock	Total	Crops	Livestock	Total
China—U. S. (U. S. = 100)						
In U. S. Prices	173.0	32.5	101.3	47.3	8.9	27.7
In Chinese Prices	91.5	35.3	70.1	25.0	9.7	19.2
At the Official Exchange Rate	70.2	15.8	42.5	19.2	4.3	11.6
India—U. S. (U. S. = 100)						
In U. S. Prices	73.2	21.3	46.8	32.2	9.4	20.6
In Indian Prices	45.5	22.7	37.3	19.8	10.0	16.4
At the Official Exchange Rate	46.8	12.3	29.2	20.6	5.4	12.8
China—India (India = 100)						
In Indian Prices	208.4	146.3	195.1	129.3	90.9	121.7
In Chinese Prices	201.4	130.1	183.2	125.1	80.7	113.7
At the Official Exchange Rate	157.5	127.8	151.2	97.8	79.6	93.9

Source: Appendix F.

In effect, then, these comparisons provide, in addition to the exchange rate distortion, a classic illustration of the index number problem and its implications for the international comparability of national incomes. All of this has, obviously, a very important bearing upon Chinese and Indian per capita product estimates, as is evident from the following table:

Table 8

Per Capita U. S. Dollar Agricultural Product of
China, (1952), India, (1949/50-1951/52), and the United States, (1952)

	Crop		Livestock		Total	
	(a)	(b)	(a)	(b)	(a)	(b)
China	54.6	22.2	10.7	5.2	65.3	27.4
India	37.3	23.8	11.3	6.5	48.6	30.3
U. S.	115.5	115.5	120.3	120.3	235.8	235.8

a) In terms of their own quantity weights at purchasing power equivalents given in Appendix Table F-4.
(b) At official exchange rates.

In appraising these figures it is important to bear in mind that they refer to gross output value per capita, rather than value added. Since there are wide divergencies in the structure of American as compared to Chinese and Indian agricultural inputs, net product relationships may be quite different. Even allowing for this, it is quite evident that if per capita farm output value is in the ranges given in Table 8, the total per capita national products of China and India quoted in United Nations and other sources as $27 and $50-60 respectively must be rather wide of the mark.

Our results thus strongly support the findings of Gilbert and Kravis. However, strictly speaking, many of the conclusions drawn above apply only to crop production, as is evident from the data in Table 7. This sector, however, constitutes about 80 percent of total farm output in India and China, as compared to 50 percent in the United States. The overwhelming importance of crop production in China and India is, of course, but a reflection of a phenomenon common to all densely populated, underdeveloped areas which are compelled to maximize the yields of high energy foods per acre. As a result, livestock husbandry under these conditions is an essentially undifferentiated, and quite imperfectly specialized "side occupation" based on multi-purpose animals. The whole nature of the inputs, the organization of production, and the quality of the output differs vastly from that of a highly developed livestock industry such as is found in the United States. All of this is further complicated by the fact that in

China and India most of the livestock is slaughtered on the farm or in the village and most of the by-products are processed there, while in the United States these functions are performed by urban manufacturing and processing industries.

These vast differences in stages of development necessarily aggravate the qualitative disparity in individual products and thus create much more serious problems than any encountered in product comparisons of Europe and the United States. Moreover, the entirely dissimilar value systems of societies such as the Chinese and Indian as compared to that of the United States will inevitably yield very different taste and preference systems. Such limitations do not hinder, to the same degree, comparisons between the farm products of India and China. Yet incomparabilities are far from negligible even in the China-India case. As a result of all of the incomparabilities combined, our comparisons do not yield the nice inverse relationships between quantity and price ratios shown in the Gilbert-Kravis scatter diagrams on pages 58 to 59 of their book. Therefore, before the conversion ratios summarized in Table F-4 can be used unequivocally even for agriculture, a number of further adjustments and more refined quality breakdowns would be required.

Abstracting from these difficulties, a comparison of farm output in India and China shows that India's livestock product per capita exceeds China's by 10 to 24 percent, depending upon whether Indian or Chinese price weights are used. Exactly the opposite relationship holds for crop production, with the Chinese per capita level being 25 to 29 percent above that for India. However, with crop production of roughly equal and overwhelming importance in the two countries, Chinese per capita farm product turns out to be about 11 per cent higher than India's regardless of whether the outputs are weighted in Indian or Chinese prices. Finally, if one were to use the ratios in Table F-4 for conversion of gross national product as a whole, Chinese per capita product would be about $80 or $120 in 1952, dependent upon whether domestic or United States quantity weights were used, as compared to about $50 at official rates of exchange.

In presenting these agricultural comparisons our purpose is primarily negative, i.e., to demonstrate the inapplicability of foreign exchange rates as converters for national products as between highly developed and very poor countries; and to show that the dollar quotations generally used greatly underestimate the per capita products of countries such as China and India in relation to the United States or other industrialized areas. At the same time, these comparative calculations again serve to emphasize the need for improving the methods currently available for interspatial comparisons of national incomes.

2. THE INTERINDUSTRY COMPOSITION OF
NATIONAL PRODUCT

A. Analysis of Industrial Structure

A study of a country's national product would hardly be complete without an analysis of economic structure examined from the point of view of value added by the different branches of the economy. This assumes particular importance in the case of Communist China, because all published figures for "total output value of industry and agriculture" are based on gross sales rather than value added. Similarly, all statements concerning the relative importance of agriculture and industry are derived on this gross basis. Given the divergent value-added ratios in different sectors of the economy, this method of presentation can yield flagrantly misleading results, as shown in Table 9-A which compares the officially given ratios with those based on the estimates in Table 9.

The estimates of gross domestic product in Table 9 were obtained in two different ways. For agriculture, it was possible to determine the gross value of output and inputs. In contrast, value added in the non-farm sectors was derived from estimated factor shares. Two converging considerations governed the choice of this method for estimating value added. On the one hand, data limitations barred the use of the more conventional approach adopted in the case of agriculture. It would have been extremely difficult to compile detailed physical output data for the non-farm sectors, than to find usable average prices, and to estimate inputs. These statistical and data obstacles were reinforced by conceptual ones, revolving around the pricing and valuation problem discussed below.

As was noted before, the data presented in Table 9 are not an independent estimate of national product. Instead, they emerge from a systematic marshalling of the relevant components in our income accounts as shown in greater detail in Appendix E and Table E-1. In general terms, the wage bill data were obtained from Table 2, except for agriculture, farm handicrafts, defense, and "other." The manpower cost in defense was adopted from Table 3 and Appendix C, while the category of "other" is based on the assumption that a wide variety of miscellaneous small items that could not be specifically accounted for might constitute about 5 percent of the total wage bill.

Table 9
Wage Bill and Gross Domestic Product
By Industrial Origin, 1952

Economic Sector	Wage Bill (Millions of New Yuan)		Value Added (Millions of New Yuan)		Percent	
1. Agriculture		(27,060)ᵃ		30,430		47.1
2. Mining and Manufacturing		(10,797)ᵃ		14,737		22.8
(a) Industry	2,910		5,980		9.2	
(b) Handicraft	(7,887)ᵃ		8,757		13.6	
(1) Farm	(6,368)ᵃ		7,075		11.0	
(2) Non-Farm	1,519		1,682		2.6	
3. Construction		(1,300)ᵃ		1,850		2.9
4. Transport and Communications		1,634		3,020		4.7
(a) Modern Transport and Communications	622		1,895		3.0	
(b) Native Transport	708		788		1.2	
(c) Hauling, Porterage and Warehousing	304		337		0.5	
5. Trade		3,236		5,384		8.3
6. Modern Banking and Insurance		220		420		0.7
7. Dwelling Services		n.a.		2,800		4.3
8. Government Services		1,675		1,675		2.6
9. Defense		1,500		1,500		2.3
10. Other		2,525		2,790		4.3
Total Wage Bill		49,947				
Gross Domestic Product at Factor Cost				64,606		100.0

ᵃ Parentheses: Wage bill imputed.

Table 9A

Comparative Importance of Industrial, Handicraft, and
Agricultural Output in Communist China in 1952

	GROSS BASIS[a]	VALUE-ADDED BASIS[b]
	IN PERCENT	
Industry	32.7	13.2
Non-Farm Handicrafts	8.8	3.7
Agriculture, Forestry, Fishing, and Farm Handicrafts	58.5	83.1
Total	100.0	100.0

[a]Official figures [Cf. HHPYK, No. 17, (1956) 39].
[b]Derived from Table 9.

As far as profits and total earnings are concerned, they are a composite of agricultural "surplus value" as defined above, of private enterprise profits estimated in Appendix C, cooperative enterprise profits estimated in Appendix D, and state enterprise profits given in the government budget, with interindustry breakdowns for the latter estimated in Appendix E.

By computing value added in terms of actually established prices, the relative weight of modern factory industry, transport, and trade in the total national product is exaggerated, for reasons to be discussed below. On the supposition, also to be examined below, that wage rates and thus the labor contribution to net product is not subject to the same biases, the wage bill and total value added by industrial origin are shown separately in Table 9. One of the problems in this context was how to estimate the wage bill in agriculture in view of the modicum of wage labor since completion of the land reform. Given the fact that the year 1952 was characterized by post-reform and precollectivization small-scale family farming, we assumed that agricultural income (in money and kind combined) can really be viewed as wage income except for an unrequited surplus collected in the form of a tax in kind. This tax in kind might in turn be considered as the now nationalized land rent.

As an indicator of economic structure, the interindustry distribution of wage income is subject to certain biases of its own. It inevitably overweights the relative importance of the labor-intensive branches such as agriculture, and conversely underweights the more capital-intensive sectors such as mining, manufacturing, and transport. On the other hand, aggregate value added yields an almost opposite bias in the Chinese case, except that it overstates one of the labor-intensive sectors as well, namely trade. The "true" interindustry distribution undoubtedly lies somewhere between these two extremes.

According to the data in Table 9, the industrial structure of Mainland China exhibits all of the typical features of an underdeveloped area with agriculture contributing almost 50 percent to national product. Only about 26 percent was derived from mining, manufacturing and construction inclusive of farm handicrafts, and 15 percent exclusive of it.

A comparison of our 1952 figures with Simon Kuznets' comprehensive studies of industrial structure indicates that China falls somewhere between his two lowest categories, in terms of both the high share of agriculture and the low share of industry. The same conclusion is reached if one notes the share of transport and communications in China in relation to that of other countries.[4] At the same time, the share of trade is significantly lower than the average for any of the categories shown by Kuznets, and "other services" fall into his last group.

These findings are confirmed by a comparative analysis of the inter-industry composition of national products in China, India and the Soviet Union, shown in Table 10, on the basis of which China and India of the early fifties would seem to be much more underdeveloped than the Soviet Union was on the eve of its first Five Year Plan in 1928. At the same time, China would appear to be somewhat behind India. This seems to be the case if we measure the stage of development in terms of the agricultural contribution to national product. While upon first sight the difference between China and India may appear slight in this respect, it must be pointed out that the Indian estimates include local farm processing in agriculture; on a comparable basis the Chinese percentage would be about 58 and India's 51. This is further reinforced by the fact that, as will be indicated later, agricultural product in China may be undervalued.

Such undervaluation certainly seems to be the case in the Soviet Union, as evidenced by the differences between columns 4 and 5 in Table 10. These divergencies are a function of the standards of valuation adopted, one in terms of established Soviet prices, and the other based on Bergson's adjusted factor cost concept. The latter comes close to a wage standard, and thus may be compared with our interindustry distribution of wage income in column 1.

The data in Table 10 would also tend to indicate that the mining and manufacturing sector as a whole (including construction) may have assumed greater importance in India than in China. Thus, excluding farm handicrafts, about 16 percent of the national product was obtained from this branch of the economy in India and 15 percent in China. Granting that these differences are sufficiently small so that they may very well lie within the possible margins of error, yet one finds them borne out by comparisons of per capita physical output of major industrial products in India and China. On the other hand, given the much more rapid rate of industrial expansion in China, if one were to compare the national products of the two countries in 1957 or 1958, it would be unquestionably apparent that the gap that may have existed between the two was not only closed, but that possibly the relation was reversed.

Yet, what is particularly striking about the economic structure of both

Table 10

Composition of National Product by Industrial Origin
In China, (1952), India, (1950-51), and the Soviet Union, (1928)
(in percent)

Economic Branch	China		India	Soviet Union	
	Wage Bill	Gross Domestic Product[a]	Net Domestic Product[a]	NET NATIONAL PRODUCT At Established Prices[b]	At Adjusted Factor Cost
Agriculture, Forestry and Fishing	54.2	47.1	51.3	37.9	41.6
Mining and Manufacturing	21.6	22.8			
Modern	—	—	6.5		
Large-scale, incl. Modern	5.8	9.2		31.5	27.7
Handicrafts and small-scale	15.8	13.6	9.6		
Construction	2.6	2.9			
Transport and Communication	3.3	4.7	—	6.8	7.2
Modern	1.3	3.0	2.3	—	—
Native	2.0	1.7	14.7	—	—
Trade	6.5	8.3		6.9	5.7
Finance and Insurance	0.4	0.7	0.7	1.2	1.3
Dwelling Services	—	4.3	4.3		
Defense	3.0	2.3	4.3	15.6	16.4
Government Services	3.4	2.6			
Miscellaneous and Other	5.0	4.3	6.3		
	100.0	100.0	100.0	100.0	100.0

[a] At Factor Cost   [b] At Market Prices

Sources: Table 8 of this study.
    Government of India, Ministry of Finance, Dept. of Economic Affairs, *Final Report of the National Income Committee* (New Delhi, 1954), Table 28, p. 106.
    Hoeffding, *Soviet National Income and Product in 1928*, Table 7, p. 46.

these countries is the modesty of the industrial sector. By contrast, the relative importance of the other sectors in the three economies can be much less clearly understood or categorized in development terms. Modern transport apparently makes a much greater contribution to national product in the Soviet Union than in the other countries, yielding a pattern that conforms to one's *a priori* expectations; but almost the opposite seems to be true of trade, with this sector looming relatively larger in India than in the Soviet Union or China. Yet, this contradiction is probably more apparent than real, since the bulk of trade in the Soviet Union was, even as early as 1928, of a largely commercial character, whereas in the case of China and particularly India, individual peddlers, small traders and shopkeepers loom very large. Thus, in India and China, the comparative importance of trade is a reflection of overcrowding and disguised unemployment in this sector, owing to the lack of alternative employment opportunities. This phenomenon was not altogether absent in the Russia of 1928, but it was of much less importance.

B. Analysis of the Pricing and Valuation Problem in Relation to Industrial Structure

We have thus far examined the composition of China's national product in terms of prevailing prices. The question to which we turn now is how meaningful these prices are. Can 1952 prices for goods and factors be considered more or less rational, in the sense that they reflect the state of factor and resource endowments in relation to planners' and consumers' scale of preferences? If not, how do departures from scarcity relationships bias our estimates of industrial structure in Mainland China? With presently available methods and data we can test only the direction of price distortions, if there are any, rather than the precise extent.

In a Soviet-type economy, saving is perforce of a preponderantly involuntary character. The bulk of it is concentrated in the hands of the government, by means of both taxation and state enterprise profits, while individual, household savings play only a minor role. In effect, the tax and the price system are designed so as to become alternative, as well as mutually supplementary, avenues for a high rate of saving. This applies both to the Soviet Union and to China, although the particular measures used differ.

In the Soviet Union this function is performed largely by the turnover tax, which constitutes an important element of price in consumer goods markets. By varying the tax rates, prices can be adjusted upward (or downward as the case may be) as a means of clearing the market, keeping consumption in check, and establishing an equilibrium between the flow of money income and consumer goods availabilities. In effect, the turnover tax neutralizes or sterilizes the growth in money income generated by an expansion in employment and output, and at the same time automatically guarantees that the financial counterpart to the real resources drawn into non-consumption accrues to the government budget.[5]

The same general purpose may be served by monopoly pricing and accumulation of large excess profits by state enterprises, which then are channeled into the government budget. Within this institutional and economic context the choice between these two forms of accumulation—two forms of drawing away resources from consumption—is more or less arbitrary, and in a sense, a matter of administrative expediency.

The Chinese Communist regime has thus far placed much greater reliance than the Soviets upon the second rather than the first method of involuntary saving. The reasons for this difference are rooted in the recent Chinese past. The victory of Chinese Communism marked the end of a prolonged period of inflation, which in the years following World War II, degenerated into a hyperinflation. This was both a symptom of, as well as a factor in, the disorganization of the Mainland Chinese economy, the disruption of the whole framework of government administration, and general demoralization of both the Nationalist regime and the people as a whole. It cut very deeply not only economically, but psychologically and politically as well. It stood as a symbol of something to be feared and avoided at all costs, thus affecting the economic—and particularly price—policies of the new regime.

One of the first and highest priority objectives of the regime was to restore fiscal and monetary stability and to restore confidence in the monetary medium. In order to attain these objectives, a battery of instruments was used, of which one is of particular significance in the present context—the linkage of bank deposits, government bond obligations, and wage and salary payments to commodity basket units, termed "parity deposit," "victory bond," (the literal translation of this term from Chinese would be "people's victory commodity equivalent bond") and " wage" units respectively. For instance, "wage units" (*fen*) were based on four or five major consumer staples such as rice or some other grain, cotton cloth, vegetable oil, salt, and coal, but exact proportions and quality differed among cities.[6]

By guaranteeing the stability of consumer purchasing power as an anti-inflationary device, the government in effect, was forced to circumscribe its freedom of action in the field of price policy. Admittedly this guarantee applied only to a limited range of goods, but it is a range that looms large in the average household budget.

Yet, as indicated earlier, indirect taxes were of considerable—though diminishing importance as illustrated by the following data: [7]

	1952	1953	1954	1955	1956
Agricultural Tax as Percent of Total Government Receipts	15.4	12.5	12.5	11.2	10.3
Industrial and Commercial Taxes as Percent of Total Government Receipts	40.0	42.3	37.8	35.6	38.7
Revenue from Government Enterprises as Percent of Total Government Receipts	32.6	35.6	38.0	41.1	46.7

The increasing reliance placed upon state enterprise profits, combined with a policy of maintaining the stability of consumer goods prices, did not present a serious problem as long as output in all sectors, including agriculture, was rising rapidly, more or less keeping pace with the expansion in money income. This was the situation during the recovery period of 1949-1952. Thus, with an excellent harvest in 1952, inflationary pressures did not become serious in spite of a near-doubling in the level of government investment expenditure. However, with levels of investment continuing to rise, while farm production remained almost stationary in 1953 and 1954, inflationary pressures began to mount to a point that forced the regime to introduce rationing of some key consumer items. This has been maintained ever since. [8]

The disadvantages of this price policy have, in recent years, become increasingly recognized by Chinese Communist planners whose hands nevertheless remained tied as long as wages and other obligations were defined in terms of commodity basket units. When monetary stability and confidence in the monetary medium were restored, the regime seemed to feel that the tie could be severed between monetary obligations and real units. The parity deposit unit was first to go; it was abolished in 1952, when prices actually declined under the impact of the "Five-Anti's" campaign. The wage unit, on the other hand, was not abrogated until 1955. [9]

Against this background, the Chinese Communist planners apparently decided to use their market power for the pursuit of a price policy based on two primary considerations: (1) maintenance of price stability in consumer goods markets, and (2) imposition of very high profit margins in state industry, trade, and transport in order to attain a high rate of involuntary saving. Logically this could be accomplished in any one or a combination of three ways: (1) by the exercise of monopoly power in final markets, (2) by capturing economies gained through improvements in productive technology and in distributive efficiency without passing these on to the consumer (in a sense a sub-case of monopoly), (3) by the exercise of monopsony power in labor and in raw materials markets.

During the first few years the regime necessarily worked with an inherited price structure which it gradually shaped to its own purposes. The inherited structure already had built into it strong monopolistic and monopsonistic tendencies occasioned by transport and communications barriers and by institutionally conditioned market imperfections (e.g., the fusion of the landlord, money lending, and marketing functions). These were reinforced by the prolonged period of inflation during which the terms of trade moved strongly against agriculture.[10] While some of the old imperfections were gradually reduced, the monopolistic and monopsonistic pricing elements undoubtedly persisted, appropriated by the state for the creation of large "excess profits" as shown in Table 11.

The data in Tables 9 and E-1 clearly show that in the case of China the greatest divergence between the wage and total factor cost basis of valuation is concentrated in modern industry, transport and communications, and trade. These are the sectors in which the wage bill constitutes the smallest share of value added. This phenomenon and its possible economic implications may be brought into sharper focus by comparing the wage shares of these economic branches in China, the Soviet Union and the United States. The differences which emerge are most striking, as illustrated by the data in Table 11. Thus while wages accounted for 70 percent of industrial product in the United States, the corresponding proportions in China and Russia were only 40 to 50 percent. For the public sector of industry in China, for which, incidentally, the estimates are more reliable than for the private sector, the percentage is lower. This tendency is even more pronounced in the case of trade, if we focus our attention on the state trading sector in China. The wage share in total trade is as high only because it includes a very large number of individual, self-employed traders who earn no more than a wage or its equivalent.

Naturally these differences are affected by a certain lack of statistical and conceptual comparabilty of the estimates for the three countries; however, these incomparabilities are not likely to alter the outcome significantly. Thus, if all three sets of estimates were expressed in terms of gross product at market prices, the wage share would necessarily be smaller in every case. For the Soviet Union, where the figures refer to net product at market prices, depreciation allowances are too small to have much of an effect. For China, these sector estimates represent gross product at factor cost, i.e., unlike the Soviet Union net of indirect taxes. Indirect taxes were of approximately the same relative importance in China in 1952 and in the Soviet Union in 1928. Therefore, on a comparable basis, the divergence between the Chinese and Soviet wage shares may be expected to become more pronounced than indicated by the data in Table 11. Similarly, conversion of the United States estimates from a net product at factor cost basis undoubtedly would yield appreciably lower wage shares. This may be expected to narrow somewhat the wage share gap between the United States on the one hand and China and the Soviet Union on the other hand, but the difference would still be of significant dimensions.

What accounts for these differences? The small wage share in China and the Soviet Union is merely a symptom of a very high rate of profit, profit here being interpreted in a broad sense as including all factor returns other than labor. In part this may be due to differences in stages of development. Given the much greater relative scarcity of capital and entrepreneurship in underdeveloped areas, one would expect profit shares to be higher in countries such as China or India than in the United States. In part, however, these differences may arise from the fact that state market power is applied to buy "cheap" and sell "dear." This power can naturally

Table 11

The Comparative Wage Share of Net Product in Industry, Transport, and Trade in China, the Soviet Union and the United States (in Percent)

Economic Branch	China[a]	U.S.S.R.[d]		U.S.[f]
	1952	1928	1937	1950
Modern Industry				
Total	48.7[b]	48.7[e]	40.5[e]	70.4
Public Sector Only	39.5	n.a.	n.a.	n.a.
Modern Transport and Communications				
Total	32.8	62.9	78.4	77.7
Public Sector Only	24.0	n.a.	n.a.	n.a.
Trade				
Total	60.1[c]	26.9	19.2	65.7
Public Sector Only	24.3	n.a.	n.a.	n.a.

[a] Gross product at factor cost.
[b] Includes large-scale mining, factory and workshop industry.
[c] Includes a large number of peddlers and self-employed small traders
[d] Net product at market prices.
[e] Includes mining, manufacturing, and construction.
[f] Net product at factor cost.

Sources: Table 8 and E-1.
      Hoeffding, *Soviet National Income and Product in 1928* (New York, 1954), Appendix Table A, p. 142.
      Bergson, *Soviet National Income and Product in 1937* (New York, 1953), Appendix Table I, p. 123.

be applied only in those sectors in which the state plays an important or dominant role. If this high rate of "surplus value" is merely a function of "cheap" purchases of the labor factor in the sense that wages are kept significantly below the marginal revenue product of labor, it will have but a redistributive effect, without necessarily affecting the interindustry composition of national product at established prices. However, if monopoly

Table 12

Agricultural-Industrial Wage Ratios in Mainland China as Compared to Other Countries

Agriculture = 100

Communist China (1952)

Public Sector:	Industry	356
	Total Non-agricultural	281
Public and Private:	Total Non-agricultural	238

Industry only

India (1953)[a]	276
Japan (1954)[b]	228
Philippines (1954)[a]	227
Chile (1953)[c]	
Based on permanent agricultural workers	149
Based on temporary agricultural workers	521
Mexico (1953)[a]	379
United States (1900-1949)	157
France (1910-1948)	110
United Kingdom (1900-1945)	154

[a] Industrial wages converted to a daily basis on the assumption of 25 working days per month.

[b] Industrial wages converted from monthly to daily basis; agricultural wages are based on males only.

[c] Both industrial and agricultural wages quoted on a daily basis.

Sources:

For China all non-agricultural wage rates based on Table 2. Agricultural wage obtained from wage bill given in Table 9 and an agricultural labor force estimate derived from an official figure of 113,683,000 for the number of farm households in 1952 and a Chinese Communist estimate of 1.51 able bodied workers per household. (Fu Jung: "Increase Agricultural Production by Means of New and Higher Labor Productivity," *Cheng Chih Hsüeh Hsi*, March 13, 1956, read in translation in *ECMM*, No. 36, p. 15.)

For United States, France and United Kingdom, Procter Thomson: *The Productivity of the Human Agent in Agriculture, An International Comparison* cited in T. W. Schultz: *The Economic Organization of Agriculture*, (New York, 1953), p. 288.

For other Countries, International Labor Organization, *Yearbook of Labor Statistics 1956* (Geneva, 1956), Tables 17 and 19.

profits reflect "cheap" purchases of inputs from other sectors or "dear" sales to these sectors, then the interindustry distribution will unavoidably be distorted, with profit margins in certain economic branches inflated at the expense of the other branches.

Which of these two conditions may have prevailed in Mainland China in 1952 can be tested, at least indirectly. In most countries, agricultural productivity and wages tend to lag significantly behind those found in the non-farm sectors. Such differentials tend to be considerably wider in underdeveloped than in industrialized countries owing to much greater overcrowding in agriculture, reinforced by frictions in mobility between rural and urban areas.[11]

Table 13

1952 Agricultural and Public Sector Non-Agricultural Productivity Ratios in Mainland China

Agriculture = 100

Industry	802
Trade	1,049
Modern Transport and Communication	1,300
Banking and Insurance	781
Government Services	244
Total Non-agricultural Sector	
Public	715
Public and private	238

Sources: Tables 2, 9, and E-1

If factor and commodity markets are reasonably free, farm/non-farm wage and productivity differentials should be more or less proportional. This is actually the case for all countries for which such data are presented in Tables 12 and 14. For Mainland China, however, while wage differentials correspond roughly to those encountered in other underdeveloped areas, productivity differentials are much higher. This would strongly suggest that the relatively high productivity in the non-farm sectors of China is likely to be a function of monopsony in farm and/or monopoly in final markets, a phenomenon which also accounts for the unusually high rate of profit shown in Table 11. All of these factors combined would therefore tend to point to price distortion rather than wage exploitation, as the explanation for the high profit rates. (This of course, does not exclude the possibility that wages in agriculture as well as in the non-farm sectors may be below

Table 14

**Comparative Agricultural and Non-Agricultural Productivity
Ratios in Mainland China and Other Countries**

Agriculture = 100

Industry

Mainland China, Public Sector (1952)	802
India, Large-Scale Industry (1948/49-1950/51)	360
Japan	
1878-1927	251
1928-1942	400
Hungary, Large-Scale Industry (1920-1941)	400-450
France (1950-1954)	145-200
Italy (1950-1954)	145-200
Netherlands (1950-1954)	115
German Federal Republic (1950-1954)	125-200

Total Non-agricultural

Mainland China, Public Sector (1952)	715
India	
Total Modern Sector	380
Total Non-agricultural	261
Japan	
1878-1927	265
1928-1942	390
Hungary (1930)	245
Argentina (1953-1955)	141
Brazil (1950)	290
Mexico (1950)	544
Chile (1952)	235
Columbia (1953)	200
Honduras (1949-1951)	243
Ecuador (1950)	163
Denmark	
1870-1952	179
1953	115
Canada (1950-1952)	145
United States (1950)	185
United Kingdom (1951)	90
New Zealand (1950)	60

Sources: Mainland China: Tables 2, 9, and E-1.

India: Government of India, Ministry of Finance, Dept. of Economic Affairs. *Final Report of the National Income Committee* (New Delhi, 1954).

Japan: Kazushi Ohkawa et. al. *The Growth Rate of the Japanese Economy Since 1878* (Tokyo, 1957), Tables 8, 10 and 12, pp. 26-29.

Hungary: A. Eckstein, "National Income and Capital Formation in Hungary, 1900-1950," *Income and Wealth, Series V,* ,(London, 1955), Tables I, V and VI, p. 165, 182, 185.

Denmark: Kjeld Bjerke, "The National Product of Denmark, 1870-1952," *Income and Wealth, Series V,* (London 1955), Table II, p. 125.

France, Italy, Netherlands and German Federal Republic: United Nations, Economic Commission for Europe, *Economic Survey of Europe in 1954* (Geneva, 1955), Table 77, Ch. 7, p. 174.

All other data from United Nations, Economic Commission for Latin America, *Economic Survey of Latin America 1956* (New York, 1957), Table 110, p. 169.

their marginal revenue products, but this would not account for the high productivity differentials).

The hypothesis of marked price distortion is strongly supported by the data presented in Tables 13 and 14. It is clear from these that productivity differentials between agriculture and the public sector of industry, transport and trade are unusually large by the standards of other underdeveloped areas. (All productivity differentials, indices and ratios in these tables are based on sectoral product [value-added] estimates divided by sectoral employment figures.) The comparison with India and Japan is particularly significant in this context, with present-day India and Meiji Japan at roughly the same stage of development as China in 1952.[12] Just as with wage levels, one naturally expects such productivity differentials to be wider in underdeveloped than in industrialized countries. However, index differentials above 300 to 500 can probably be explained only in terms of monopolistic and/or monopsonistic pricing in non-agricultural sectors.

As was indicated earlier, we cannot draw unequivocal conclusions from these data as to whether these differentials are a function of underpricing in the farm market or overpricing in the non-agricultural markets. In either case, the relative weight of agriculture would be understated in the interindustry composition of national product.

3. PATTERN OF RESOURCE USE

A. Comparative Resource Use Patterns in China, India, and the Soviet Union

A number of analytically significant conclusions emerge from an examination of the data in Table 15. First of all, as one might perhaps expect, in contrast with India, Chinese and Soviet pre-plan resource use patterns were very similar. Thus the burden of non-consumption seems to be just about the same in China in 1952 and in the Soviet Union in 1928. Given the fact that by any index of development China seems to be much more backward than Russia on the eve of its first Five Year Plan, this burden weighed much more heavily upon China. At the same time we must recognize the possibility that our estimates somewhat overstate the weight of this burden, inasmuch, as is indicated below, consumers' goods may have been undervalued in China in 1952, particularly the mass consumption staples. Thus, on an adjusted factor cost basis, personal consumption in China might loom larger than shown in Table 15.

On the other hand, the Indian rate of personal consumption may be overstated since the figures for that country make no allowances for increases in working capital. As will be brought out in greater detail below, it is conceivable that inventory accumulation may have been unimportant in 1950-51, in which case the margin of error would be small. In any case there is no question that a much larger share of national product went into household consumption in India than in China. Surprisingly, however, the gross rate of investment in fixed capital was not too different in the two countries. This, of course, may be less true in later years since the Chinese rates of investment in fixed capital probably were rising at a more rapid rate than the Indian. Yet, until we have carefully worked out national income and investment estimates for both countries for different years we can not be sure of this. The contrary impression which generally prevails rests on the comparison of dissimilars, *total* investment in China (including fixed and working capital), with investment only in *fixed* capital in India. On this basis, for the last pre-plan years the rates would be about 5 to 6

Table 15

Comparative Patterns of Resource Use in China, India and the Soviet Union (in Percent)

Item	China[a] 1952	India[a] 1950-51	Soviet Union[b]			
			1928		1937	
			At established prices	At adjusted factor cost	At established prices	At adjusted factor cost
Household Consumption	70.1	(88.5)	69.4	66.3	62.9	55.7
Government Consumption						
Community Services	1.7	⎰ 3.5	4.9	5.2	9.4	10.6
Govt. Administration	3.0	⎱	2.5	2.7	2.5	3.1
Military Outlays	6.2	1.9	2.3	2.5	6.0	7.7
Gross Investment (Total)	(16.0-18.0)	n.a.	20.8	23.2	19.2	22.9
In Fixed Capital Only	10.3	9.3	(17.6)	n.a.	(13.7)	17.6

[a] Gross Domestic Product at Market Prices.

[b] Gross National Product

Sources: Table 5 of this study.
    Government of India, Ministry of Finance, Dept. of Economic Affairs, *Final Report of the National Income Committee* (New Delhi, 1954), Table 34, p. 11.
    United Nations, *Economic Survey of Asia and the Far East, 1956*, Special Table 0, p. 194.
    Hoeffding, *Soviet National Income and Product in 1928* (New York, 1954), Table 6, p. 46 and Appendix E, Bergson, *Soviet National Income and Product in 1937* (New York, 1953), Table 8, p. 75 and Appendix Table 3, pp. 136-137.

percent for India, and about 15 percent for China. These wide discrepancies reflect the high levels of investment in working capital and the lower capital consumption allowances in China.

For India, unfortunately, there are no working capital or inventory accumulation estimates for 1950-51. However, on *a priori* grounds at least, one would expect this type of investment to be considerably higher in China during this period, and probably subsequently as well. In 1950-51, and during the early years of the first Five Year Plan, Indian industrial plant was operating well below capacity, while Mainland Chinese plant was, even in 1952, and particularly toward the latter half of the year, being utilized very intensively. This was evidenced, for instance, by multi-shift operations over wide ranges of industry. At the same time, much of the new investment in fixed capital went into rehabilitation of damaged or dismantled equipment, with most of new plant construction taking place in later years. In such circumstances, the labor-capital ratio—in industry at any rate — must have been higher in China than in India, and corresponding working capital requirements per unit of fixed capital must have been higher too. Working capital requirements must have been high also for the large mass labor projects in railroad and highway construction, and in irrigation, flood control, and drainage projects for which there are no exact counterparts in India. All of this was further reinforced by the bumper harvest of 1952 in China, which prompted the government to augment significantly its central reserves and stocks.

In the final analysis, these differences in working capital investment in China and India are a function of the different patterns of planning in the two countries. Thus, under *ceteris paribus* assumptions the more rapid the rates of growth, the higher will tend to be the working capital requirements. Beyond this, fixed and working capital are substitutable within certain ranges. On the basis of all of the available evidence, the Chinese planners seem to be much more conscious of this than the Indians. One finds for instance, that practically all of the discussions in India of investment and capital requirements are confined to fixed capital, and that the Indian Five Year Plans make no explicit allowance for working capital needs. In China, the high rates of investment in working capital are a consequence of the planners' commitment to high rates of growth in the economy as a whole, while assigning highest priority to the expansion of producers' goods industries. This necessarily means that in the initial and early stages of development, when fixed capital resources are scarce, a large share of them must be channeled to the investment goods industries. As a result, the other industries, and particularly the other economic branches, are kept on a short investment ration of fixed capital. If they are to expand as well, considerable reliance must be placed upon working capital and labor-intensive methods.

One of the striking features of Table 15 is the high rate of military expenditure in China, not only as compared with India, but even with the Soviet Union in 1928. In part, this is undoubtedly due to China's involvement in the Korean War; but more fundamentally it is an expression of the much more active and aggressive foreign policy pursued by Communist China even in its early stages of development, as compared to the Soviet Union, which concentrated primarily upon internal reconstruction and development until the Nazi threat in the thirties led to a reorientation.

Actually, investment and military outlays combined seem to have been relatively the same in China in 1952 and in the Soviet Union in 1928, but as the military pressures diminished with cessation of the Korean hostilities, the Chinese could, through a process of reallocation, raise the rate of investment in fixed capital without necessarily increasing the aggregate non-consumption burden. In reality, the total was also raised in recent years to the point that it may approximate Soviet 1937 rates. At the same time, available data point to more rapid increases in fixed than in working capital investment, so that in this respect, too, the differences between the Chinese and Soviet investment patterns seem to be narrowed more and more.

B. The Valuation of Consumption and Investment

In examining the valuation problem in relation to industrial structure we found that the particular price policies pursued in Communist China tend to distort the share of the different economic branches in the national product. Is there a similar bias in the pricing of consumers' as against producers' goods which might lead to an overstatement (or understatement) of consumption or investment?

In analyzing the relationship of consumers' and producers' goods prices in 1952 it is important to reassert that up to 1953 there was no formal price control and rationing. Nonetheless, state trading organs exercised considerable price leadership, using their market power to enforce price stability for consumer necessities. This was particularly true for the staple food grains, vegetable oils, cotton cloth, and coal or some other fuel, which in varying proportions constituted the different commodity basket units, e.g., victory bond, wage, parity deposit units. On the other hand, until 1953 capital goods prices were permitted to fluctuate freely. As a result, these prices rose much more rapidly between 1949 and 1952.

Producers' goods prices may have reflected fairly accurately prevailing scarcity relationships. By the time of the Communist victory, the output of producers' goods industries had been drastically curtailed, while farm output had dropped only an estimated 25 percent below its peak levels. At the same time, reconstruction needs on the one hand, and military requirements for the Korean War on the other, imposed a very heavy demand upon the producers' goods industries. Thus, the supply-demand relationships probably favored a more rapid rise in the prices of producers' goods relative to consumers' necessities.[13] This tendency was, however, artificially accentuated by virtue of the controls exercised over consumers' goods prices. As a result, the prices of consumers' goods in general and of necessities in particular were unquestionably undervalued.[14]

Obviously we witness a rather different situation from that encountered by Bergson and his associates in the Soviet Union, where producers' goods were undervalued while consumers' goods were deliberately overpriced and the turnover tax was relied upon to establish equilibrium in consumers' goods markets.[15] As a consequence, our estimates expressed in terms of Bergson's adjusted factor cost standard would probably show a higher rate of consumption and a lower rate of investment.[16]

These conclusions are based on articles dealing with price problems and price policy in the Communist Chinese economic literature and the price indices shown in Tables 16 and 16A. The Nankai Index, initiated in

Table 16

Nankai Wholesale Price Index for Tientsin
July 1936 to June 1937 = 1

Item	1947	1949[a]	Year 1950	1951	1952[b]
Food	42,285.7	2,961.5	20,576.2	21,260.9	22,682.7
Textiles	44,308.3	3,523.9	23,749.4	28,936.8	30,067.6
Metals	56,335.4	5,132.4	32,140.1	48,827.6	57,662.1
Construction Materials	58,677.6	5,345.9	30,050.8	38,404.9	41,533.2
Fuel	54,900.4	3,765.9	20,220.7	25,855.9	25,881.1
Chemicals	114,670.7	4,307.9	28,181.6	41,959.0	42,124.6
Miscellaneous	42,966.4	3,114.4	26,354.5	33,102.1	35,561.4
Total	48,819.2	3,589.3	23,815.6	28,852.8	30,841.3

[a] Feb.-Dec.　　[b] Jan.-March.

Note: The apparently sharp dip of prices in 1949 and the relatively lower price level after 1950 as compared to 1947 is due to changes in the monetary units on the basis of which these indices are computed, rather than in the price level. Between 1947 and 1950, for instance, there were two such changes according to the above-cited source (Appendix II, p. 324). Nevertheless, the table as presented is serviceable for our purposes, pointing up the disparate price rise of investment goods and consumers goods.

Source: Nankai University, Institute of Economic Research, *Nan-kai chih-shu tsu-liao hui-pien* (Collections of Nankai Indices) (Peking, 1958).

the 1920's by the Nankai Institute of Economics, was kept up until April 1952. It was then discontinued by the Communist authorities and replaced by an aggregate wholesale price index .Given the commodity group breakdowns and the comparative reliability of the Nankai Index, it is particularly useful for our purposes.

Table 16A

Nankai Wholesale Price Indices for Tientsin
Converted to a 1950 Base

Item	1951	1952
Food	103.3	105.4
Textiles	121.8	126.5
Metals	151.9	179.4
Construction Materials	127.8	138.2
Fuel	127.8	127.9
Chemicals	148.8	149.4
Miscellaneous	125.2	134.9
Total	121.1	129.4

Source: Nankai University, Institute of Economic Research, *Nan-kai chih-shu tsu-liao hui-pien* (Collections of Nankai Indices) (Peking, 1958).

The 1947 data clearly show the price shifts resulting from the prolonged period of inflation. It is clear from these that the prices of metals, construction materials and particularly chemicals rose much more rapidly than foods and textiles, tendencies markedly accentuated after the Communist rise to power. The data in Table 16A clearly show that while food prices rose only by 5 percent between 1950 and the first quarter of 1952, metals increased by 80 percent and construction materials by almost 50 percent. Unfortunately, with the index terminating in March, corresponding data are not available for 1952 as a whole. That these discrepancies in price trends characterized 1952 as a whole, although perhaps to a lesser degree, is confirmed by Fan Jo-yi in the article cited above.

These policies were reversed by the Chinese Communist authorities in 1953 when prices of both producers' and consumers' goods began to be subjected to direct control. Whether price controls led to an over—or undervaluation of consumption during China's first Five Year Plan period can be determined only after a most careful and detailed study of price trends and changes in the price structure between 1953 and 1957. This would carry us well beyond the scope of our present study.

4. SOCIALIZATION OF THE ECONOMY

As was noted in earlier chapters of this study, the economy of the Chinese Mainland was, in 1952, still far from fully socialized. In a sense, it was a "mixed" economy in the process of transition from a state in which it was preponderantly private in character to one in which, gradually, more and more sectors were brought within the purview of nationalization. In this respect, the economy was very similar to that of the Soviet Union in 1928. Moreover, this similarity seems to have been not only one of kind, but also of degree, as the quantitative indicators in Table 17 reveal. These indicators are intended to gauge (a) the contribution made by public enterprises to total national product, (b) the weight of government in total national expenditure, and (c) the importance of public investment.

Table 17

Statistical Indicators of the Government's Role in the Stream of Economic Activity in China, India, and the Soviet Union (in Percent)

	China 1952	India 1950-51	USSR 1928
The share of government in:			
Generation of product	20.7[a]	7.6[c]	n.a.
National expenditure at market prices	19.5[b]	8.2[d]	24.5[f]
Gross capital formation	68.1[e]	27.8[e]	71.0

[a] Gross domestic product a factor cost.
[b] Gross domestic expenditure.
[c] Net domestic product at factor cost.
[d] Net national expenditure.
[e] Fixed capital only.
[f] Gross national expenditure.

Sources: Tables 4, 5, 9 and E-1 of this study.
Government of India, Ministry of Finance, Dept. of Economic Affairs, *Final Report of the National Income Committee* (New Delhi, 1954), Table 31, p. 109.
Hoeffding, *Soviet National Income and Product in 1928* (New York, 1954), Tables 1 and 2.

As of 1952, practically all of Chinese agriculture was still based upon private peasant landholding. During this year the land redistribution program was completed while state farms and collectives were as yet of negligible importance. Large segments of industry—particularly consumers' goods industries—and retail trade were in private hands. On the other hand, virtually all of transport, communications and banking were nationalized. This was for the most part also the situation in the Soviet Union in 1928.

As a matter of fact, one of the things that emerges very clearly from the comparative analysis in this chapter is that, in spite of the fact that in terms of stage of development and economic structure China of 1952 lagged considerably behind the Soviet Union on the eve of its plan era, in pattern of resource allocation and degree of socialization China closely paralleled its senior partner. Thus, while the Indian and Chinese economies exhibit roughly the same structural characteristics, by 1952 the outlines of a sovietized path of development were so indelibly imprinted upon China's Mainland economy, that in all other respects the contrast between India and China appears very sharp even at this relatively early stage.

Actually, one of the more notable features of the Indian situation is the very low degree of socialization—this in spite of a commitment to a "socialist pattern of society." At least in average terms the state plays a comparatively modest role in India's economic life, though an examination of the figures for the later plan years would undoubtedly show some growth in the importance of the public sector. Yet even for recent years the state's function is less significant than in most so-called free enterprise economies. Admittedly, this is so partly because large segments of the Indian economy are non-monetized; but, as the Chinese example amply illustrates, this need not be a barrier to socialization in one form or another. This does not mean that the government sector in India may not be of greater importance in dynamic terms than these avearges would indicate. It certainly does signify, however, that the Indian brand of socialism is an unusually mild species of the genus, much milder than the pronouncements of many Indian leaders would lead one to suspect.

Appendix A

MAINLAND CHINA'S FARM PRODUCT IN 1952

I. AGRICULTURAL PRODUCT

AGRICULTURAL PRODUCTION as defined here includes food and oil-bearing crops, plant and animal fibers, sugar crops, tea, tobacco, fruits and vegetables, and the products of livestock husbandry. The latter in particular is frequently considered a "subsidiary" or "side occupation," along with farm handicrafts and other miscellaneous sources of farm income. In effect, we have excluded the other categories of "subsidiary," in our concept of gross agricultural product. However, as may readily be seen from Table A-1, the bulk of China's agricultural product (i.e., 80 percent) is derived from crop production, while animal husbandry contributes only about 20 per cent. Close to half the total is obtained from cereals which, as in all other agrarian countries, constitutes the major food staple for men and animals.

It should be noted in this connection that the terms "grain" and "food crops" are used interchangeably in China, thus giving rise to considerable confusion. Actually "liang-shih" literally means food grain and is generally translated as grain. However, in Chinese statistical and economic usage, in contrast with colloquial practice, it always refers to food crops or food-stuffs, specifically to all the grains, soybeans, pulses and potatoes.[1]

It is interesting that the relative weight of crop versus livestock production seems to have been roughly the same in India as in Mainland China for the years from which detailed Indian national income estimates are available, i.e., 1948/49 - 1950/51.[2] On the other hand, cereals seem to occupy a less important place in India than in China, contributing only about one-third to the agricultural product, as compared to just under half in China.

The principal components of agricultural product and the inputs that were "used up" in the process of production are shown in Table A-1, and the detailed data on which these estimates are based presented in Table A-2. Subsequent sections of this appendix provide the basic documentation from which each of the figures in Table A-2 is derived.

Theoretically these tables should include an allowance for the production of fodder crops, green manure, night soil, and animal manure. However, since these are intermediate products entirely consumed within agriculture and since there are no reliable ways of calculating their output or assigning price weights to them, we decided to omit them. Similarly, on the output side, there should be a revenue item in animal husbandry for services of draft livestock in crop production, but there should then be a corresponding charge on crop output. Since these two items cancel each other out, there is no need to go through the difficult and unreliable procedure of distinguishing between feed consumption by draft animals and by other livestock. This would be of importance if we wanted to set up a separate crop and livestock account. However, even if we were interested in doing so, there would be a serious problem in allocating joint costs such as those incurred in maintenance of farm buildings and installations.

Table A-1

Mainland China's Agricultural Product Account in 1952
(Millions of New Yuan)

Output		Input	
Crops			
Food Crops:		Seeds	1,553.2
Cereals	15,748.7	Fertilizer	505.6
Pulses	480.0	Insecticides	50.0
Soybeans	1,370.9	Expenditures for	
Tubers	2,612.0	farm capital,	
Total Crops	20,211.6	plant repair, etc.	564.4
Oilbearing crops	1,135.6	Animal feeds	2,686.1
Fibers	2,423.8	Total Inputs	5,359.3
Tea	97.1		
Tobacco	257.4		
Sugar cane and beets	157.0		
Tung seed	36.7		
Vegetables and fruits	2,861.1		
Other minor crops	1,430.5		
Total Crops	28,610.8		
		Gross Value Added	30,099.2
Silkworm production	129.9		
Livestock and products			
Increment in numbers	916.6		
Meat production	4,322.5		
Animal fiber	93.9		
Misc. animal products	763.7		
Hides and skins	285.1		
Misc. minor products	336.0		
Total	6,717.8		
Total Agricultural Product	35,458.5	**Total**	35,458.5

1. Crop Production

(a) PADDY RICE, WHEAT, TUBERS, SOYBEANS, TOTAL FOOD CROPS, COTTON, JUTE AND AMBARY HEMP, CURED TOBACCO, AND SUGAR CANE AND BEETS

Data for these crops are published in "Condensed Tables of the First Five-Year Plan," *HHYP,* (September, 1955), 132-137. It should be noted that the bulk of tubers is sweet potatoes; also that the figure of 16,325,000 metric tons is rather misleading since this is not the actual potato production. In most Chinese Communist sources, potato production is given in terms of its grain equivalent. According to an article by Wang Shou, Deputy Director of the Production Bureau in the Ministry of Agriculture, on "Food Crop Production of Our Country and Its Problems" in *Ko-hsueh Tung-pao* (Science Bulletin), No. 5 (1954), 17-20, the potato-grain ratio used is 4:1. Therefore, 1952 tuber production may be estimated as 65,300,000 metric tons.

(b) CORN, MILLET AND KAOLIANG

These were derived from the above cited article of Wang Shou, in which he gives the percentage share of each of the more important crops in the food crop total. The figures for these grains can be computed from the food crop total given in the Five-Year Plan Tables cited above.

(c) OTHER FOOD CROPS

The combined production data for rice, wheat, corn, millet, kaoliang, soybeans and tubers leaves a food crop residual of 12,017,000 metric tons that is not identified in detail. Since in Chinese usage the term *liang-shih* (food crops) includes all cereals, soybeans, tubers and pulses, the residual may be assumed to include barley, oats, and other minor grains, broad beans and peas. We broke this residual down as between minor grains and pulses on the basis of the prewar ratio given by T. H. Shen, in his book *Agricultural Resources of China* (Ithaca, New York, 1951), p. 379.

(d) RAPESEED, PEANUTS AND SESAME

The official 1955 *Communique* of the State Statistical Bureau gives the 1952 production for rapeseeds and peanuts (*HHYP* [Nov., 1955], p. 84). On the other hand, an article on "Basic Conditions of Agricultural Produc-

Table A-2

Calculations of Gross 1952 Agricultural Production Value

Crop	Quantity (Q)	Price (P)	Value (PQ)
	(000's MT)	(in New Yuan/MT)	(Millions of New Yuan)
Paddy Rice	68,425[a]	108.0	7,389.9
Wheat	18,125	166.0	3,008.8
Corn	16,883	110.0	1,857.1
Millet	11,474[b]	160.0	1,835.8
Kaoliang	11,146	83.0	925.1
Pulses	(4,000)	120.0	480.0
Barley, oats and miscellaneous minor grains	(8,017)	91.3	732.0
Soybeans	9,520	144.0	1,370.9
Potatoes[c]	16,325	160.0	2,612.0
Food crops, total	163,915	—	20,211.6
Rapeseed	930	240.0	223.2
Peanuts	2,315	192.0	444.5
Sesame	525	300.0	157.5
Cottonseed	(2,610)	100.0	261.0
Other oilseeds	(260)	190.0	49.4
Oilbearing crops, total	6,640	—	1,135.6
Cotton	1,305	1,600.0	2,088.0
Jute and hemp	305	560.0	170.8
Ramie	(100)	1,400.0	140.0
Flax and other fibers	(100)	250.0	25.0
Fibers, total	1,810	—	2,423.8
Tea	82.4	1,178.0	97.1
Tobacco, cured	220.0	1,170.0	257.4
Sugar cane	7,115.0	20.0	142.3
Sugar beet	480.0	.30.7	14.7
Tung seed	(340.0)	108.0	36.7
Miscellaneous crops, total	n.a.	n.a.	548.2
Vegetables and fruits	n.a.	n.a.	2,861.1
Miscellaneous minor crops	n.a.	n.a.	1,430.5
Crops, total	—	—	28,610.8
Silkworms:			
Domesticated cocoon	62.2	1,400	87.1
Wild cocoon	61.1	700	42.8
			129.9

Table A-2 (Cont'd)

Livestock

Increase in Livestock Numbers:

Species	Number (in 1,000 heads)	Price/head (in New Yuan)	Value (Millions of New Yuan)
Pigs	9,035	45	406.6
Sheep and goats	10,054	7	70.4
Cattle	4,039	69	278.7
Horses	391	130	50.8
Donkeys	808	73	59.0
Mules	287	178	51.1
Livestock Increment Total	—	—	916.6

Meat Production	Quantity (in 1,000 MT)	Price/MT (in New Yuan)	Value (Millions of New Yuan)
Pork	4,308.7	740	3,188.4
Mutton	370.7	842	312.1
Beef	849.0	740	628.3
Chicken	172.3	851	146.6
Ducks	58.9	666	39.2
Geese	14.6	544	7.9
Meat Production total	—	—	4,322.5

Other Livestock Products

	Quantity	Price/MT (in New Yuan)	Value (Millions of New Yuan)
Pork Fat	359.10	740	265.7
Hog bristles	14.36	7,068	101.5
Wool	25.82	2,200	56.8
Goat hair	14.94	2,200	32.9
Camel hair	0.81	5,148	4.2
Feathers	12.00	1,420	17.0

	Number (in Millions)	Price/unit (in New Yuan)	Value (Millions of New Yuan)
Eggs	14,471.65	0.022	318.4
Pork casings	71.81	0.50	35.9
Sheep and goat casings	21.02	1.20	25.2
Other Livestock Products Total	—	—	857.6

Hides and skins	Number (in 1,000 Sheets)	Price/sheet (in New Yuan)	Value (Millions of New Yuan)
Sheepskins	11,064	3.60	39.8
Goatskins	9,960	2.16	21.5
Cattle hides	5,660	36.00	203.8
Other hides and skins, including furs	n.a.	n.a.	20.0
Hides and Skins Total	—	—	285.1

Table A-2 (Cont'd)

Miscellaneous minor animal products (5% of total)	n.a.	n.a.	336.0
Livestock, Total	—	—	6,717.8

Note: All figures in parentheses are estimates rather than official figures.
^a Presumably includes glutinous rice.
^b Presumably includes glutinous proso-millet.
^c These are preponderantly sweet potatoes; production and price is stated in terms of millet equivalents, i.e., 4:1.

tion Work in the Past Four Years and Future Tasks" (*HHYP* [Nov. 1954], pp. 131-135) indicates that planned 1957 production for rapeseeds, peanuts and sesame combined is 116 million piculs, supposedly 53.7 percent above the 1952 level. Calculating the 1952 production of the three oilseeds in this way, and deducting the figures for rapeseeds and peanuts, we can derive the 1952 production figure of 525,000 MT for sesame.

(e) OTHER OILSEEDS

There are no published data for 1952 cottonseed and other oilseed production. Cottonseed production was derived from the 1952 raw cotton figure on the assumption that the prewar raw cottonseed ratio would not be much altered. This ratio in turn was computed from figures given by T. H. Shen, *op. cit.,* p. 248. In the absence of sufficient information which would permit an estimate of 1952 production for other oilseeds, the prewar (1931-37) average given by Shen was used.

(f) MINOR PLANT FIBERS

Both prewar and postwar data for the minor plant fibers, such as ramie, flax and other miscellaneous species, are very scant. The ramie figure is based on scattered prewar estimates by various international and British Commonwealth agencies, and that for flax and other fibers combined, on Chinese Communist reports of flax production. According to these, the 53,000 tons of flax produced in Heilungkiang province of Manchuria in 1954 (*NCNA* Daily Bulletin No. 1176, London [November 12, 1954]), constituted an appreciably higher output than that of 1952. Taking account of this, of flax production in the other provinces of Manchuria, and of the production of other miscellaneous fibers all over China, 100,000 MT seemed to constitute a plausible guess as to the combined production total of flax and other fibers.

(g) TEA

Data for 1952 are given in SSB, *Communique* for 1955, p. 34

(h) TUNG SEED

This is derived from an estimated tung oil production—obtained from Hong Kong trade sources—of 85,000 MT. Tung seed production was calculated on the assumption of a 25 per cent extraction rate as given by Shen, *op. cit.,* p. 269, and by Ou Pao-san in his study on *China's National Income* (Shanghai, 1947).

2. Silkworm production

1952 domesticated and wild cocoon production was published in SSB, *Communique for 1955,* p. 34.

3. Livestock production

(a) INCREMENT IN LIVESTOCK NUMBERS

According to published livestock statistics, livestock numbers, badly depleted during World War II and the civil war following it, have been recovering at a rapid rate, as is illustrated by the data in Table A-3.

Since the published livestock tables do not give the exact date on which livestock censuses were taken or sample surveys made, it is not absolutely certain whether these refer to end or mid-year estimates, but all of the available indications point to the latter. This presumption is supported by an article on the "National Livestock Situation in 1956," published in *TCKTTH* (Statistical Bulletin), No. 23 (1956), and reprinted in *HHPYK,* No. 1 (1957), 88-90, which refers to a "national livestock census conducted on July 1, 1956." The figures cited in this connection are those officially released by the SSB. Comparative data given in the same article for 1955 and annual percentage increases given by livestock category for 1952 to 1955 yield the same figures as those given above. Thus, in order to derive the 1952 increment in livestock numbers, we converted these figures to an end-year basis by averaging the 1951-52 data, on the one hand, and the 1952-53 data, on the other.

(b) OUTPUT OF LIVESTOCK PRODUCTS

In contrast with livestock numbers, there are no officially published data on the output of livestock products, which had to be estimated. The data given in Table A-2 come from estimated slaughter rates, meat, hide and skin, wool, feather, casings, bristles, eggs and fat produced per head, as given in a detailed technical study of animal husbandry in China published in Shanghai in 1953.[3] The author does not indicate clearly how his data and estimated rates were obtained; they would seem to be in the nature of theoretical averages based on prevailing practice, and are probably not the result of careful sampling studies. The margin of error in these estimates may therefore be considerable.

As far as casings is concerned, each head of cattle, sheep, goat, and pig slaughtered would yield one. Pigs would produce an average of 0.2 kg of bristle and 5 kg of fat per head. In the absence of information on poultry numbers for 1949-1954, we have adopted the poultry meat, egg, and feather production data given in the book cited in footnote 3 of this Appendix on animal husbandry, these data being based apparently on information assembled prior to 1949. For this reason, all of the poultry output figures must be considered highly arbitrary.

On the basis of the 1952 livestock numbers given in Table A-3 and the estimated slaughter rates and weights given in Table A-4, the meat production figures given in Table A-2 were derived as follows:

	Livestock Numbers in 1952	Number of Livestock Slaughtered	Meat per head (Kg)	Total Meat Production (in 1000 MT)
	. . . . . (in 1000 heads)			
Pig	89,765	71,812	60	4,308.7
Cattle	56,600	5,660	150	849.0
Sheep	36,880	11,064	20	221.3
Goat	24,900	9,960	15	149.4

Table A-3

Livestock Numbers in Mainland China, 1949-1954

(In 1,000 heads)

	1949	1951	1952	1953	1954
Horses	4,875	5,730	6,130	6,512	6,939
Cattle	43,936	51,930	56,600	60,008	63,623
Donkeys	9,494	10,600	11,806	12,215	12,700
Mules	1,471	1,070	1,637	1,645	1,717
Sheep	{ 42,347	{ 51,915	36,880	{ 72,023	{ 81,304
Goats			24,900		
Pigs	57,752	78,060	89,765	96,131	101,718
Camels	—	—	285	—	—

Sources SSB, *Communique for 1955*, p. 33; number of sheep and goats were given separately for 1952 in the *First Five-Year Plan for the Development of the National Economy of the People's Republic of China* (Peking, 1955), p. 88; 1951 livestock figures were derived from the published 1952 data on the basis of percentage increases given in the State Statistical Bureau's "Communique for 1952", HHYP (Oct. 1954), 229-230 and in HHPYK, No. 1 (1957), 88-90.

Table A-4

Average Estimated 1952 Livestock Slaughter Rates
and Weights in Mainland China

	Livestock		Wool	
	PERCENT SLAUGHTERED	MEAT PRODUCED PER HEAD (KG)	PERCENT SHEARED	PRODUCED PER HEAD (KG)
Camel	—	—	95	3
Sheep	30	20	70	1
Goat	40	15	60	1
Pig	80	60	—	—
Cattle	10	150	—	—

4. Prices

Many data problems were encountered in the compilation of state farm procurement prices, which were, for the most part, culled from the Chinese Mainland provincial press. A number of newspapers carry urban wholesale price quotations for most of the important processed and unprocessed foodstuffs. Unfortunately, there is no corresponding information for prices received by the farmer, and it had to be obtained from a wide variety of scattered news items, articles, texts of speeches, administrative directives, and even "letters to the editors" columns in the newspapers.

The farm price information is usually presented in a didactic context designed to serve any one or several of the following purposes:

(1) To discourage private trading by criticizing merchants' practices, by trying to prove that prices paid by private traders are below those offered by the state trading companies.

(2) To demonstrate continuing improvement in farmer purchasing power and standard of welfare by showing that prices paid to farmers were higher, or at least no lower, than in the preceding year or some other reference period.

(3) To step up the rate and efficiency of farm procurement by criticizing local collection and marketing practices.

Contexts (1) and (2) may yield an upward bias, and context (3), a downward one. To minimize these biases, great care was exercised in the choice of price weights. Since for most commodities, and particularly the more important ones, a number of price quotations were available with a wide range between extreme values, any one or a combination of the following considerations entered into the selection of the price weights:

(1) The context within, and the purpose for, which the price was given.

(2) The desirability of giving greater weight to post-harvest prices, i.e.,

prices at which the bulk of the crop is marketed, than to prices later in the year.

(3) The desirability of giving greater weight to prices in major producing and marketing areas.

(4) The desirability of giving greater weight to average unit prices based on large bulk contracts than to isolated quotations.

On the basis of these considerations, farm prices could be found for the majority of agricultural products. For the others, only wholesale prices in small market towns or in large urban centers could be located. In the case of the small towns, the wholesale price was used as a substitute for the farm price on the assumption that the transport and trading margin between the farm and the local market center would be rather narrow. Yet unquestionably this procedure tends to overvalue those products for which it had to be used. In contrast, urban wholesale prices were used merely as a basis for deriving an imputed farm price. This was done by relating the urban wholesale price of the commodity, for which the farm price was missing, to the corresponding price of one of the important products in the same commodity group, for which a farm price was available as well. For instance, the farm prices for millet, corn, koaliang and soybeans were derived by relating their wholesale prices in Tientsin to the wheat price in the same market, and then multiplying this relative by the farm price for wheat.

Implicit in this procedure is the assumption that the trading and transport margins of these products are proportionate. This assumption may be more or less valid for wholesale trade mark-ups, but is not applicable to transport costs which are largely a function of weight and bulk. Since for cereals weight and bulk are quite similar, their absolute transport costs are about the same, but proportionately they are greater for the lower priced commodities and *vice versa*. This means that this procedure tends to overvalue those products which are expensive in terms of wheat. On the extreme assumption that the size of the marketing margin for kaoliang, corn, and soybeans is the same as for wheat, the combined value of these three grains would be overstated by about 25 percent; however, as compared to the value of aggregate cereals output, the margin of error would be only about 4 per cent. If one takes into account that this procedure yields an opposite bias in some of the other agricultural commodity groups, and that for each group the margin of error in relation to total agricultural output is small, the effect upon aggregate agricultural output value may be considered negligible. There may, however, be some distortions in the structure of the product thus estimated.

In the light of these qualifications, the price weights in Table A-2 are derived as follows:

(a) PADDY RICE

While in 1952 private traders were still theoretically free to buy and sell agricultural products at prices different from those of the state trading companies, in reality, this right was circumscribed by the market power these companies 'were able to exercise. Yet, the very presence of private traders undoubtedly tended to maintain a certain element of competition in the market, particularly in view of the fact that fierce competition was one of the means through which the state trading companies tried to drive out private traders from the agricultural scene.

Altogether 23 farm price quotations were obtained by us for paddy. These are all for the post-harvest period when prices were at a seasonal low, but also when the bulk of the purchases was made. The geographic distribution and the range of these prices are shown below:

PROVINCE	PRICE RANGE in yuan/catty	NO. OF QUOTATIONS
Kwangtung	.038-.080	9
Szechuan	.032-.058	5
Hunan	.045-.050	2
Kirin	.056	1
Kuangsi	.035-.065	2
Kiangsu	.060	1
Anhwei	.060	1
Fukien	.059-.061	2

Sources: FKJP, Nov. 8, 20, 1952.
        NFJP (Canton), July 12, August 2, 12, 27, 1952.
        HHJP (Chungking), August 18, Sept. 22, Oct. 24, 1952.
        JMJP, April 10, August 26, 1952.
        TKP, Aug. 9, Oct. 10, 1953.

To select an average or representative price from this range is difficult and inevitably involves a certain element of subjective judgment. This judgment, in turn, was based on the following considerations:

(1) The two largest rice producing provinces are Kwangtung and Szechwan. In the former, none of the purchases by state trading companies was at a price lower than Y0.050/catty or higher than Y0.060/catty. In Szechwan, state trading company purchases were at Y0.046/catty. At the same time, the general price level in Szechwan, as illustrated by a wide range of agricultural and non-farm commodities, was below that for the rest of the country.

(2) Most of the state trading company purchases in the other provinces for which we have quotations were made at around Y0.060/catty.

(3) The unweighted average of all quotations amounts to Y0.054/catty. In face of the wide scatter of price quotations even within the provinces, and in the absence of information about the quantities sold at each price, it was not possible to compute a weighted average. In view of all of these factors combined, it seemed that this last price would be most plausible and reasonable, with the resulting weight of Y108.0/metric ton as given in Table A-2.

(b) WHEAT

Just as in the case of rice, the state played a preponderant, though not yet an exclusive, role in the marketing of wheat. For instance, the state trading companies purchased 70 per cent of the total quantity of wheat marketed in June 1952. In contrast with rice, the range of price variation for wheat, seems to have been narrower as is illustrated by the following data:

PROVINCE	PRICE RANGE in yuan/catty	NO. OF QUOTATIONS
Shensi	.092-.093	22
Shantung	.090-.091	4
Kiangsu	.080-.085	3
Anhwei	.073	1
Hupei	.070-.080	2
Fukien	.082-.085	3
Kwangtung	.070	1
Kansu	.065	1

Sources: CCJP (Wuhan), June 15, 1952; Ch'un-chung Jih-pao (Sian), June 9, Sept. 26, 1952; CFJP (Shanghai), June 15, July 8, 1952; NFJP (Canton), April 19, 1952; Foochow Jih-pao, July 19, 1952; JMJP, July 23, Aug. 2, 1952.

Using prewar quantity weights based on 1931-37 production data broken down by provinces as given by Shen (Appendix Table 2), we computed a weighted average price for the provinces for which we have quotations. In terms of prewar relationships, just about half of the total wheat crop was grown in these areas. Considering that the range of quotations was not very wide, and that it was possible to calculate a weighted average, the wheat price used in Table A-2 is probably fairly representative.

(c) MILLET, CORN AND KAOLIANG

In the newspapers and publications available to us, we could find no farm price quotations for these cereals. However the *Hopei Jih-pao* (Paoting) for May to November 1951 gives weekly prices for these commodities and for wheat in Paoting, Peking, Tientsin, and four small market centers in Hopei. For Tientsin, we have also 1952 quotations, but only for wheat and millet. The sources used were *TTJP* and *CPJP*. On this basis, the 1952 farm price for millet, corn and kaoliang was estimated by calculating the 1951 and 1952 price ratio of these to wheat in Tientsin, and then applying this ratio to the average farm wheat price as derived above. It should be noted that the millet price thus arrived at is for unhusked millet. While it is not absolutely certain whether the production figure refers to the husked or unhusked grain, the available evidence would suggest that we are justified in assuming that it is unhusked.

(d) BARLEY, OATS, BUCKWHEAT AND OTHER MISCELLANEOUS GRAIN

Also in this case, the farm price had to be derived indirectly. For July 1951, barley and wheat prices were available for five small market centers in North Kiangsu, i.e., Yang-chou, Tai-chou, Nan-tung, Hwai-yin, and Yen-cheng. (Source: *SPJP*, July 8, 1951.) For January to May, 1951, and January 1952, one can find Yang-chou prices. (Source: *SPJP,* June 30, 1952.) In these three periods in different places one obtains a barley-wheat ratio of about 60:100, 67:100, and 55:100, respectively. Since this group includes a number of coarse grains of lower quality than barley, the lowest ratio was applied to our farm price for wheat. For pulses we used the price ratio between millet and Kalgan broad bean in the Tientsin wholesale market; the price of the latter being about 75 percent of the former. The sources used were the 1951 and 1952 issues of the *TTJP* and the *CPJP*.

(e) SOYBEANS

The farm price for soybeans was calculated by applying the soybean-millet price ratio in Tientsin to the farm price for millet as derived above. For this purpose, price quotations were available for millet and soybeans for most months in 1951 and 1952. The sources used were the *CPJP* and the *TTJP*. From these it appears that in Tientsin the wholesale price for soybeans was 10 percent below the millet price.

(f) SWEET POTATOES

As was indicated in the crop production notes above, the quantity figures are expressed in terms of millet equivalents, the conversion ratio being 4:1. Thus the farm price for millet was considered as applicable to the quantity given in Table A-2

(g) RAPESEED

The price information obtained for this oilseed is rather inconclusive. Altogether nine farm price quotations were assembled for Anhwei, Shanghai and Kiangsu.

Kiangsu	.1140	yuan/catty
Shanghai	.1235	yuan/catty
Anhwei		
March 1951	.1700	yuan/catty
May 1951	.0795-.0848	yuan/catty
July 1951	.1000-.1374	yuan/catty

Sources: *HWJP* (Shanghai), May 30, June 7, 1952.
Wan-pei Jih-pao (Ho-fei), May 23, July 12, 1951.

The information given does not permit the assignment of relative weights to these different prices; for this reason the prewar wheat-rapeseed relative of 100:145 emerging from prices used by Ou Pao-san was adopted. As may be readily seen, this price of .12 yuan/catty falls within the range of quotations given above.

(h) PEANUTS

Farm price quotations could be found for two provinces only, Szechwan and Kwangtung. These ranged between .045 and .055 yuan/catty in the first case (*HHJP*, Nov. 11, 1952), and .09-.12 in the second case (*NFJP*, Aug. 27, 1952). In the face of such a wide range in the data, it seemed most appropriate to base the farm price for peanuts on the Tientsin millet-peanut wholesale price ratio multiplied by the farm price for wheat. The .096 yuan/catty that emerges from such a calculation tends to be supported by a press statement to the effect that "100 catties of peanuts could exchange for 125 catties of millet." (Source: *CPJP*, Oct. 7, 1951.) On this latter basis, the peanut price would be Y0.10/catty.

(i) SESAME

The *Honan Jih-pao* for April 1, 1951, published in the province with the largest production of sesame, reported that the price of sesame ranged from one and a half to more than twice that of wheat. This is supported by November 19, 1950 to October 1951 wholesale market quotations for Kaifeng, which ranged from 0.1020 to 0.1085Y/catty for wheat, and from

0.1652 to 0.2782Y/catty for sesame. One of the most striking things about these price data is that the price of wheat, being closely controlled by open market operations of the state trading companies, remained quite stable during the crop year, while sesame exhibited wide seasonal fluctuations. Our price is based on the post-harvest relation between wheat and sesame of 1:1.8.

(i) COTTONSEED

The farm price for cottonseed had to be arrived at very indirectly. This was done by first calculating the cottonseed oil-peanut oil and cotton-seed oil-rapeseed oil ratios in Shanghai on the basis of mid-month whole-sale price quotations for February, August, October, and November, 1952. Then the oil extraction rates for cottonseed, peanut and rapeseed were compared. Finally, the farm price for a metric ton of cottonseed was calculated, based on peanuts and on rapeseed separately. Thus: (price of cottonseed oil/price of peanut oil) x (cottonseed extraction rate/peanut extraction rate) x (Farm price for peanut) = 90% x 60% x 192 = Y103.68 per metric ton. Repeating the same procedure for rapeseed yields the following result: 96.4 x 43 x 240 = Y99.4 per MT. The price used in Table A-2 represents an average of these two (Y101.5/MT) rounded to Y100.0/MT.

(k) OTHER OILSEEDS

The farm price for other oilseeds is based on the 1951 hempseed-sesame wholesale price ratio in Tientsin (source: *CPJP*) applied to the farm price of sesame as derived above.

(l) COTTON

From its very inception the Chinese Communist regime devoted a great deal of attention to the production and market regulation of cotton. Up to 1953, strenuous efforts were made to encourage the expansion of raw cotton acreage and output. With this object in mind, in March 1952, the government announced the following grain exchange equivalents for 1 catty of medium grade lint cotton of ⅞ inch staple length:

REGION	NO. OF CATTIES OF GRAIN FOR 1 CATTY OF COTTON
Hopei, Pingyuan, Shantung	8-9 millet
Central Shansi	8.5-9.5 millet
Southern Shansi, Shensi, Honan	7.5-8.5 wheat
Hupei, Kiangsi, Hunan	8-9 rice ("chung-shu mi")
Kiangsu, Anhwei, Chekiang	8-9 rice ("chung-shan mi")

Source: JMST (People's Handbook), 1952, p. 296.

Later in the year (i.e., in August), the government announced the following purchase prices for the new cotton in the different market centers:

REGION	PRICE RANGE (yuan/catty)	SOURCE	NO. OF MARKET CENTERS QUOTED
North China	.805- .860	(JMJP, Aug. 4, 1952)	8
Central-South	.740- .850	(CCJP, Aug. 10, 1952)	12
East China	.825- .920	(CFJP, Aug. 10, 1952)	19
South-West	.878-1.025	(HHJP, Aug. 16, 1952)	8
North-West	.795- .805	(CCJP, Aug. 3, 1952)	4

In the light of all these quotations, and paying particular attention to the prices in the small market towns in the major cotton-producing areas, and, at the same time, taking account of the grain-cotton exchange ratios given above, we took a farm price of Y.80/catty to be most reasonable for cotton.

(m) JUTE AND AMBARY HEMP

The *Hopei Jih-pao* of September 6, 1951 gives the price of medium grade jute as equivalent to 3.5 catties of financial millet, such millet being valued at Y0.095/catty according to the July 15 issue of the same paper. Applying this ratio to our 1952 farm price for millet yields the jute price used in Table A-2.

(n) RAMIE

The *HHJP* of August 20, 1952 gives a native jute price for the South-West of Y0.19/catty and of Y0.50/catty for white fiber (ramie). Applying this 0.19:0.50 ratio to the national jute price calculated above yields a ramie price of Y0.70/catty.

(o) OTHER FIBERS

The *TPJP* (Mukden) of July 31, 1950 indicated that the state trading company purchased special grades of flax on the basis of a flax-soybean exchange ratio of 2:1. Assuming that this ratio remained unchanged and using the farm price of soybeans given in Table A-2, the 1952 flax price would be Y0.144/catty. Since the original quotation referred to special grades of flax, this price was reduced to Y0.125/catty.

(p) TEA

The available farm price information is very scattered and fragmentary, and is further complicated by the many varieties of tea. Quotations range from Y.19/catty for Grade C white tea in Hupei (*CCJP*, Sept. 6, 1952) to 1.3/catty for very high quality tea quoted in Shanghai (*CFJP*, May 22, 1952). The price used in Table A-2 is computed from the average collection price for the whole 1952 spring tea crop of Y0.589/catty, given in the September 14, 1953 issue of the Hong Kong *TKP*.

(q) TOBACCO

The price used in Table A-2 is based on Hsuchang VI (Honan) tobacco which was assumed to be the national standard because it is the brand and grade most commonly quoted. However, for this grade we have only 1952 urban wholesale prices for Tientsin (Y1.04/catty on February 17 and Y0.985/catty on April 20 from *CPJP*, Feb. 17, 1952 and April 20, 1952) and Shanghai (Y1.085/catty in January to March and Y1.020/catty from April to December). But we do have official farm purchase prices for October 1951 in Shansi (*Shansi Jih-pao*, Oct. 31, 1951); these Shansi prices are for the following six grades:

Grade 1	for high grade cigarettes	.61 yuan/catty
2		.56 "
3	for medium grade cigarettes	.51 "
4		.46 "
5	for low grade cigarettes	.38 "
6		.29 "

The same source indicates that the two top grades correspond to Hsuchang VI. We took an average of these as our farm price for tobacco.

This is, of course, only a late 1951 price, but it is evident from the urban wholesale quotations that tobacco prices have not changed appreciably between 1951 and 1952.

(r) SUGAR CANE

Farm price information for sugar cane is very difficult to come by. According to a news item in the *HHJP* of September 14, 1952, the prevailing price for sugar cane was Y0.01/catty in 1951. In the absence of other information this single price had to be used. It should be added that it is eminently plausible in terms of prewar price relationships, as is illustrated by the prices used in Ou Pao-san's study. According to this source, the sugar cane price was 11.4 percent of the wheat price, which on the basis of the 1952 farm price for wheat, would amount to Y0.0095/catty.

(s) SUGAR BEET

The 1952 farm price for sugar beets was derived from the following information:

(1) The official 1950 purchase price in Manchuria, practically the only region in which sugar beets are grown on any significant scale, was based on an exchange ratio of 1 ton of sugar beets to 1.42 *shih* (volume) of soybean. (*TPJP*, July 31, 1950.)

(2) *1 shih* of soybeans weighs 400 catties (*TPJP*, September 6, 1950*).*

(3) Soybean wholesale price in the city of Kirin was Y0.425/catty (Northeast currency), or Y0.045/catty. The source for price is *TPJP*, July 31, 1951; for rate of conversion, *Jen-min Shou-ts'e* (People's Handbook) for 1952, p. 276.

(4) The Tientsin wholesale price of soybeans rose by 20 percent between the last quarter of 1950 and the last quarter of 1952. In the absence of corresponding information for Kirin, we have assumed that price trends there followed the national trend, so that the 1952 wholesale price of soybeans in Kirin would be Y0.045 x 1.20 equals Y0.054. On this basis, then, the 1952 price for sugar beets may be estimated as 400 x 1.42 x .054 or Y30.672 per MT.

(t) TUNG SEED

Owing to lack of any current price information, we adopted the wheat-tung seed price ratio used by Ou Pao-san in his prewar estimates as a basis for arriving at the 1952 price.

(u) FRUITS AND VEGETABLES

There are no comprehensive national data for fruit and vegetable production either prewar, postwar, or Communist. There are some statistics for a few provinces, for the prewar period, and there are some scattered data for some of the Communist years. From these it would be very difficult, if not impossible, to reconstruct P and Q for individual varieties of fruit and vegetable. Even if it were possible, the margin of error would undoubtedly be so large that one could not justify the energy and labor expended. There was no choice left but to make a rather rough estimate of gross output value based on the following considerations:

(1)   Both Ou Pao-san and T. C. Liu supply figures for fruit and vegetable production. They both calculated total output of fruits and vegetables in physical terms, using somewhat different methods. Then they applied average price weights to these quantities. Of the two, Liu's estimate seems to be more comprehensive and more carefully done (CF. T. C. Liu, *China's National Income, 1931-36,* 24-26), and was therefore adopted as a basis for our computations.

(2)   While Liu's fruit and vegetable estimates may be better, crop output values (excluding fruits and vegetables) given by Ou seem the more thorough of the two. We proceeded to relate the former to the latter, obtaining an output figure for fruits and vegetables close to 14 percent of gross crop output value (exclusive of fruits and vegetables) in 1933.

(3)   We assumed that this percentage would be reduced for recent years, since there was a sharp decrease in fruit production during the war and civil war. On this basis, it was concluded that 10 percent of total crop value (including fruits and vegetables) may be a more reasonable ratio for 1952.

(v) OTHER CROPS

Buck's land use survey shows that 3.0 percent of the total area cropped in the thirties was in opium, flowers, and other ornamental crops as well as certain by-products used for fuel, not included in our crop total (J. L. Buck, *Land Utilization in China,* II, Table 2, 178). Taking account of this, and of the fact that there is a wide variety of minor crops that were not included in our table, we considered it reasonable to allow 5 percent of gross crop value for this whole category.

(w) SILK COCOONS

The fresh silk cocoon price used in our table was based on the following schedule of 1952 purchase prices (*CFJP,* May 24, 1952) for improved spring cocoons for East China (standard reeling equivalent 250-260 catties in Y1.0/picul):

Grade	Reeling· Equivalent[a]	Chekiang	S. Kiangsu	N. Kiangsu	Shantung	Anhwei
				(in yuan/catty)		
Special	280	.0095	.0095	.0092	—	—
1	300	.0089	.0089	.0086	.0083	.0083
2	320	.0083	.0083	.0080	.0077	.0077
3	340	.0078	.0078	.0075	.0071	.0072
4	360	.0074	.0074	.0071	.0065	.0068
5	380	.0070	.0070	.0067	.0060	.0064
6	400	.0066	.0066	.0063	.0055	.0060

[a] Reeling equivalent refers to the number of catties of fresh cocoons required to produce 1 picul of raw silk.

The most important province for cocoon production is Chekiang, contributing about one-third to the country's total in 1952. Of the total cocoons purchased in this province in 1952, about 85 percent were in Grades 1 to 6 (*JMJP,* July 24, 1953). The unweighted average of the prices given above for Chekiang would be about Y7.67/picul. It is however, evident that the price in Chekiang is higher than in· the other provinces; this is particularly true if one takes account of prices in Southwest China. For this reason, we used Y7.0/picul as the national average.

There are no price data for wild cocoons, but some scattered information would tend to indicate that they were sold at roughly half the fresh cocoon price level.

(x) LIVE PIGS

The 1952 prices paid to farmers for live pigs varied widely depending upon quality and weight. The four quotations available to us indicate a range from Y31.5 to Y51.5 per pig. In addition, it was possible to locate 12 quotations given in terms of catty of live weight; these varied from Y0.17 to Y0.35. Various studies of animal husbandry in China indicate that 180 catties represents a reasonable estimate of average weight for pigs. Our price information shows that for pigs of this weight Y0.25/catty seems to be a representative price. Thus, the price given in Table A-2 is based on 180 x .25 equals Y45.0, (Sources: *JMJP,* April 2, 1952; *NFJP,* April 29, 1952; *HWJP,* May 29, 30, July 7, 1952; *HHJP,* September 14, 1952).

(y) LIVE CATTLE

Altogether six quotations could be unearthed for this category of livestock: three for oxen, ranging from Y49.0 to Y140.0; one for a cow at Y60.0, one for a buffalo at Y35.0, and one for a calf at Y30.0. In the face of such variation, our price is based on Ou Pao-san's live pig-ox and live pig-buffalo relative, assuming that buffalos comprise 26 percent of the cattle stock. This assumption is, in turn, based upon the data given in the volume on animal husbandry cited earlier. (Sources: *JMJP,* April 10, 1952; *CCJP,* October 31, November 13, 1952; *CPJP,* September 10, 1951; *HHJP,* October 8, 1952.)

(z) SHEEP

We have five quotations ranging from Y5.4 to Y11.8 per head. One of these represents an average price of a sale of 4,000 sheep in Shansi (*JMJP,*

August 27, 1952). This is the price adopted by us. It is incidentally a figure that is quite close to Ou Pao-san's live pig-sheep price relative, i.e., 7.0 vs 7.4.

(aa) HORSES, DONKEYS AND MULES

The price information for these is particularly scanty. We have a single quotation for horses and none for the others. For this reason the prices used in Table A-2 are based on Ou Pao-san's price relatives applied to our live pig price. It should be pointed out that all these prices which are based on Ou Pao-san's price relatives are probably overstated, since most of the increase in livestock inventory would be made up of young animals of lower value than the average. This may be counterbalanced to the extent of the increment derived from superior livestock imported for breeding purposes.

(bb) MEAT PRICES

(1) Pork — These are based on average January to December, mid-month live pig per catty and fresh pork per catty ratios in Shanghai applied to farm price per live catty as estimated above. (Source: *HWJP*, 1952.)

(2) Beef — On the basis of the Tientsin beef-pork retail price relationship, we have assumed that the beef price is the same as that for pork.

(3) Lamb — Only retail price quotations could be found. The farm price was therefore estimated by applying the Tientsin mid-month pork-mutton retail price ratio for January to December, 1952 to the farm price of pork as calculated above.

(cc) POULTRY

This is derived by the same method used for lamb except that Shanghai wholesale prices were used for chickens, ducks and geese. (Source: *HWJP*, 1952.)

(dd) WOOL

We have about ten price quotations for different grades of wool ranging from Y1.08 per catty to Y1.51 per catty. The price adopted by us is based on the following considerations:

(1) The grazing tax which is levied on wool in Tsinghai province was accounted for at Y1.3/catty in 1952 *(CCJP*, December 16, 1952).

(2)   The wholesale price for Ho-hsi wool, which is of lower quality than Tsinghai wool, was quoted in Paotow at Y1.15/catty *(CCJP,* July 18, 1952). Thus the farm price must have been somewhat lower.

(3)   In Tientsin there was a 20 percent wholesale price differential between Tsinghai wool and Ying-tse wool, the latter being the lowest quality wool purchased.

In the light of this evidence, a price of Y1.1 per catty for the average farm purchase price of all grades of wool seemed most reasonable.

(ee) CAMEL HAIR

Based on the Tientsin camel hair-wool wholesale price ratio, the price of camel hair seems to have been 2.35 times that of wool *(TTJP,* 1952).

(ff) HOG BRISTLES

The price adopted by us is based on the value at which 360 tons (720,000 catties) of hog bristles were purchased in late 1951 by the state trading organs in Hopei *(HPJP,* October 30, 1951). This general price range of Y3.534/catty seems to be borne out by the Shanghai wholesale price quotations for 1952, which average Y5.063 per catty. With proper allowance for trading and transport margins, the price used in Table A-2 does not seem unreasonable.

(gg) LARD

There is very little information on lard prices. Only Shanghai retail quotations for June to December, 1952, could be found *(HWJP,* 1952). Comparing these to corresponding pork prices, the ratio thus computed was applied to the farm price of pork.

(hh) EGGS

Egg prices used in Table A-2 are based on an item in *JMJP* of April 25, 1952, indicating that "this year (i.e., 1952) the price of 16.6 eggs equals the price of 1 catty of pork." From this we derived an egg price on the basis of our farm price for pork. In this same source there is a reference to Y0.018-0.020 per egg being paid by peddlers in the villages. However, prices in this type of transaction were probably below what might be considered as the national average.

(ii) CASINGS

Hog casings were priced between Y0.50 and Y0.60 in the producing areas, according to the *HPJP* of October 20, 1951. The average 1952 wholesale price in Tientsin was Y0.70. This seems to be roughly six times the average wheat wholesale price. Applying this ratio to the farm price for wheat, a 1952 price of Y0.50 for hog casings would emerge.

The average 1952 wholesale price for medium-grade sheep and goat casings in Tientsin was Y1.68 (*CPJP,* January-April 1952, and *TTJP* for October-November, 1952). This, related to the Tientsin price and the farm price for hog casings, yields the figure used in Table A-2.

(ii) FEATHERS

The wholesale price of duck and goose feathers in Shanghai was quoted as Y.98 and Y1.331 per catty respectively (*CFJP,* January-June 1952). Given the much larger number of ducks than geese, one could estimate the weighted average price of feathers in Shanghai as Y1.0/catty. Comparing this with the Shanghai wholesale price and the farm price of pork, we calculated the farm price of feathers as Y.71/catty.

(kk) HIDES AND SKINS

(1) Cowhide—The average Tientsin wholesale price for two kinds of cowhide (Dry, South and Dry, North) for February-April, 1952 was Y1.65/catty (CPJP, 1952). This is roughly the same as the average Tientsin wholesale price of sheep casings. On this basis, the farm price for cowhide would accordingly be the same, i.e., Y1.2/catty. The previously cited book on animal husbandry in China gives the average weight of cowhide sheets as 30 catties. The computed farm price of a sheet would thus be Y36.0.

(2) Sheepskin—The average Tientsin wholesale price for a sheet of sheepskin was between Y5.0 and Y5.5 Taking the lower figure and relating it to the price of a cowhide sheet, we can calculate the farm price for sheepskin.

(3) Goatskin—The same newspapers give the average Tientsin wholesale price for goatskin as Y2.9. From this the farm price can be derived by the same method as for sheepskins. (Sources: *CPJP,* January-April 1952; *TTJP,* October-November, 1952).

(4) Other—This is a purely arbitrary estimate designed to take account of all the other types of animal hides, skins, and furs used.

(II) MISCELLANEOUS MINOR LIVESTOCK PRODUCTS

Just as in the case of crops, an arbitrary allowance was made for a wide variety of livestock products that could not be individually accounted for. For this purpose, 5 per cent was added to the livestock total.

5. Inputs

(a) FERTILIZER

According to published reports 300,000 tons of chemical and 2,000,000 tons of cake fertilizer valued at Y406.12 million were distributed in 1952. *(HHYP,* No. 2 [1954] p. 162.) A later issue of the same journal gives a figure of 290,000 for the former and 2,600,000 for the latter. *(HHYP,* No. 101 (1954), p. 231). Still other sources give 330,000 tons for chemical fertilizer consumption.

It was possible to obtain scattered price quotations both for chemical fertilizer and for cake. Nine quotations available for the former indicate a range of Y0.17 to Y0.27 per catty, while five quotations for the latter exhibit a range of Y0.061 to Y0.090. One of the nine prices for chemical fertilizers derived from a large transaction, indicates a unit value of Y0.183 per catty or Y366.0 per metric ton. Similar considerations suggest Y0.074 per catty or Y148.0 per metric ton as most reasonable for cake fertilizer.

On the basis of these prices, 2,000,000 tons of cake and 330,000 tons of chemical fertilizer would be valued at Y405.8 million, i.e., almost the same figure as that given in the original source. Applying these prices to the larger quantities (i.e., 2,600,000 and 330,000) would give us a fertilizer input figure of Y565.6 million. Our inclination is to adopt this higher figure, partly because it is based on later information— it was pointed out in Chapter III that statistical accounting and reporting were improving constantly — and partly because cake distributed may be less than cake consumed. Some locally processed cake may not have entered processing channels and thus would not be accounted for.

(b) SEED

The total value of seed required for 1952 crop production may be estimated as Y1,553.2 million. This figure was arrived at by first calculating seed requirement per unit of land area based on prewar data given in T. H. Shen's *Agricultural Resources of China,* Appendix Tables 3 and 4, pp. 376-379. This seed factor was then applied to the 1952 crop acreage figures given in the publication on the Five-Year Plan and in Wang Shou's article in the *Science Bulletin.*[4] The values were then obtained on the basis of the farm prices for the different crops given in Table A-2, except in the case of jute seed which was not given there. The details of this calculation are presented in Table A-5.

Table A-5
Seed Required in Mainland China's Crop Production in 1952

	Area Planted in 1952 (1,000 ha.)	Seed Required (Kg./ha.)	Total Seed Requirement (1,000 MT)	Price (Y/MT)	Value (Y million)
Rice (including glutinous rice)	28,382	74.5	2,114.0	108.0	228.3
Wheat	24,780	105.0	2,602.0	166.0	431.9
Corn	12,770[a]	70.0	894.0	110.0	98.3
Millet (including proso millet)	9,920[a]	36.0	357.0	160.0	57.1
Kaoliang	9,550[a]	55.0	525.0	83.0	43.6
Minor grains	10,930[a]	105.0[c]	1,148.0	91.3	104.8
Pulses	7,280[a]	98.0[d]	713.0	120.0	85.6
Soybeans	11,679	105.0	1,226.0	144.0	176.5
Potatoes	8,688	480.0	4,170.0	40.0[e]	166.8
Rapeseed	1,863	31.2	58.0	240.0	13.9
Peanuts	1,804	90.0	162.0	192.0	31.1
Sesame	931[b]	35.2	33.0	300.0	9.9
Cotton	5,576	42.8	239.0	100.0	23.9
Jute	158	15.0	2.4	1,600.0[f]	3.8
Total	134,311[g]				1,475.5
Other crop seed requirement unaccounted for (5 percent of total)					77.7
Adjusted Total					1,553.2

Notes and Sources:

All data on cropped area from SSB, *Communique for 1955,* p. 30, unless otherwise specified below.

[a] "Miscellaneous food crops" have an acreage of 50,450,000 hectares according to *Communique for 1955,* of which the cropped area for corn, millet, and kaoliang can be derived on the basis of the percentages given in Wang Shou's article in *Ke-hsueh T'ung-pao,* (1954), 17-20. The residual, 18,210,000 hectares, are divided between minor grains and pulses at the ratio of 6:4. (This ratio is based on the prewar data given by T. H. Shen, *Agricultural Resources of China,* (Ithaca, N.Y., 1951).

[b] Derived by dividing the average yield per hectare for the period 1931-37 and for 1946 and 1947 into the estimated 1952 production. (Shen, op. cit., pp. 248-249.)

[c] Barley is used as a representative of this group.
[d] Average of broadbeans and field peas.
[e] Based on the previously cited assumption of a millet-sweet potato ratio of 4:1.
[f] Li Tsung-tao, *Huang Ma* (Jute) (Shanghai, 1952), p. 115.
[g] The total 1952 cropped area was 141,256,000 hectares according to the SSB *Communique for 1955.* The cropped area included in this table accounted for about 95 percent of the total.

(c) FEEDSTUFFS

The National Agricultural Research Bureau conducted, in the thirties, surveys of crop utilization in Chinese agriculture. The results of these surveys were published in *Nung Ch'ing Pao-kao* (Crop Reports), II, No. 8, and were used by Ou Pao-san, *China's National Income,* I, 39, for estimating feed allowances in his study. In the absence of reliable prewar livestock statistics, as a basis for comparing livestock numbers in 1952 with those in the thirties, it is difficult to assess precisely whether these allowances would still be applicable. However, in the circumstances we had no choice but to adopt this procedure.

Thus, applying the feed allowances given below, to the production figures given in Table A-2, we converted these into value terms by using the prices paid to farmers as given in the same table.

CROP	PROPORTION OF OUTPUT USED AS FEED	CROP	PROPORTION OF OUTPUT USED AS FEED
Rice	4%	Barley	33%
Wheat	5%	Soybeans	25%
Corn	19%	Broad beans	12%
Kaoliang	24%	Field peas	24%
Millet	7%	Other pulses	6%
Oats	22%	Sweet Potatoes	34%
Buckwheat	11%		

(d) INSECTICIDES AND OTHER RAW MATERIAL PURCHASES

These cannot be estimated with any degree of reliability. According to available information, 2.3 percent of total producers' goods purchases were for this purpose in 1953, 14.4 percent in 1954, 10.9 percent in 1955 and 16.5 percent in 1956. (Ch'u Ch'ing and Chu Chung-chien, "Variations in the Commodity Turnover in China's Rural Markets," *CCYC* [Economic Research], [June 1957], 100-126 and C. M. Li *Economic Development of Communist China* Table XXX p. 132). Using the 1953 percentage and applying it to estimated producers' goods purchases of Y2,240 million gives us a very crude estimate for this input of about Y50 million.

(e) COSTS OF REPAIR AND MAINTENANCE OF FARM CAPITAL PLANT

Under this item should be included, theoretically, expenditures for repair and maintenance of roads, irrigation facilities, farm buildings, fences, farm equipment, etc. Needless to say, farm equipment in China does not imply tractors, combines or other complex farm machinery, except in the case of a few state and model farms. Obviously, some simple tools and similar durable equipment are used. Simple tools with a life span of less than a year and outlays on maintenance of more durable equipment and structures should be charged against current output. Unfortunately, there is no direct way of estimating these.

As indicated in Chapter III, it is possible to estimate total farm purchases of producers' goods, including outlays on fertilizer, insecticides, and other raw materials going into production of current output on the one hand, and purchases of investment goods on the other hand. These estimates can be derived in alternative ways: from rural cash expenditure and from agricultural loans.

In a speech at the Second Session of the First National People's Congress, the Minister of Agriculture gave figures for rural cash expenditure on commodities in 1952, 1953, and 1954. (*HHYP*, [Aug. 1955], 107.) An article on "Variations in our Rural Market Commodity Turnover" (*CCYC*, [June 1957],116) indicates that the following share of total rural cash expenditure was used for purchases of production requisites:

1953	14.5%
1954	14.4%
1955	12.1%
1956	16.0%

Unfortunately, the 1952 percentage is not given. However, assuming that the 1952 share was between 14 and 15 percent, the corresponding outlays on production requisites would be between Y2,159 and Y2,313 million. If we assume the same share for 1952 as for 1953, i.e., 14.5 percent, the expenditure figure would be Y2,236 million.

An article on "The Way to Finance Agricultural Development in China" (*CCYC*, [Jan. 1958], 32) gives year-end balances of agricultural loans for 1952 to 1956, as well as the following percentages of such credits channelled into retail sales of production requisites in rural markets for 1953 to 1956:

1953	25.0%
1954	26.1%
1955	32.3%

Assuming that 1952 outlays may have been around 20 to 25 percent of the total, farm purchases of production requisites may be estimated at Y1,926 to Y2,408 million.

Proceeding on the basis of these alternative approaches, one may consider as reasonable, a figure of Y2,240 million for 1952. For our purposes, this total needs to be broken down into purchases of capital equipment and raw material inputs currently consumed. Such breakdowns are given in the above cited *CCYC* article [June 1957], as follows:

1953	59.7:40.3
1954	51.7:48.3
1955	52.2:47.8
1956	50.3:49.7

The equipment purchases here include adult livestock, while we consider all livestock increments under inventory investment. For this reason, and on the basis of these ratios, a 50:50 division between these two categories may perhaps not be too unreasonable for 1952. Accordingly, total raw material and maintenance outlays would be Y1,120 million. Deducting from this, fertilizer purchases of Y506 million and other raw material purchases of Y50 million, leaves a residual of Y564 million, which may be considered as an approximation of cash outlays on capital repair and maintenance.

II. FARM INCOME FROM
PROCESSING AND HANDICRAFTS

This is a composite of five types of activities which are defined in Mainland sources as follows:

(1) Collecting, fishing, and hunting; gathering of medicinal herbs, wild fruits, firewood, and grasses, felling of bamboo and of trees, hunting, and fishing, exclusive of commercial fishing which is included under fisheries production.

(2) Preliminary processing of farm produce, e.g., husking rice, milling flour, ginning cotton, shelling peanuts.

(3) Self-supplying handicrafts, e.g., home spinning of yarn and weaving of cloth, and the making of clothing, shoes, bedding, etc., by the farmers themselves for home consumption.

(4) Processing of materials for consumers; this refers to the same types of activities as under (3) above except for the fact that the raw materials are provided by the consumer, while the farmer or members of his family provide only the labor.

(5) Farm handicrafts for sale, or what in official Mainland statistical usage is referred to as "farmers' sideline handicrafts of commodity nature" *(nung-min chien-ying shang-p'ing hsing shou-kung-yeh)*. This is distinguished from (4) above by the fact that the latter involves work on specific orders by consumers who supply their own materials, while the former probably involves production activities similar to those of self-supplying handicrafts, except that it is for sale rather than self-consumption.

Mainland sources usually treat the first four categories together under so-called "farmers' subsidiary production." The 1952 figure for this item given in all official sources is Y9.9 billion. (See for instance an article by

Chao Ch'ing-hsin, "Seasonal Variations in our Market after the Agricultural Cooperation," *CCYC* [Economic Research], [1956] No. 5, 25). Official sources give Y7.6 billion as the value of "self-supplying handicrafts and processing." This figure actually refers to items (2) and (3) combined, as can be definitely established if one compares Chao's figures for 1952 to 1955 with detailed breakdowns given for each of the above categories in another source. (Wang Keng-chin "My Views on the Method of Calculating the Gross Value of Agricultural Output," *TCKT*, [1957], No. 4, 4).

By the very nature of the activity, category (2) is entered into the composite figures on a net basis. This is made explicit by Yueh Wei in an article on the "Gross Value of Industrial and Agricultural Output." (*Hsüeh Hsi*, [April, 1956], 25). However, category (3) is gross. Fortunately (2) + (3) can be derived on a net basis from other sources. From Niu Chunghuang's study of *Accumulation and Consumption in the National Income of Our Country* (Peking 1957), one can derive the official figure of Y36,-197 million for net product in agriculture and subsidiary production. In another source, the net value of agricultural and subsidiary production exclusive of income from self-supplying handicrafts and preliminary processing is given as Y32,276 million (Li Shu-teh, "Conditions and problems of peasants' burden in 1956" *Ts'ai Cheng* [Public Finance] [Aug. 1957], 3). Thus, the difference between these two figures represents the combined value added in (2) + (3). Conceptually, this figure presents something of a problem since the official national income estimate is calculated from NNP at market prices. However, a study of Mainland statistical and methodological articles indicates that only the urban sectors are valued at market prices, while the rural product is valued either at farm procurement prices or at factor cost. Thus, in price terms it is comparable with our sector products, but it is net rather than gross of depreciation. This, of course, introduces an element of error.

Summarizing the information from these different sources, we can now reconstruct value added in this subsector as follows:

(a) Total subsidiary production: (1) to (4)	Y9,900 million
(b) Preliminary processing and gross product of self-supplying handicrafts: (2) + (3)	Y7,600 million
(c) Preliminary processing and net product of self-supplying handicrafts: Y36.2 — 32.3 billion	Y3,900 million
(d) Collecting, fishing and hunting, and processing of materials for consumers, (1) + (4) = Y9,900 — Y7,600 million	Y2,300 million
(e) Total value added in subsidiary production: (1) to (4) = Y3,900 + Y2,300 million	Y6,200 million

The Y2,300 million for (1) and (4) was originally estimated on a net basis, therefore no further adjustment is required.

The 1952 value added in "farm handicrafts for sale" can be estimated only indirectly and crudely. The sources indicate very explicitly that this and "farmers subsidiary occupations" are two distinct items, and that the production value of the former should be included in individual handicrafts, while the latter should be assigned to the agricultural sector. (Data from China Academy of Sciences, Institute of Economic Research, *National Survey of Individual Handicrafts in 1954,* [Peking, 1957], p.1). On the other hand, the handicraft employment figures given in Appendix B, on which our computation of handicraft product is based, exclude farm handicrafts. This item therefore, needs to be separately estimated.

According to the 1954 national survey of individual handicrafts, "farm handicrafts for sale" gross output value was "around Y2.5 billion." (Wei I: *On the Establishment of the Preliminary Foundations of Socialistic Industrialization,* [Peking, 1956], p. 117). In the absence of a 1952 estimate, how shall we determine output trends in this sub-sector between 1952 and 1954?

The aforementioned report on the 1954 handicrafts survey gives the following comparative data for "farm handicrafts for sale" in millions of yuan:

	1952	1954
Chekiang	88.5	81.5
Kiangsi (cotton weaving)	17.7	8.2
Honan (21 crafts)	71.3	70.5
Heilungkiang	16.5	15.5
East Kwangtung Region	40.4	42.5
Liaoning	33.0	31.0

These fragmentary data amounting to about 10 percent of total output value in 1954 would indicate a slight decline since 1952. In the face of this, one may be justified in assuming that output value in this sub-sector remained more or less stationary between 1952 and 1954.

With gross output at Y2.5 billion, what was net output? It was indicated above that the net output of "preliminary processing" combined with the gross output of "self-supplying handicrafts" amounted to Y7.6 billion in 1952. At the same time, these two on a net basis are officially estimated at Y3.9 billion, the difference of Y3.7 billion representing the inputs of "self-supplying handicrafts." Given the similar character of output and productive organization in this sub-sector and in "farm handicrafts for sale," the input-output ratio of the former may be applicable to the latter.

With inputs of Y3.7 billion, what portion of the Y7.6 billion is the gross output of "self-supplying handicrafts" alone? Breakdowns by individual categories in "subsidiary occupations" are given in official sources only for 1955. (Wang Keng-chin, "My Views on the Method of Calculating the

Gross Value of Agricultural Output," *TCKT,* [Feb. 1957], 4). On the assumption that the ratio between these two segments has not changed appreciably between these two years, we applied the 25:75 ratio of the later year to 1952. We find the following relationships emerging in billions of yuan:

"Preliminary farm processing" (net)	1.9	(25%)	1.9 (net)
"Self-supplying handicrafts" (gross)	5.7	(75%)	2.0 (net)
	7.6		3.9

On this basis, the net-gross ratio of "self-supplying handicrafts" is about 35 percent. Applying this to gross output value of "farm handicrafts for sale," net product of the latter may be estimated at Y875 million (Y2,500 million times 35%).

III. FARM MONEY INCOME

As indicated in Chapter III, our figures for farm money income derive from the following series for "total purchases of farm products by the society," in billion yuan:

1951	11.64
1952	15.61
1953	17.04
1954	18.06
1955	18.89
1956	19.55

It is, however, unclear whether this includes or excludes the agricultural tax in kind. The problem may perhaps be investigated from two points of view: (a) terminological and conceptual and (b) statistical.

(a)   There are three relevant terms used in Mainland sources, namely "purchases" or *ts'ai kou* which is the term applied to the series above, "levy and purchase" or *cheng kou,* and "commodity" or the "commercial value of agricultural products." The first, when used for grain or food crops, specifically refers to purchases exclusive of tax, while the second naturally includes tax. Moreover, these first two terms are very rarely used for farm products other than grain. In reference to farm output as a whole, the third term is most generally used. This concept, on the other hand, probably refers to all farm products entering marketing channels, regardless of whether they are collected through purchase or tax.

The question that needs to be answered is whether the term "purchase," *ts'ai kou,* as applied to total farm product in the above series, is equivalent to the "commercial value of argicultural products." On this point Chinese

Mainland sources contradict each other. According to Hsu Chien et. al., *Lectures on Economic Statistics,* "the agricultural tax while in substance not commodity circulation, *is included in purchases of agricultural product* both because it is an important source of supply of agricultural products collected (centralized) by the state and because it will be sold by the commercial departments." On the other hand, a textbook on commercial statistics compiled by the Ministry of Commerce does not include, according to the reviewer of the book, a tax in kind in the purchases of agricultural products, because of a difference in character, the latter belonging properly in the sphere of commodity circulation (Hsiung Chen: "Review of Com· mercial Statistics," *TCYC,* [July 23, 1958], 37).

Thus far the evidence is inconclusive. In addition to these definitions, we must also consider the context in which the above-cited series appeared. The primary objective of the *TCKT* article on the "Price Gap Between Industrial Products and Farm Products: Their Changes in the Post-liberation Years," is to show that the real income position of the farmers has greatly improved in recent years, since the price terms of trade have moved in favor of the farmer between 1952 and 1957. Inclusion of the tax in kind in such a calculation would be strange indeed. On this basis one might conclude that the series of "purchases . . . by the society" excludes tax in kind.

(b)   An examination of the figures, however, leads one to a different conclusion, although here, too, the evidence is far from unequivocal. Chao Ching-hsin, in an article in *CCYC* of October, 1956, gives the value for production of commercial commodities in 1954 as Y16.3 billion in 1952 prices. The 1954 figure given in the above cited *TCKT* series is Y18.06 billion in current prices, which, deflated by the price index given in the same *TCKT* article, yields Y16.2 billion in 1952 prices. This could be taken as proof that "purchases" and "commercial value" are equivalents and that, since the latter presumably includes taxes in kind, the former do also. This is, indeed, the evidence on which Hollister bases his conclusions with respect to this point.[5] In another article, published a few months earlier (*CCYC,* [February, 1956], 43), Chao Ching-hsin gives the "commodity ratios" for both 1953 and 1954. The 1954 ratio yields the same figure of Y16.3 billion. The 1953 ratio enables us to compute the figure for that year which comes to Y12.5 billion in 1952 prices. The *TCKT* series gives Y17.09 billion for the value of purchases in current prices, the deflated equivalent being Y15.35 billion, almost 3 billion more than indicated by the 1953 commodity ratio. Therefore, in this case, too, the outcome is inconclusive.

There is one other way in which the composition of the *TCKT* series may be tested. From the *TCKT* article one can derive the following "purchases of farm products by the state and cooperatives:"

1952	Y10.31 billion	1955	Y12.97 billion
1953	Y 8.19 billion	1956	Y12.97 billion
1954	Y12.10 billion		

From the annual Communiques of the SSB, the *SSB Communique on the First Five Year Plan,* an article by Chin Chih in *HHYP,* No. 11 (1955), 172 and from *Purchasing Work* (Peking, 1956), 7, a book published by the Chinese Cooperatives, for 1954, the actual purchases can be reconstructed in detail as follows:[6]

1. Purchases by cooperatives
   a. On their own account .... Y1,828 million
   b. On behalf of the state .... Y6,119 million
2. Purchases by the state
   a. Through its own agencies .... Y1,530 million
   b. Through cooperatives .... Y6,120 million
3. Total [1(a) + 1(b) + 2(a)] .... Y9,477 million

The discrepancy of Y2.6 billion between the foregoing figure and the Y12.10 billion derived from *TCKT* may be accounted for by the agricultural tax. This calculation would suggest that the *TCKT* series and the 1952 figure for "purchases of agricultural products by the society" include the agricultural tax in kind, which is the view we finally adopted.

The implications of this conclusion for 1952 may be summarized as follows (in billion yuan):

1. Value of agricultural and subsidiary product
   collected by state trading and cooperative organs 10.31
   a. Collected as tax in kind 3.30
   b. Purchased 7.01
2. Value of agricultural and subsidiary product
   purchased by private traders or commercial organizations 5.30
3. Total 15.61

This view of the problem seems to be confirmed by a recent statement that the "commodity rate accounted for about one-third of the total value of farm and subsidiary products during each year. In 1957 the commodity figure was 23 percent above 1952."[7] On the one hand, the Y15.61 billion represents almost one-third of 1952 gross argricultural output value; on the other hand, 1957 "purchases by the society," when expressed in 1952 prices, seem to be quite close to the percentage rise given.

The figure of net money income given in Table 1 was obtained by deducting total tax payments, in kind and money, and cash purchases of production requisites estimated in the preceding section, from the Y15.61 billion.

Appendix B

THE NON-AGRICULTURAL WAGE BILL
INCLUDING INCOMES OF SELF-EMPLOYED

THERE ARE TWO special problems involved in Chinese labor force data. First of all, the sources do not indicate clearly whether employment figures are year-end estimates or annual averages, although certain indications would point to the former as a more likely possibility.[1] If this, indeed, is the case, then the labor force data may have an upward bias, since economic activity was more brisk in the second half of 1952 than in the first. The second difficulty is that all employment figures refer only to so-called registered workers. According to prevailing regulations, all long-term, seasonal, and temporary employees of an enterprise must be registered, except for "those who have been engaged in major productive activity of the enterprise for less than one day or those who have been engaged in subsidiary activity for less than five days."[2] Unfortunately, there are no reliable data for unregistered workers. According to one source, there were 587,000 of these in 1952.[3] They were employed only part-time, and since data for converting this figure to a man-year basis are not available, a wage bill for this category cannot be calculated. However, according to official sources, "the wage bill of unregistered workers was very small."[4]

With these two exceptions noted, labor force data for the public sector probably can be used with a fair degree of confidence for several reasons. This sector encompasses chiefly large enterprises and organizations which, presumably, are in a better position to keep good records, and are expected to do so. Moreover, the government planning and control authorities have direct and automatic access to these records which, of course, they are much less likely to have in the private sector. The least one can say is that there is every reason to suppose that, for the public sector, the labor force statistics at the disposal of the government authorities are quite good. Unless one assumes deliberate falsification in the process of publication, these data can be held to be fairly reliable.

However, even these statistics do present a problem in occupational or inter-industry classification. Thus, the labor force in enterprises under the

[124]

jurisdiction of the Ministry of Trade, for example, may all be counted under trade, although some processing establishments might be included.

In general, the reasonableness or the plausibility of the non-farm labor force totals may be gauged by comparing them with total non-farm population. In these terms, about 40 to 45 percent seem to be actively engaged in the labor force, i.e., a ratio very much in accord with those prevailing in other underdeveloped areas. (See International Labor Office, *Yearbook of Labor Statistics, 1956,* [Geneva, 1956], Table 4, 10-43.)

The non-agricultural wage bill total was built up, sector by sector, from the sources and with methods outlined below.

I. MINING AND MANUFACTURING

1. Labor Force in 1952

Table B-1
Number of Workers and Employees

		NUMBER	PERCENT
(a)	State Industry	2,761,882	
(b)	Cooperatively Operated Industry	130,000	25.1
(c)	Handicraft Producers Cooperatives	218,018	
(d)	Joint Industry	247,800	2.0
(e)	Private Industry	(2,019,600)	16.3
(f)	Handicraftsmen's Supply and Marketing Cooperatives	4,288	
(g)	Handicraftsmen's Teams	5,480	56.6
(h)	Individual Handicraft	7,002,932	
	Total Industry	(12,390,000)	100.0

This table was compiled on the basis of the following information:

On pp. 57-61 of *HHPYK,* No. 2 (1957), the following percentage breakdown for industrial employment is given:

Socialist-state and cooperatively operated	25.1
Semi-socialist, joint public-private	2.0
Private capitalistic industry	16.3
Individual handicraft	56.6
Total Industry	100.0

The same source gives the figure for item (d) in Table B-1 (i.e., Joint Industry) on p. 68. This figure appears also in two other sources: Chao I-wen: *Hsin-chung-kuo ti kung-yeh* (Industry in New China), (Peking, 1957), 75, and Ch'ien Hua et al.,: *Transformation of Private Industry and Trade of Our Country During the Past Seven Years, 1949-1956* (Peking, 1957), p. 112. The data for Joint Industry combined with the percentage breakdowns given above enabled us to compute the actual number in each of the major categories as shown below:

Socialist Industry	3,109,900
Semi-socialist	247,800
Private	2,019,600
Individual Handicraft	7,012,700

The figure for Cooperative Industry (b) item in Table B-1 is given in the *First Five Year Plan* (Peking, 1955), p. 128; and for Handicraft Producers' Cooperatives, item (c) in Table B-1 in Chao I-wen, *op cit.,* 111. Deducting these two from the Socialist Industry total, the labor force in State Industry is derived as a residual.

Similarly, labor-force data for Handicraftsmen's Supply and Marketing Cooperatives, item (f) in Table B-1, and for Handicraftsmen's Teams, item (g) in Table B-1, are also published in Chao I-wen's book on p. 111. Deducting these from the Individual Handicraft total given above, one can derive the figure for item (h) in Table B-1.

The question arises, however, as to how one can ascertain that items (b) and (c) should be treated as part of the socialist sector, while items (f) and (g) should be assigned to individual handicrafts. Data concerning industrial output value provide a clue.

Table B-2

Total Value of Industrial Output, 1949-1952

Type of Industry	GIVEN IN PUBLISHED SOURCES In millions of Yuan (1)		In Percent (2)		PERCENTAGE BREAK-DOWN DERIVED FROM COL. (1) (3)	
	1949	1952	1949	1952	1949	1952
Socialist Industry	—	—	26.7	44.7	—	—
State	3,683	14,258	—	—	26.273	41.537
Cooperative	65	1,109	—	—	0.464	3.231
Semi-socialist Industry						
Joint State-Private	220	1,367	1.6	4.0	1.569	3.982
Private Industry	6,828	10,526	48.7	30.7	48.709	30.665
Individual Handicraft	3,222	7,066	23.0	20.6	22.985	20.585
Total Industry	14,018	34,326	100.0	100.0	100.000	100.000

Sources: Value data in column (1) in SSB, Communique for 1955, p. 22.
Percentage data in column (2) in HHPYK No. 2 (1957), pp. 57-61.

A footnote to the original value data in SSB, *Communiqué for 1955,* p. 22, specifically indicates that the output value of Cooperative Industry includes processing by Supply and Marketing Cooperatives and Handicraft Producers' Cooperatives; also that Individual Handicraftsmen's Supply and

Marketing Cooperatives and Handicraftsmen's Teams are treated as Individual Handicrafts.

Converting these value data into percentage terms in column (3) shows that these correspond to the breakdowns in column (2). These, in turn, are given in the original source in the same table as the percentage data in Table B-1, on which our labor force calculations are based. Except for private industry, these also are the figures which in more summary form we used in Table 2 of Chapter III. For this sub-sector Chien Hua et.al., *op. cit.*, p. 8 cites 2,056,689, which is the figure we used since it is explicitly given rather than derived. It should also be noted that public sector employment in Modern Industry shown in Table 3 includes Joint and Co-operative Industry.

2. Wage Rates

(a) MODERN INDUSTRY

Chao I-wen's book cites on page 32, an average monthly wage figure of Y355 for state, joint state-private, and cooperatively operated industry in 1950. Other sources (NCNA news release, April 15, 1956; "National Wage Conference," *HHPYK*, [May 21, 1956], 71, and Chu Hsueh-fan "Report to the National Congress of the People's Representatives" *HHPYK*, [1957] No. 16, 51-54), state that "the average money wage of industry for the country has increased by 57.7 percent between 1950 and 1952." With this information the average 1952 monthly wage for publicly operated industry may be computed as Y560.

For private industry the same wage rate was adopted, primarily on the basis of wage quotations obtained for the textile industry, which as of 1952 was still preponderantly in the private sector, and by far its most important branch of manufacture.

Actual wage quotations culled from the Chinese Mainland press would indicate a somewhat higher average wage for Modern Industry in 1952, possibly around Y600 to Y650. However, the individual quotations cited for illustrative purposes below do not include a wide range of consumer goods industries, such as agricultural processing. Also the quotations undoubtedly are weighted in the direction of the more highly skilled and highly paid workers. With these qualifications, wage information for modern industry generally tends to be more consistent, more readily available, and probably more reliable than for any of the other economic branches. Wage information is outlined below under three headings: coal mining, heavy industry, and light industry.

(1) Coal Mining

This is clearly the most important branch of mining in Mainland China, overshadowing all other branches both in terms of employment and value of output. On the basis of the following wage quotations, the average monthly wage may be estimated as Y50.

1. Average 1952 wage workers in the Ta T'ung mine (Shansi Province) was Y50 per month. (*JMJP*, Sept. 14, 1952, p. 4.)

2. The average monthly wage in the Wang-chia-yuan unit of the P'ing-hsiang coal mine (Kiangsi province) was Y56 in 1952. (*CCJP*, Oct. 12, 1952, p. 2.)

3. In 1952, the average monthly wage in the No. 3 mine of the Ping-kuei Mining Bureau was Y49.47 (*JMJP*, Sept. 2, 1953, p. 2.)

4. The average monthly wage in the Nan-fen mine of the Pen-hsi Iron and Steel Co. was Y66 in 1954. (*JMJP*, July 7, 1955, p. 3.) This of course means that it must have been considerably less in 1952.

5. The average monthly wage of administrative personnel in the production sectors of the Fuel Industry Department was Y60 in 1954-1955. (*HHYP*, No. 10 [1955], p. 182.)

(2) Heavy Industry

(*i*) *Iron and Steel.* Wage quotations in this industry exhibit considerable variation, depending upon the level of skill and responsibility. In one plant — i.e., in Shih-ching-shan — the average wage for 1952-1953 may be derived as Y57.4 per month. (*JMJP*, Feb. 20, 1953, p. 2.) At the same time, the average wage for the Anshan Iron and Steel combine was apparently about Y74 per month. (*JMJP*, March 3, 1953, p. 1.)

According to a new wage contract entered into between workers and entrepreneurs in private machine and iron casting plants in Tientsin, monthly wage rates of "primary workers" were set as of December 18, 1952 (*TJP*, Dec. 2, 1952, p. 1) as follows:

GRADE	FEN (1 fen = Y0.2343)	YUAN
1	186	43.5798
2	203	47.5629
3	220	51.5460
4	237	55.5291
5	256	59.9808
6	276	64.6668
7	299	70.0557
8	322	75.4446
9	349	81.7707
10	378	88.5654
11	406	135.7258

This basic classification applied to other categories of workers as well, but with certain modifications. The minimum wage of salaried employees was to be 197 fen, while casual labor was to start with 135 fen but could not rise above a maximum of 254 fen. Apprentices were to be outside this classification with their monthly wages ranging from 80 to 169 fen.

A sample survey covering 700 plants in Tientsin with 11,000 employees showed that the new wage standard exceeded the old by about 8-10 percent in the machine shops, and by 14-16 percent in iron casting plants. It is, of course, the latter that are relevant for the iron and steel industry. On the basis of the scattered wage rates for individual workers and the two averages in the large plants cited above, the modal groups seem to be represented by grades 5, 6 and 7; according to the old standard, this would have entailed monthly wages of about Y52, Y56, and Y61 respectively.

(*ii*) *Engineering Industry*. The average wage of piece workers at the government motor vehicle repair plant in Harbin was in 1952, Y67 per month. (*JMJP*, April 21, 1954, p. 2.)

Average wage of production workers at the No. 2 plant of the Northeast Mechanics Bureau was Y41.25 before April and Y54.2 after April, 1952, (*KJJP*, May 28, 1952, p. 2.)

The average wage in the privately operated T'a-li Machinery Plant (Shanghai) was Y62.47 in 1952. (*HWJP*, Jan. 6, 1952)

In the privately operated Ta-jen Machinery Plant of Tientsin, the average monthly wage was Y62.8 (*TJP*, Dec. 21, 1952, p. 2.)

According to the official Machine Industry Journal the following would represent a model wage structure: (*Chi-ch'l Kung-yeh* (Machine Industry) May 21, 1954, pp. 22-26.)

Primary workers	Y50 per month
Subsidiary workers	Y40 per month
Technical personnel	Y80 per month
Office workers	Y45 per month
Miscellaneous workers	Y25 per month
Apprentices	Y20 per month

On the basis of this combined evidence for mining, iron and steel, and engineering, an average wage of about Y60 per month or Y720 per year would seem to be indicated.

(3) Light Industry

There are more wage data for the textile industry, the largest single industrial branch in China, than for any other consumer goods branches. The information available would suggest that the average textile wage in 1952 may have been around Y50 a month or Y600 a year. The following are some of the salient data on which this conclusion is based:

The average wage of state textile plants in the East China Region, the most important center of production, was Y55 per month. This was not quoted as such, but can be derived on the basis of an item given in *HWJP* of Feb. 27, 1952, p. 4.

The average wage of state textile plants in Tsingtao was Y54 a month. The original item in *KJJP* of March 28, 1952, p. 2, refers to 1951, giving the monthly wage as Y48. However, on the basis of a textile wage index for state plants (1950=100), one could convert this into 1952 terms. (*HHYP,* No. 11, [1954], pp. 122-123.)

The average monthly wage in the joint public-private Hua-hsin plant in Tangshan (Hopeh) was about Y52.

About twenty scattered quotations referring to individual workers fluctuate within the general range of Y40 to Y60 a month, with most being between Y40 and Y50.

While there is no comparable information for the other consumer goods industries, the scattered data that are available suggest lower wages in these than in the textile industry. It is these unaccounted branches of manufacture which undoubtedly pull the all-industry average down to Y560, because the average for the industries reported would seem to be Y600 or more.

(b) NON-FARM HANDICRAFTS

The wage of non-farm handcrafts used in Table 3 is based on the over-all average for members of handicraft production cooperatives, given in published sources as Y209 per year. (*TKP* Tientsin, Sept. 24, 1954, p. 6)

II. CONSTRUCTION

Although employment data are given for the public construction sector in Table 2, they were not used in our wage bill calculations. Actually, it was possible to compile fairly good wage information for this sector, showing an average annual wage of Y480. We did not feel justified in using it because construction activity is notoriously seasonal and casual in character. Thus, without additional information, one could not take it for granted that 1,021,000 workers engaged in publicly managed construction enterprises would be employed all year around. On the other hand, the wage bill as estimated by us may relate to a broader category of workers than those included in this employment figure. Moreover, there are no employment data for private construction. This raises some additional difficulties, since the income items in our household and private sector account are all in terms of gross product net of indirect taxes, while a construction figure thus derived is net, and at market prices. The margin of error on this account is probably not very large. On the one hand, indirect tax rates on construction materials were among the lowest even in 1952 (5 to 10 percent commodity tax rate on construction materials and 1 to 1.5 percent rate on business turnover). On the other hand, depreciation may be expected to be rather low since the construction industry in China is highly labor-intensive.

Both Niu and Yang Po[5] state that national income in 1952 (based on constant 1952 prices) was Y61,130 million with the following composition (in percent):

Industry	18.0
Agriculture	59.2
Construction	3.0
Transport, Postal & Telecommunications	4.0
Commerce	15.9

Therefore, Y61.3 billion times 3% is Y1.834 billion. We rounded this to Y1,850 million and used it, on the basis of the following cost breakdown, for our wage bill calculation:

Construction materials	60%
Direct cost	15%
Indirect cost	15%
Profits	10%

Sources: *HHYP*, No. 9 (1954), p. 123; *TTKP*, March 31, 1955, p. 3; *JMJP*, May 8, 1954, and June 4, 1955, p. 2.

In effect construction materials are inputs and the bulk of the remainder combined constitute gross product. A textbook on *State Enterprise Accounting* by Yü Chao-chih, pp. 102-124, defines direct costs as wage costs in the narrow sense, while indirect costs refer to wages of management, enterprise rewards, depreciation and certain other fixed charges. Some of these fixed charges, such as electric power and some types of administrative expenditures represent inputs. Available data do not permit a more refined cost breakdown. Assuming therefore that about one-third of indirect costs are inputs and most of the remaining two-thirds constitute wage elements, we get a wage: non-wage product ratio of 70:30. We estimated the wage bill as Y1,300 million. If one were to assume that depreciation, interest, and insurance constitute a larger element of indirect cost than the 70:30 ratio suggests, and that a 60:40 ratio would be more realistic, the wage bill would be Y1,110 million.

III. TRANSPORT

1. Modern Transport

(a) LABOR FORCE

Data for this sub-sector can be considered as fairly trustworthy, generally of the same order as those for Modern Industry. Published sources give 1,130,000 as the aggregate labor force figure for modern transportation and communication (Data Office of *TCKT*, "Statistical materials concerning the improvement of standard of living for workers and employees," *TCKT*, [July 29, 1957] p. 13, and 716,000 for the public sector alone (*The First Five Year Plan*, p. 78). This leaves 414,000 for the private sector, all of which may be assumed to be in transport, since communication was nationalized in China even before the advent of the Communist regime.

(b) WAGE RATES

Since more than 500,000 of the 596,000 workers engaged in the publicly operated segment of transport were employed by the railroad system, we feel justified in using railroad wage rates for modern transport as a whole. The railroad wage was derived from some operational data for the Changchun Railroad in Manchuria, and from wage information for the Peking-Tientsin Railroad.

In November 1952, the *JMJP* published a series of articles on the operation of the Changchun Railroad (Nov. 6, 1952, p. 2; Nov. 10, 1952, p. 2; Nov. 13, 1952, p. 2) These indicate that in 1951 the average cost of operating the railway was Y0.00731 per ton-km; that out of this total outlay 26.7 per cent went into wages, and that the average labor product was 259,000 ton-km. Hence, the average wage of this railroad may be estimated as Y0.00731 x 0.267 x 259,000 = Y505.

Published sources give the 1951 minimum wage on the Peking-Tientsin Railroad as 134 wage units ("fen"), which on the basis of Peking-Tientsin area "fen" values is equivalent to Y375 per year. From what we know of the wage structure in state industries, the average wage may be expected to be 30 to 50 percent above the minimum.

This conclusion is drawn from a 1955 survey of the frequency distribution of industrial workers in the different wage grades under the eight grade system. (Cf. "China's Workers in 1955: Their Number, Composition and Distribution," translation of an article from the*TCKTTH*, No. 23, [Dec. 14, 1956] in *ECMM* No. 68 [Feb. 4, 1957] 27-34). Assuming that this relationship also applies to the railroad system, the average annual wage on this railroad may be calculated at Y488 to Y563.

At least for these two railroad lines, an average wage of about Y500 seems most reasonable for 1951. However, in 1952, the average money wage in state industry was raised by 11 percent. If the railroad wage was similarly raised, the average annual railway wage for 1952 may be estimated as Y550.

2. Native Transport

(a) LABOR FORCE

Native means of transportation still plays an important role in the vast hinterland and on the waterways of Mainland China. For instance, according to reports of recent years, in Shansi province 76 percent of total transport was by animal-pulled carts. (Chung I, *Ti-i-ke wu-nien chi-hua ti yun-shu ho yu-tien yeh* [Transportation, Posts and Telecommunications in the First Five Year Plan], Peking, 1956, 21.) Similarly, as of 1953, native boats still supposedly accounted for more than 74 percent of total tonnage and 46 percent of traffic (in ton-km) on inland rivers. (*JMJP*, Nov. 19, 1953 and *JMJP*, Oct 29, 1953.)

Unfortunately, labor force data for this sector are quite poor and represent only crude approximations from the following information:

(i) *Native Shipping*. One source gives the number of native boats on inland rivers as 600,000 (*JMJP*, Nov. 19, 1953). Typically, these boats represent households, with the family living on the boat and participating in its operation. One might therefore assume two full-time workers per boat. Ou Pao-san in his national income study assumed three workers per boat for China proper and two for Manchuria. However, presupposing an average family size of about 5, and considering the size of these boats and the nature and seasonality of the cargos carried by them, two workers per boat would seem a more reasonable figure. On this assumption, the total number of persons engaged in native inland river shipping would be 1,200,-000. To this must be added an allowance for coastal shipping. The source just cited also indicates that the total tonnage of native inland river boats may be placed at about 3,000,000 and that "if coastal vessels are included the total tonnage would be close to four million." However, other sources, while giving the total junk tonnage, both inland and coastal, as 4,000,000 show a lower percentage of coastal vessels in the total. (*JMJP,* Oct. 29, 1953; and *HHYP* No. 12,[1952], 150-151.) Assuming that coastwise tonnage is about one-fourth of that for inland shipping, and that the same ratio obtains for labor force, we estimated the total labor force in native shipping to be about 1,500,000 persons.

(ii) *Native Land Transport.* According to the previously cited article of November 19, 1953 in *JMJP,* there were in 1953 about 2.2 million animal-pulled carts in the country. A more recent and reliable source gives the number as 1.1 million. (Ch'ou Ch'i-hua, *Wo-kuo fa-chan yun-shu ho yu-tien ti ti-i-ke wu-nien chi-hua,* [Our First Five Year Plan on the Development of Transport and Posts and Telecommunication] Peking, 1956, p. 35.). A third source, reporting on cooperative organization of animal-drawn transport, refers to 320,000 carts with a labor force of 540,000, thus indicating an average of 1.7 persons engaged per cart. (Wang Shou-tao, "Do Well the Task of Communication and Transport, Support the Movement of Agricultural Cooperativization," *HHYP,* [Dec. 1955], p. 220). On this basis, employment in cart transport may be crudely estimated as 1,870,000, derived from 1,100,000 x 1.7.

(b) WAGE RATES

In the absence of wage or income information for this subsector we use the average wage rate for non-farm handicrafts.

3. Warehousing, Porterage and Pedicab Drivers

(a) LABOR FORCE

This category includes dock workers, porters on railway stations, movers and haulers in urban areas, and pedicab drivers. A 1951 survey encompassing 432 urban centers found a total of 800,000 workers engaged in this branch. (*JMJP,* October 5, 1951, p. 2). Our figure is based on the assumption that there was no marked change in the economic status of this sub-sector between 1951 and 1952.

(b) WAGE RATES

In assigning wage rates to this group of workers it seems desirable to make a distinction between pedicab drivers on the one hand, and dockers, porters and haulers, on the other. From what we know of the earnings of pedicab drivers it would seem justifiable to apply to them the wage of modern transport (Y550).

For the haulers, etc., all the available wage data are on either a daily or monthly basis; and considering the highly seasonal or irregular nature of this kind of work it would be inappropriate to calculate annual wage figures on the basis of these data. Inasmuch as this category of work requires little skill, and since there still was considerable urban unemployment in 1952, there is reason to believe that the earnings of haulers, etc., probably were not much higher than those of handicraft workers. We might, therefore, take Y210 as the annual wage of haulers, dockers and porters.

On the assumption that pedicab drivers account for about half of the total workers in this sector, the average wage for the group as a whole would be Y380.

IV. POST AND TELECOMMUNICATIONS

The *JMST* (People's Handbook), 1953, p. 252, gives an employment figure of 120,000 in Post and Telecommunications for 1952. There are no wage quotations for this sector, but given the close interrelationships between transport and this sub-sector, use of the average transport wage rate of Y550 may perhaps be justified.

V. TRADE

1. Public Sector

(a) LABOR FORCE

The *HHPYK* in its December, 1956, issue reprinted an article on "The Development of Our Commercial Network and its Basic Condition in 1955" from *TCKTTH* (No. 18, 1956) which gives the following labor force data for 1952:

State trade	535,000
Cooperative trade	711,000
State and cooperative trade	1,246,000

This differs from the following data given in the *Five Year Plan*

State trade	492,000
Cooperative trade	641,000
Total state & cooperative trade	1,133,000

There is no explanation of this discrepancy, but we used the former data since they were given in a later source.

(b) WAGE RATES

Wage information is much more scattered as evidenced by the data cited below, on which the average public sector wages for trade shown in Table 2 is based.

"According to a survey of 46 private cotton, silk, and general stores in Tsingtao, the average wage in 1953 was Y60.8 which is ... *44 percent* higher than those for state operated general stores." (Ch'ien Hua et. al., *Transformation of Private Industry and Trade of Our Country During the Past Seven Years, 1949-1956* [Peking, 1957], pp. 148-149.)

"The average wage of the centrally and locally operated state enterprises has increased 5 per cent between 1952 and 1953." (*JMJP,* May 3, 1954, p. 1.)

On this basis, average wages in Tsingtao's state operated general stores in 1952 may be estimated as Y40.2 ($60.8 \times \frac{100}{144} \times \frac{100}{105} = Y40.2$) per month or Y480 per year.

"According to a 1954 survey of four types of trade (general stores, drugs, tea, oil and salt) in Peking ... the monthly wage in state trade was Y43.93."

"The average money wage of employees of various departments of the country has increased 20.2 per cent from 1952 to 1955." (*JMJP,* June 30, 1956, p. 9.)

"The average wage of our country's employees has increased 3.9 per cent compared with 1954." (SSB, *Communique for 1955,* p. 11).

Given the second, fifth and sixth items above, the percentage rise in money wages between 1952 and 1954 may be derived as 115.7 per cent, and the average 1952 wage of four types of state stores in Peking as Y37.88 per month or Y455 per year.

Given the lower wages in state trading establishments in smaller cities and towns, it seemed more reasonable to use the Peking rather than the Tsingtao rate.

2. Private Sector

(a) LABOR FORCE

Because of differences in character, capitalization and wage rates, it is necessary to distinguish among four types of private trading establishments: "*tso*" trade, "hsing" trade, stalls and small merchants, and catering trades including restaurants, cafeterias, etc. *The Practical Dictionary of National Economy* (Shanghai, 1953), p. 4018, gives the following definitions for these types:

"*Tso*" trade, as the word "*tso*" implies, encompasses all establishments with a fixed site—store or office—but probably excluding small merchants.

"*Hsing*" merchants are itinerant traders without a definite business site. They travel constantly within a fixed radius, selling and shipping commodities.

"Small merchants" are those who depend wholly or primarily upon retail trade for their livelihood, operating with little or no capital and without employees. Small merchants who do not operate at a fixed site, but move around, are "peddlers."

Based on these categories, a recent study of private industry and trade provides the data for 1952 presented in Table B-3 (Ch'ien Hua et. al., *op. cit.*, p. 52 and p. 123).

Table B-3

Number of Units, Number of People Engaged, Total Capital, and Trade Volume of Different Types of Trading Establishments

TYPE OF TRADE	NO. OF UNITS	NO. OF PEOPLE ENGAGED in 1,000	TOTAL CAPITAL	TRADE VOLUME in millions of yuan
1. "Tso"	1,820	4,012	1,860	15,360
2. "Hsing"	300	329	80	870
3. Stalls and small merchants	2,180	2,427	80	2,940
4. Catering trades	850	1,450	100	1,360

These data are clearly not of uniform reliability. Of the four categories, undoubtedly the information concerning the number of establishments and employees for "*tso*" merchants and all others with fixed sites is relatively the best, and that for the itinerant " *hsing*" and peddlers, the poorest. The different columns for each of the categories are not equally reliable. With respect to capitalization the data must be mere guesses for categories 2 and 3, and for part of 4, while for 1, it is reported, rather than actual, capitalization.

(b) WAGE RATES

(i) *"Tso" Trade.* According to the wage survey made by the All-China Federation of Trade Unions in eight types of trade in Peking, including 106 establishments with 910 employees, "the average wage in 1954 was Y51.3." (Ch'ien Hua et. al., *op cit.,* p. 148).

Another survey in 1954 in Peking, cited above (Section 1.b) indicated an average wage in private trade of Y52.65 per month. The Tsingtao survey cited above in the same source indicated a wage of Y60.8 per month.

If one were to take these wage rates as the average for "*tso*" trade, they would be Y600 or more per year. However, all of these surveys covered relatively large establishments in large cities. For instance, while in "*tso*" establishments as a whole, as shown by Table B-3, there were only 2.2 people engaged per unit, the more comprehensive of the two Peking surveys showed 8.6 people per unit. At the same time, the average capitalization per unit, and the value of sales per person was lower in private "*tso*" trade than in public trade. For all of these reasons combined, we assumed that the average wage in "*tso*" trade in the country as a whole was about 10 percent below the public trade average.

(ii) *Other Trades.* In attempting to estimate wage rates for the "*hsing*" and the "small merchants," it is important to consider that these are preponderantly self-employed categories so that, in this respect, their status may be comparable to that of individual non-farm handicrafts. While many of the catering establishments— particularly in the large cities—have employees, the average sales per person in these establishments is very close to those found in handicrafts as illustrated by the data below.

CATEGORY	SALES PER PERSON ENGAGED		WAGE RATE DERIVED
	VALUE IN YUAN	INDEX	IN YUAN
"Hsing"	2,644.4	260	550
Stalls & small merchants	1,211.4	120	250
Catering trades	937.9	93	195
Handicrafts	1,007.6	100	210

In computing the average wage rates, we assumed a paralellism between average wage and sales value per person, using the average handicraft wage of Y210 as the base. This, obviously, is a very crude procedure which makes sales per person serve as an index of productivity, and implies that wages are proportional to productivity. Highly simplified assumptions such as these had to be adopted owing to lack of data. The resulting figures show a high wage rate for "*hsing*" merchants. This may not be as unreasonable for an almost entirely self-employed category, in which the Y550 represents income with concealed non-wage elements in it.

VI. BANKING AND INSURANCE

For this sector, no wage information could be found, but labor force data are given in the *Five Year Plan*. The wage rate given in Table 2 is the same as that estimated above for heavy industry on the assumption that average incomes of banking employees will tend to be in the higher ranges. From what information we have, it would seem that there are no radical differences in the wage and salary structures of the various economic branches. Roughly the same system of grades from apprentice to manager, prevails with approximately the same wage or salary per grade. The frequency distribution of the grades differ widely, however, between the different branches. In these terms, one would expect to find in banking and insurance a considerable concentration in the upper grades. This has been the case with salaried personnel in pre-Communist China, and given the literacy, accounting and other skills, and the financial responsibility required of banking personnel, there is no reason to suppose that this situation would be very much altered by 1952.

VII. GOVERNMENT SERVICES

For this sector also, labor force data were obtained from the *Five Year Plan,* while wage rates had to be derived.

Employees of state organs, government bureaus and popular organizations were paid in two ways. A large number, constituting probably the majority in 1949 and 1950, but declining since, were under the so-called "supply system", i.e., they were paid only in kind. They were supplied with room and board and the other ingredients of subsistence. As late as 1955, when the system was abolished, one-third of all government employees were still paid in this way. (Editorial, *JMJP,* Sept. 15, 1955). The other form of remuneration was the usual one of fixed money wages or salaries, although a combination of the two systems was also used.

Those under the "supply system" received an average annual wage of 1,800 catties of millet in 1950. (Ti Ch'ao-pai: "Financial and Economic Prospects for 1950," *CCCP,* [March 9, 1950] 4). In terms of the 1952 value of so-called financial millet in Tientsin, this would be equivalent to Y200. The 1952 numbers of the *CPJP* and the *TTJP* give mid-month quotations for financial millet in Tientsin as 1,069 old yuan (equal to 0.1069 new yuan) per catty in January, 1,098.5 old yuan in February, with the February level remaining unchanged for the rest of the year. Thus, 1,098.5 $\times$ 1,800 catties = 1,977,300 old yuan or 197.73 new yuan, which comes to Y200 in round numbers. Between 1950 and 1952, definite efforts were made to raise the real wages of this category of workers. In Manchuria, it was apparently increased by 50 percent, and in 1952, all workers in state organs received an average salary increase of 15 percent. (An Tzu-wen's report on the work of the cadres, *HHYP*, [Oct., 1952] 25; and "Communiqué of the State Statistical Bureau for 1952," HHYP, [Oct., 1954], 232). It is likely that those under the "supply system" were raised more, the others less. The average wage or salary of employees under the "supply system" may have been raised by 25 to 50 percent between 1950 and 1952, so that the 1952 average may have amounted to Y250 to Y300 in money terms. That it was probably closer to the higher figure is borne out by another source. A news item in the *HWJP* of January 7, 1952, 2, indicates that in Shanghai 14 million old yuan (equal to 1,400 new yuan) was needed to maintain 58 cadres in the city government for a month. This would be equivalent to an average wage of 290 new yuan per year. To allow for the higher prices prevailing in Shanghai this should perhaps be adjusted downward, and we use for this purpose the wage unit values in Peking as compared to Shanghai. The average 1952 value of the wage unit in Shanghai was 2,534 old yuan as compared to 2,311 in Peking according to *JMST, 1953* (The 1953 People's Handbook), 300. Therefore, 2,311/2,534 x 290 = 264. On this basis, the annual wage or salary of employees under the "supply system" may be roughly estimated as Y264 in early 1952. Assuming that these workers received at least the average 15 per cent salary raise extended to government employees in 1952, the 1952 figure would come to Y304.

The average salary of government employees paid in money terms was said to be equivalent to 4,200 catties of millet in 1950. (Ti Ch'ao-pai in *CCCP*, [March 9, 1950], p. 4). Assuming at least 10 percent increase in the real wages of this group between 1950 and 1952, and using the 1952 financial millet quotations in Tientsin for conversion purposes, their average 1952 money wage may be estimated as Y500.

In the absence of information on the proportion of employees paid under each system, we have no choice but to use the ratio cited above, referring to 1955. This entails a certain margin of error since it is likely that a larger proportion of the total were under the supply system in 1952 than in 1955. By using the 1955 ratio, we overstate the average wage rate. With this qualification, taking Y500 for the money wage and Y300 for the supply wage, the aggregate average may be estimated as Y430 by using the 1955 ratio of 2:1.

VIII. MISCELLANEOUS SERVICES

The estimate for this category is based on the supposition that the wage bill in the various services and occupations would constitute 5 percent of the total wage bill in the economy, including an imputed wage bill for agriculture. The percentage is computed from the relative weight of these types of services in the national product of other underdeveloped areas, particularly India.

Appendix C

THE HOUSEHOLD AND PRIVATE SECTOR ACCOUNT

I. INCOMES

1. Incomes of Farm Households

(a) NET MONEY INCOME

See Appendix A.

(b) NET INCOME IN KIND

See Table 1 and Appendix A.

(c) IMPUTED RENT ON FARM DWELLINGS

The estimate in Table 3 is based on a study by J. L. Buck. In a sample survey of 2,666 farms conducted in the early twenties, he collected data on farm family income (in cash and kind), including "estimated rental value of farm residence".[1] These data show that estimated rental value constituted about five percent of total farm income. Applying this percentage to our estimate of agricultural product in 1952 yields an imputed gross rental income figure of Y1,875 million. From this total we must deduct an allowance for cost of repair and maintenance. In India these costs were placed at 28 percent of gross rental income in rural areas. Ou Pao-san in his study of China's national income for 1931-36 used a 30 percent allowance, which, however, includes depreciation.[2] On the basis of these two estimates, and considering that ours is a gross rather than a net concept, a 25 percent deduction seemed most reasonable.

Clearly, this is a crude procedure. While Buck's survey was a careful one, his sample is confined only to seven provinces and his sampling procedures were not up to current standards. Moreover, since the information obtained from his survey is now thirty years old, its applicability to 1952 conditions may be limited. On the other hand, one should take cognizance

[142]

of the fact that the provinces covered include some of the most densely populated regions of China, and the type and quality of rural housing as well as the pattern of cultivation and of farm location are not likely to have changed appreciably. between 1921-25 and 1952. Therefore, while the actual level of imputed rental income must have risen, rent as a fraction of total farm or agricultural income need not have changed appreciably.

Buck's data, on the basis of which we estimated our imputed farm rent may be summarized as follows (all data in 1921-25 Chinese dollars):

Total farm receipts (including increase in capital)		376.24
Farm expenses	136.64	
Decrease of capital	−7.44	
	129.20	−129.20
Farm earnings		247.04
Income from other than farm sources		24.06
Total farm household income		271.40
Estimated rent of farm residence		12.50

Rent in relation to farm earnings is thus about 5 per cent; in relation to total earnings exclusive of rent, it is about 4.7 per cent and, inclusive of rent, it is 4.4. per cent.

2. Non-farm Wages and Salaries
Including Incomes of Self Employed

(a) DIRECT WAGES, SALARIES AND INCOMES

See Appendix B.

(b) SUPPLEMENTARY WAGE PAYMENTS IN KIND

In effect these represent sickness, death, and similar benefits extended in kind by private and public enterprises, to workers covered by labor insurance. All these payments as well as contributions to the labor insurance and trade union funds are financed exclusively by the managements of state and private enterprises. In effect, these supplementary payments in kind represent benefits paid to the workers directly by the enterprises over and above their regular contributions to labor insurance and trade union funds.

With this background information in mind, we can estimate these payments on the basis of the following specific items of information:

(i) The state, its organs and enterprises, spent in 1952 a total of Y160 million on labor insurance. This was ten percent of the total wage bill of employees covered (Cf. *JMJP* [May 1, 1955] p. 2).

(ii) According to the labor insurance regulations, the enterprises and organs covered must contribute three percent of the total payroll to the labor insurance fund.

(iii) This, then, means that out of the total state expenditures on labor insurance, which according to item (i) represented about ten percent of the payroll, approximately 70 percent must have been paid to the workers directly, and 30 percent to the labor insurance fund. The state organs and enterprises must have paid directly Y112 million worth of benefits to the workers in 1952. To this must be added direct payments by private enterprises.

(iv) Chu Hsueh-fan, then Vice-Chairman of the All-China Federation of Trade Unions stated in a speech (Cf. *JMJP*, May 8, 1953, p. 2) that the total labor insurance payments, including direct payments by managements, constituted 8.66 percent of the total wage bill of the organs and enterprises covered.

(v) According to officially published data, total contributions to the labor insurance fund amounted to Y65.938 million in 1952. (SSB, *Communique for 1954*, p. 37). On the basis of items (i) and (iii), we know that the state sector must have contributed Y48 million to this total (160 − 112 = 48). Therefore, it may be assumed that the remainder, i.e., Y17.938 million, was contributed by the private sector. According to the labor insurance regulations, this sum may be considered as equivalent to three percent of the wage bill in the private enterprises covered, from which the wage bill of Y597.9 million can be computed.

(vi) From item (iv) we know that the labor insurance fund benefits paid to the workers directly constitute 8.66 percent of the wage bill. Therefore, in terms of millions:

$$\frac{160 + 17.938 + X}{1,600 + 597.9} = 8.66\%$$

Then $X + (2,197.9 \times 8.66) - 177.938 = $ Y12.4 million which represents the direct payments made by private enterprises. The figure in Table 3 combines this Y12.4 and the Y112 million estimated above.

In addition to these benefits in kind, wage earners and salaried personnel receive certain special cash awards and bonuses for plan fulfillment and overfulfillment, for the introduction of technical or organizational improvements, etc. Such payments are made by public enterprises out of the "enterprise reward fund," the size of which is estimated below as part of the public sector account. Besides financing these awards and other worker welfare measures, the "enterprise reward fund" is used also for covering the cost of safety and sanitation equipment and other expenditures designed to improve production. Unfortunately, data on breakdowns of how the fund is used are not available so that there is no way of estimating what proportion of it goes into supplementary wage or salary payments and what proportion into plant improvement. Therefore no attempt was made to include it under this item in Table 3, which for this reason must be viewed as an understatement.

3. Private Business Earnings

These were particularly depressed in 1952 primarily because of the "Five-Anti's" campaign which was rampant in the first half of the year. Its effect upon profits is well illustrated by the situation in private modern industry for which the data are comparatively good.

PROFITS IN PRIVATE INDUSTRY, 1950-1955
(in million Yuan)

1950	348
1951	817
1952	371
1953	913
1954-55	658

In general, private sector profits were one of the most difficult items to estimate in our accounts. For private industry earnings, estimates for 1950 to 1953 are either directly provided or can easily be computed as indicated below. These figures show that in relation to total volume of sales the profit rate was 8.07 percent in 1951 and 3.53 percent in 1952.

According to prevailing accounting practice in China, these earnings were, in principle, net of depreciation and before payment of direct taxes. Since the accounts in Tables 3 to 5 are in terms of gross product, depreciation allowances should be added to these net earnings, but unfortunately, there are no data. Theoretical depreciation rates based on the value of fixed assets may prove quite erroneous in this case, since, given the unfavorable climate for private business operations in 1952, it is possible that no funds were allocated to depreciation reserves.

In the case of construction, modern transport, native transport and trade, handicrafts, and miscellaneous small establishments, there are no published data for any year and very crude methods of estimation had to be used. For construction, net earnings were computed from both value added and the wage:non-wage ratio in value added. In modern private transport, it was assumed that the wage bill:net earnings ratio would be the same as in private trade, these two branches being closely linked. Native transport and trade, handicrafts, and miscellaneous small establishments all fall within the purview of what in Chinese Communist terminology is referred to as individual economies with a preponderance of self-employed. In this respect their position is similar to that of the peasant farms in agriculture.

A priori, in all of these individual economies, one would expect the non-wage share of net product to be comparatively small and very difficult to distinguish from the wage share. In agriculture, as shown in Table 9, we assumed, in effect, that the agricultural tax absorbed the non-wage share, and what remained to the individual farmer represented a reward for his labor. On this basis, his reward seemed to constitute about 90 per cent of agricultural product. While conditions in handicraft, small scale trade, etc., are admittedly different from those in agriculture, their similarity in this respect may warrant a 90:10 ratio for their non-wage share as is shown below.

Net earnings estimates for the different sectors are summarized in the following table:

Modern Industry	Y370 million
Trade	380 million
Construction	175 million
Modern Transport	25 million
Other	540 million
Total	Y1,490 million

These profit estimates were computed on the following bases:

(a) PRIVATE INDUSTRY

(i) Total profit of private industry was Y913 million in 1953, which is 2.62 times that of 1950 and 11.9 percent higher than that of 1951. (Ch'ien Hua et. al., *Transformation of Private Industry and Trade . . .* [Peking, 1957], p. 90)

(ii) Private industry profits have increased by 146 per cent between 1952 and 1953 (Chao I-wen, *Industry in New China* [Peking, 1957], p. 67).

(iii) In 1951, profit of capitalistic industry in the country was about Y817 million (Chao I-wen, *op. cit.,* p. 64).

(iv) According to a preliminary survey, the estimate of profit of capitalistic industrial enterprises from 1950 to 1955 totaled Y3,107 million. (Data Office of *TCKT*, "From Dividing Profits into Four Shares to Fixed Interest Policy," *TCKT*, [March 1957], 30-32)

(v) From items (i) and (ii), 1952 profits may be estimated as Y371,138,200.

(b) PRIVATE TRADE

(i) Estimated profit in capitalistic trade (excluding catering) was Y475 million in 1951 (Ch'ien Hua, *op. cit.*, 53).

(ii) In 1951, the ratio between capital in private industry and private trade was 1.00:1.17, their profit ratios being 1.00:1.43. In this case, trade includes catering (Wu Chen-min, "The characteristics of Chinese national capital," *CCYC*, [1956] No. 6, 133).

(iii) Value of output or sales in private industry and trade (in billions of yuan):

	1951	1952
Industry	10.12	10.53
Trade	24.22	19.17

From items (i) and (iii) we can see that in 1951 the rate of profit in private trade (excluding catering) was 3.08 percent.

Comparing the private industry profits estimated above with the gross output values given in (iii), industrial profit rates seem to have been 8.07 percent for 1951 and 3.53 percent for 1952. If it is assumed that the rate of decline in profits was the same in trade as in industry, the profit rate in trade would be around 1.35 percent in 1952, but since trade was much harder hit by the Five Anti's campaign than industry, we estimated the earnings rate as only 1 percent. On this basis, private trade net earnings would be Y191.7 million in 1952.

Finally, to determine profit in private catering, item (ii) and the private industry profits estimated above, were used; accordingly, 1951 profits of trade including catering were estimated as Y817,000,000 x 1.43 = Y1,168,310,000. Deducting from this the 1951 trading profits (excluding catering) of Y745 million, catering profits may be placed at Y423,310,000. Assuming here the same declining rate of profit as in industry, catering profits in 1952 would be Y190 million.

(c) CONSTRUCTION

As is shown in Appendix B, the non-wage share in total construction product was estimated as Y550 million. Assuming that the construction equipment ratio and the profit rate is the same in private as in public construction, the relationship between private and total investment in fixed capital could serve as a basis for a breakdown between public and private construction. As to the first assumption, since, in 1952, private investment was largely in agriculture, it was probably more construction-intensive; on this account the method used understates earnings in private construction. On the other hand, profit rates in private construction may have been lower than in the public sector, so that from this point of view the estimate may contain an upward bias.

From the assumptions outlined above and according to the investment estimates in our expenditure accounts, private construction earnings may be computed as follows: (Y2,362,000 ÷ Y7,362,000) x Y550,000,000 = Y176,000,000.

(d) MODERN TRANSPORT

There are no data on transport earnings in the private sector. We estimated these on the assumption that the wage and non-wage shares in transport product would be the same as in trade. On the basis of the estimates in Table 3, the latter ratio seems to have been around 90:10 in 1952 so that modern transport earnings would be Y25 million.

(e) MISCELLANEOUS EARNINGS

As indicated in the text, these were derived from the estimated wage bill in those individual economies for which earnings were not estimated elsewhere, on the basis of an assumed 90:10 relationship. The relevant wage categories are the following:

Private handicraft	Y1,473 million
Native transport	708 million
Hauling	304 million
Miscellaneous occupations	2,400 million
	Y4,885 million

The corresponding non-wage share then would be about Y540 million.

4. Rental Income

With an estimated average farm population of 478.9 million in 1952, imputed rural rental expenditure estimated by us above comes to Y3.915 per capita.[3] According to Ou Pao-san's estimates for the prewar period, the urban-farm rental ratio per capita was 3.2:1, which would make urban per capita rental Y12.5. According to workers' cost of living suveys in Peking and Shanghai, the average monthly rent was Y1 per capita (including utilities) in the former, and Y1.1911 (excluding utilities) in the latter.[4] The annual Shanghai rent (exclusive of utilities) would be somewhat higher than the Y12.5·mentioned above, and the Peking rent would be lower. While these figures do not appear to be unreasonable, since workers' housing costs were kept deliberately low through varying forms of rent control, they may not necessarily be representative of the urban rents at large.

For this reason, it seemed more appropriate to adopt the Indian urban-rural ratio of 4.4:1[5] which would yield an urban per capita rental of more than Y17 with aggregate rental outlays of Y1,550 million.[6] This constitutes close to 9 percent of the aggregate wage bill as estimated above, i.e., a rate of expenditure for housing which appears rather reasonable in terms of household budget data for underdeveloped areas.[7] To derive a net rental income estimate, a 10 percent allowance was made for costs of housing repair and maintenance. In the absence of Chinese Mainland data, the latter was also based on Indian estimates.

5. Payment and Subsistence of Armed Forces

Owing to the nature of this item, there are no published figures. According to a number of press reports, both Chinese and American, the size of the Chinese Communist army has been placed at around five million in 1952. For 1950 there is a specific Chinese Mainland report to this effect.[8] The average cost of maintaining a soldier is given by an official source as 2,700 catties of millet in 1950.[9] The Tientsin papers give the monthly quotations for so-called financial millet; according to these the average value per catty was Y0.109 in 1952.[10] Therefore, the 1952 pay and subsistence of the armed forces may be estimated as 5,000,000 x 2,700 x 0.109, which when rounded, gives us the figure shown in Table 3. This calculation is based on the implicit assumption that the real cost of maintaining a member of the armed forces has remained the same between 1950 and 1952.

6. Transfer Receipts

(a) RURAL RELIEF

This item did not have to be estimated since it is given as such for 1952 in an article by Feng Chi-hsi in *TCKT,* (June 29, 1957), 32. The figure actually published is Y144.26 million, which we rounded to Y145 million.

(b) STATE UNEMPLOYMENT RELIEF

This includes relief for unemployed workers and intellectuals. Theoretically, relief funds for unemployed workers are drawn from three sources in Mainland China: (i) in cities covered by unemployment insurance, all state and private factories, workshops and commercial enterprises must contribute one percent of their aggregate payroll to an unemployment relief fund; employees of these enterprises contribute an equivalent amount; (ii) relief appropriations by central and local governments, (iii) charity. Unemployed intellectuals are completely dependent upon central government relief. (Cf., *CYTC*, 1st series [Peking, Aug. 1950], pp. 761-769).

We have no way of estimating relief contributions by agencies or funds other than government for which the total, including state relief to both workers and intellectuals, is given in the above cited issue of *TCKT*, (June 29, 1957), 32, as Y37.14 million, rounded to Y40 million.

(c) VETERANS' BENEFITS

This item is also given in this same source, p. 31, as Y208.1 million, which we rounded to Y210 million.

(d) STUDENT STIPENDS

Unlike the preceding three items, this one had to be estimated. The computation was made from data of the student population and the rates of stipend extended to the different categories of students. The *JMST* (*People's Handbook*) for 1953 (pp. 370-372) indicated that the monthly stipends for junior high school students was to be Y8.5 and for those in senior high school Y9.5. In these cases, the state makes only a partial contribution to the support of the student. In contrast, stipends of students in schools of higher education, in technical high schools and in teacher training institutes, are supposed to take care of all of their board, cloth-

	1951-52	1952-53
Schools of higher education	155,570	194,000
High schools		
Specialized schools	162,940	} 536,000
Teacher training institutes	219,787	
Senior high schools	184,393	260,000
Junior high schools	1,383,691	2,233,000

ing purchases, expenditures for books, etc. Accordingly their average monthly stipend should be Y32.

Since our interest is in total stipends received during 1952, we need data for the student populations of both 1951-1952 and 1952-1953.
On the assumption that the stipends would be paid only for the months during which the students were in attendance, the total may be estimated as follows:

[Y30 x 6 x (155,570 + 382,727)] + (Y9.5 x 6 x 184,393) + (Y8.5 x 6 x 1,383,691) + [Y30 x 3 x (194,000 + 636,000)] + (Y9.5 x 3 x 260,000) + (Y8.5 x 3 x 2,230,000) = Y316,947,102, rounded to Y320 million in Table 3.

This estimate may be too high, in that we assumed all high school students to be recipients of stipends, but according to the regulations only the needy ones would be subsidized. Moreover, the rates we used were promulgated as of December 1952; the rates prevailing prior to that time are not known. This upward bias is counterbalanced, at least to some extent, by the omission, for lack of information, of subsidies to students of industrial and agricultural elementary schools. Furthermore, university and high school students in serious economic difficulties would be given aid over and above their regular stipends, which we also left out of account.

(e) PENSIONS, ALLOWANCES, AND OTHER BENEFITS

There are no data on pensions, allowances and other benefits actually paid out, but we know that such payments are made out of the Labor Insurance Fund. The size of this Fund was Y65.938 million in 1952 (SSB, *Communique for 1954*, p. 37). A portion of this Fund is deposited to the account of the All-China Federation of Labor to be used for the construction of workers' hospitals, sanatoria, etc. The rest, deposited to the account of local trade union units, is used for the payment of pensions, health benefits, etc. The first part is given in official sources as Y13.78 million in 1952, (*JMJP*, May 15, 1953, p. 2), so we can derive the portion available for payment as a residual: Y65,938,000 − Y13,780,000 = Y52,158,000. Rounding this to Y50 million, we assume, in effect that this sum was actually paid out, though this was not necessarily the case.

(f) AMORTIZATION AND INTEREST ON BONDS AND INTEREST PAID ON BANK DEPOSITS

(i) *Bonds.* There were several bond issues in 1950: the so-called

People's Victory Bonds sold in China proper, with a total value of sales of Y260.12 million, (Ke Chih-ta, *China's Budget during the Transitional Period* [Peking, 1957], p. 84) and two bond issues in Manchuria, the so-called Northeast Production and Construction Bond, and the Northeast Yu-tao Railroad Repair and Construction Bond. These two combined had a total sale of Y42 million, (*ibid*), which were to be amortized over a five year period: 10 percent of the total to be amortized in 1951, with five percent to be raised each subsequent year. The official regulations provided also that a five percent rate of interest was to be paid on this internal loan. (Cf. *CYTC* [First Series], p. 105.)

From these data we can estimate the portion of the internal loan repaid in 1952 as follows: (Y260,120,000—Y42,000,000) x 15% = Y45,-317,000. The interest payment on the loan may be estimated as Y13,595,-400, on the assumption that 10 percent of the issue was repaid in 1951, leaving Y271,908,000 as the outstanding portion of the loan at the beginning of 1952.

(ii) *Interest on saving deposits*. The total value of savings deposits was Y543.37 million in 1951 and Y860.88 million in 1952. (Wang Wei-ts'ai, "Develop Further the Work of People's Savings Deposits," *HHYP*, [March 1955], 146-148). Assuming that these are end-year figures, we can estimate average deposits for 1952 as Y702 million. The interest rate on savings deposits for not more than one month was reduced on June 25, 1952, from 1.05 percent per month to 0.75 percent per month (Wang Wei-ts'ai in the article just cited). The next higher rate is for deposits for three months. The average number of days for saving deposits was 33 days in 1951 and 112 days in 1954 (Wang, *ibid.*). In 1952, the average may be assumed to have been longer than in 1951, but short of 90 days (i.e., three months). Accordingly, the average interest rate for 1952 may be estimated as 0.9 percent per month.

On this basis the interest paid on deposits in 1952 may be calculated as 702 x 0.9 x 12 = Y75.8 million. This order of magnitude is borne out by the statement that "since 1952, the Bank has paid out from Y80 million to Y100 million annually, as interest on saving deposits." (Wang, *ibid.*)

To sum up, then, the total given in Table 4 is made up of the following items:

Amortization of bonds	Y45.3 million
Interest on bonds	13.6 million
Interest on savings deposits	75.8 million
	Y134.7 million

II. EXPENDITURES

1. Retail Sales to Households for Consumption

The problem here is how to estimate retail sales exclusive of "group" consumption. Wu Ting-cheng in an article on "Clarification of certain problems in the program for calculating social purchasing power" (*CHCC,* [Sept. 1957] 27), states that "residents' purchasing power" comprised 84 percent of total retail sales. Unfortunately, this article does not specify during which years was this the case.

Po I-po in his "Report on the Implementation of the National Economic Plan for 1956 and on the Draft National Economic Plan for 1957" (*HHPYK,* [July 25, 1957], 30,35), indicates that "total purchasing power" in 1956 was Y46.5 billion while Y47.32 billion is planned for 1957. At the same time he indicated that "group purchasing power" was to be reduced by Y0.98 billion between 1956 and 1957.

Huang K'o in an article on "How to Solve the Problem of Disequilibrium between Social Purchasing Power and the Commodity Supply in 1958" (*CHCC,* [November, 1957], 31), states that group consumption in 1957 was to be 17 percent below the 1956 level.

Group purchasing power for 1956 may, therefore, be estimated as Y5.76 billion (0.98 billion ÷ 17 percent) or 12.4 percent of total consumption (5.76 ÷ 46.5). The corresponding figure for the 1957 Plan may then be placed at Y4.78 billion (5.76-0.98) or 10.1 percent of the total (4.78÷ 47.32).

With these percentages for 1956 and 1957, the 16 percent cited above may refer to earlier years. If this is so, 1952 retail sales for household consumption may be derived as follows:

Retail sales of society	Y27,665 million
Consumption of government and social groups (27,665 × 16 percent)	− 4,430 million
Sales of production requisites to farm households (See Appendix A and Table 1)	− 2,240 million
	Y20,995 million

It should be borne in mind that this figure probably includes sales by peasants in small town markets, but it is doubtful that it encompasses local village sales.

2. Farm Consumption in Kind

This item was derived from farm income in kind as follows:

Farm income in kind	Y26,315 million
Tax in kind	−3,300
Increment in livestock	−917
Increment in farm inventories	−500
Farm consumption in kind	Y21,598 million

Farm income in kind was calculated in Table 1. The tax in kind is discussed below under transfer payments, while the livestock increment is estimated in Appendix A. Both of these may be considered to have a fair degree of reliability, greater than that for farm inventories which were estimated on the basis of a statement in the first *Five Year Plan* that the farmers, "own accumulation" was expected to be Y10 billion, Y6 billion in fixed capital and Y4 billion in inventory accumulation. These figures can be considered as no more than informed guesses by the planning authorities. The inventory figure would represent an average of Y800 million a year, which was adjusted downward partly because 1952 farm output was about 10 per cent below the planned average for the Five Year Plan period, and partly because it includes young livestock, with older animals counted as fixed assets. Since we had already deducted livestock accumulation, if no adjustment were made there would be a double deduction. Unfortunately, none of the sources reveal what the livestock component in fixed and/or in liquid capital is; this makes the adjustment itself subject to a considerable margin of error.

With the adjusted figure for inventory accumulation and the estimated investment in fixed capital, total self-financed capital formation in agriculture would be Y1,620 million. This would constitute a 5.4 percent rate of gross capital formation in relation to gross agricultural product, and 4.3 percent in relation to total farm product. These figures are in keeping with the 3 percent net rates given in Chinese Communist studies of national income.

3. Expenditure on Housing Services

See text in Chapter III.

4. Consumption of Subsistence by Armed Forces

The assumptions and methods on which this estimate is based are outlined in Chapter III.

5. Trade Union and Other Dues

(a) TRADE UNION DUES

According to published information, the All-China Federation of Trade Unions received from its member unions and local units a total of Y3.79 million in dues payment. The same source indicates that in 1951, the sum paid to the Federation constituted 10 percent of the total trade union dues collected. (Speech by Li Tsai-wen, ACFTU official, *JMJP*, May 16, 1953, p. 2.) Assuming that this percentage did not change between 1951 and 1952, trade union dues paid in the latter year may be estimated at Y37.9 million.

(b) PEASANTS' ASSOCIATIONS

In the four regions of East China, Central South, South West, and North West, the membership of peasants' associations reached 88 million in 1952. (Cf. *San-nien lai hsin-chung-kuo ching-chi ti ch'eng-chiu* [New China's economic achievements in the past three years] compiled by the Commission for Promoting China's International Trade [Peking, 1952], p. 116.) If one includes North and Northeast China and at the same time considers that the total of farm households was 110 million, one might estimate the membership for the country as a whole at around 100 million. The "Organization Rules for Peasants' Associations," adopted by the State Administrative Council on July 14, 1950, (*JMST* [People's Handbook] 1951) indicates that annual membership dues should be 1 catty of rice. On the basis of Y0.1 as the wholesale price of milled rice, the total dues payments may be placed at around Y10 million.

(c) COMMUNIST PARTY

In 1951, the party had a total membership of 5.8 million, out of which more than 2.7 million were in the army, the government, and factories and mines, while more than 3 million were in the villages.

(*Chung-kuo kung-ch'an-tang ch'eng-li san shih chou-nien chi-nien chüan-chi* [Special volume for the thirty years' establishment of the Chinese Communist Party] [Canton, 1951],1.) Assuming that 1952 membership was about 6 million, divided evenly between country and city, total dues payments may be estimated as Y6.9 million. This estimate, in turn, is based on the supposition that party members would contribute at least the same share of their average income as the members of the New Democratic Youth League, i.e., 0.5 percent. (Cf. *Tsen-yang chien-li hsin-min-chu-chu-i ch'ing-nien-t'uan* [How to establish new democratic league] Peking, 1950). Using the non-farm wage data in Table B-1 and pay and subsistence data of the armed forces, average non-agricultural income may be placed at about Y360. With an estimated 110 million rural households and a money income of about Y11.2 billion (Table 1), average rural household money income may be computed at about Y100. Party dues may therefore be tentatively put at (360 x 3,000,000) + (100 x 3,000,000) x 0.005 = Y6.9 million.

(d) OTHER MASS ORGANIZATIONS

These would include the New Democratic Youth League, the All-China Federation of Democratic Women, and a number of other smaller organizations. For these we make an arbitary allowance of Y10 million.

(e) TRADE UNION AND OTHER DUES TOTAL

Trade union dues	Y37.9 million
Peasants' associations	10.0 million
Communist party	6.9 million
Other	10.0 million
	Y64.8 million

By rounding this total, we get the figure in Table 4.

6. Expenditure on Miscellaneous Services

The first nationwide and comprehensive household budget survey was conducted in 1954. It embraced "more than 16,000 farm households in 25 provinces".[11] As for urban family budget studies, the original survey program was said to have provided for the inclusion of 6,000 households in 27 cities, but, in practice, the number of households surveyed was supposedly doubled.[12] In conducting these surveys, the sample was required to "meet the condition that while the number of households to be investigated should be limited, they must, above all, be representative of the nation as a whole." How adequately this stipulation was actually met is difficult to judge from available information.

The most detailed household budget data are given for 1955. These indicate that "non-commodity" outlay constituted 5 percent of the total in farm households, and 20 percent of the total for families of workers and employees.[13] Workers' and employees' non-commodity outlay includes 6 percent for remittances to rural areas for the maintenance of dependents there, and another 6 percent for rent, utilities, and transportation. The first of these items is a transfer payment, and the second has already been estimated by us on the basis of different methods. This leaves 8 percent for other services, including payments of fees and dues already accounted for and cash gifts at weddings and funerals (which are transfers), but excluding public utilities and transport expenditures.

Our estimate of miscellaneous service expenditures by urban households is based on this 8 percent for other services, on the assumption that the transfer and double-counted items just about cancelled out the omitted outlays. Therefore, with a wage bill including incomes of self-employed of Y14.89 billion, miscellaneous service outlays in 1952 would be about Y1.19 billion. This method of calculation assumes in effect that the total of wage and self-employed incomes are spent. While this was not completely true, given negligible individual saving, this assumption cannot be too far off the mark.

The survey leaves out of account miscellaneous service outlays by businessmen. This, however, could not be a significant figure, considering that only a part of profits would be spent and only a small part of that would go into this channel.

The same survey showed that of total farmers' outlays 5 percent went into "non-commodity" expenditure, but in this case it is difficult to define total farmers' outlays. Moreover, with the uncertainties surrounding published figures for aggregate farm expenditure, it may perhaps be safest to apply this 5 percent to total net income of farm households, exclusive of imputed rent and agricultural tax paid. Thus, farm outlays on miscellaneous services would be about Y1.71 billion, so that total outlays, both urban and rural, may be estimated at Y2.9 billion.

7. Gross Investment in the Private Sector

See Chapter III and discussion under public investment in Appendix D.

8. Transfer Outlays

(a) INCREASES IN BANK DEPOSITS OF HOUSEHOLDS

The total value of savings deposits in Mainland China was Y543.37 million in 1951 and Y860.88 million in 1952, an increase of Y317.51 million between the two years. (Wang Wei-ts'ai: "Develop Further the Work of People's Savings Deposits," *HHYP,* [March, 1955], p. 147).

(b) DIRECT TAXES

See "Indirect Taxes" in Appendix D.

(i) *Agricultural tax.* In the annual budget reports the agricultural tax refers to collections in kind during the fall harvest of the preceding year and the spring harvest of the current year, plus the cash tax payments made from the harvests of the current year. The probable reason for this procedure is an inevitable time lag between the collection of farm products as tax and their sale; from a budgetary point of view, these taxes become revenue only when they enter marketing channels. In contrast, the agricultural tax figure used throughout this study and appearing in Table 3 represents the farm procurement value of the agricultural taxes collected during the fiscal year, and thus differs from the official budget figure.

Some authors have suggested that these values are based on wholesale rather than on farm procurement prices (Hollister, pp. 111-117), but this contention cannot be really documented. The figures for agricultural tax collections on a fiscal year basis are quoted both in terms of so-called "fine grain" and in *JMP.* From these, the average "fine grain" price can be derived (Y0.85 per catty or Y170 per ton). The definition of "fine grain" is not clearly stated in official sources. By all indications it is an imaginary unit which serves as a common denominator for all the crops collected. It almost certainly represents a processed grain equivalent such as milled rice, wheat flour, or some combination thereof. Therefore, it necessarily incorporates the processing margins, but there is no evidence that it also includes transport costs and wholesale trade markups, since the price of wheat flour and even milled rice was, in 1952, appreciably above Y0.85 in all wholesale markets. As a matter of fact, it would seem rather illogical for the regime to value the tax grain at wholesale rather than at farm prices, since it is always eager to show how small a tax burden the farmers carry.

Sources: Total agricultural tax in 1952, including surtax, was given as 38.8 billion catties of "fine grain" by Li Hsien-nien in his 1956 budget report (*HHPYK,* [July 25, 1956], 6).

The principal tax actually collected in 1952 was 35.2 billion catties of "fine grain" according to Li Shu-teh, "Conditions and Problems of Peasant's Burden in 1956", Ts'ai Cheng, (August 1957, 3.)

The difference between the 38.8 and 35.2 billion catties may then be assumed to be the surtax.

These quantities of "fine grain" may be converted into value terms on the basis of unit prices given by Li Hsien-nien in his 1957 and 1958 budget reports. In the first, he gives the value of two billion catties of "fine grain" as Y170 million (*HHPYK,* [July 25, 1957], 21,) while in the second (*HHPYK,* [May 10, 1958] 6), he indicates that 770 million catties was equivalent to Y66 million. Both of these yield a unit price of Y0.085 per catty.

These results may be summarized as follows:

	FINE GRAIN (billions of catties)	VALUE (millions of Yuan)
Principal tax	35.2	2,992
Surtax	3.6	306
Total Agricultural Tax	38.8	3,298

The rounded figure of Y3,300 million needs to be compared with Li Shu-teh's total 1952 tax burden of Y3,380 million. The latter, as explicitly stated in his article, includes "all other taxes collected in the rural areas," in addition to agricultural taxes. These other taxes, apparently amounting to Y80 million, are local village taxes, such as the slaughter tax, etc.

(ii) *Business income taxes.* See Appendix D.

(c) GIFTS

For 1952, these were the "donations" to the Korean Arms Fund, collected over a period of twelve months, from June 1, 1951 to May 31, 1952, totalling Y556.5 million (*JMST,* [1953], p. 6). Out of this amount, Y502.47 million was collected in 1951 (*JMST,* [1952], pp. 15-16), so that Y54 million comprises the 1952 share of these "donations."

(d) PRIVATE ENTERPRISE CONTRIBUTIONS TO SOCIAL INSURANCE

(i) *Labor insurance fund.* The official labor insurance regulations provide that enterprises covered shall contribute to the fund "a sum equivalent to three percent of the total payroll of all workers and employees." (*CYTC*, 3rd series, pp. 970-982). According to officially published information, state enterprises spent Y160 million on social insurance in 1952, which constituted about 10 percent of the wage bill in these enterprises. (*JMJP*, [May 1, 1955], p. 2) From this we can calculate the portion that was paid into the labor insurance fund alone: (160,000,000 ÷ 10) × 3 = Y48,000,000. At the same time, the aggregate size of the labor insurance fund is given in published sources as Y65,938,000. (*SSB, Communiqué for 1954*, p. 37.) Therefore, the private sector contribution to the fund can be calculated by deducting the state enterprise payments from the total.

(ii) *Trade Union Fund*. The Trade Union Law promulgated in 1950 provides that "factories, mines, business establishments, farms, institutions, schools and other productive or administrative units shall allocate each month to their respective trade union organizations as trade union funds . . . two percent of the total wages of all workers and staff members." The bulk of this, i.e., 1.5 percent of the total wage bill, is to be used for financing cultural and educational activities for workers and staff members (*JMST* [1953], p. 213). In 1952, Y45.4 million was spent out of the Trade Union Fund for this latter purpose. (Speech by Li Tsai-wen, ACFTU official, published in *JMJP* [May 16, 1953], p. 2.) On this basis, then, one can estimate total 1952 payments into the Trade Union Fund: (45,400,000 × 2) ÷ 1.5 = Y60,530,000. There is no information from which one could derive the private sector contribution to this total. However, we may not be too far wrong if we assume that private enterprises and organizations made the same relative contributions to this Fund as to the Labor Insurance Fund. On this assumption, private sector payments may be estimated as: (17,938,000 ÷ 65,938,000) × 60,530,000 = Y16,464,000.

Appendix D

PUBLIC SECTOR ACCOUNT

I. INCOMES

1. Earnings of Government Enterprises and Organizations

(a) PAID INTO THE BUDGET

According to an article in *Ts'ai Cheng* (August 5, 1957), and several other sources (e.g., Wang Tzu-ying, "Public Finance of our Country," Tientsin *TKP* [January 27, 1955]) "enterprise and operating revenues" amounted to Y5,728 million. As is indicated in the text, from this must be deducted the "operating receipts," while incomes of the insurance system must be added.

An article by Feng Chi-hsi in *TCKT* (June 29, 1957) gives a 1952 government revenue total of Y17,560 million (including proceeds of foreign loans) broken down as follows:

State economic organizations	Y10,181 million
Cooperatives	189 "
State-private enterprises	184 "
Peasants	2,809 "
Private industry and trade	3,722 "
Other sources	474 "

Operating receipts must be concentrated in revenues from "other sources." Admittedly there might be some economic organizations outside the *khozraschét* system, but the bulk of operating receipts would undoubtedly be obtained from non-economic organs. Therefore, revenues from "other sources," after deduction of Soviet loan proceeds which are probably entered in this item, may represent an approximation of "operating revenues" which need to be deducted from the budget figure for enterprise receipts. This leads, then, to the following derivation of public enterprise earnings paid into the budget:

Budget receipts from enterprises and establishments	Y5,728 million
Less revenues from "other sources" exclusive of Soviet loan proceeds	−307 "
Public enterprise earnings	Y5,421 million

However, the official budget figure for enterprise revenues excludes net earnings of the insurance companies, listing these instead under "income from credit and insurance." Originally, the latter item referred to net earnings from banking and insurance. According to the revised budget methods, bank revenues are treated as part of the public enterprise totals, while "income from loans" really means proceeds from foreign and domestic loans. For some unexplained reason, insurance was left in the latter category; however, it can be separately estimated and combined with the net earnings of other public enterprises and organs. This is the procedure followed in Table 4.

These insurance earnings were derived on the following basis:

(i) Li Hsien-nien in his 1957 budget speech stated that total 1953 budgetary revenue, exclusive of foreign loans, was Y21,324 million.

(ii) The above mentioned *Ts'ai Cheng* article indicates that 1953 revenues, exclusive of foreign loans, were 122.6 percent above the 1952 level. Therefore, total 1952 revenues, exclusive of loans, may be derived as Y17,393 million.

(iii) The same *Ts'ai Cheng* source gives Y17,560 million as total budgetary revenue, including foreign loans. On this basis, foreign loan revenues would be Y167 million. However, the *Ts'ai Cheng* article gives a figure of Y193 million for this category, including insurance income and proceeds from domestic loans, so that it may be safe to assume that these items account for the difference in the two figures. In 1952 there was no domestic bond issue, so that the total difference of Y26 million may be accounted for by insurance. Adding this to the original enterprise earnings gives us the figure in Table 4.

(b) RETAINED EARNINGS

(i) *The enterprise reward fund.* As indicated in Chapter III, the size of this fund was estimated on the assumption that out of total enterprise earnings in mining and manufacturing, in transport, and in telecommunications, an amount equivalent to 10 percent of the wage bill would be set aside for this fund. According to Table 3, the public sector wage bill in these branches was as follows:

Mining and manufacturing	Y1,804 million
Transport	328 "
Telecommunications	66 "
	Y2,198 million

Ten percent of this, rounded, gives us the figure in Table 4.

(ii) *The major repair fund.* According to the first Five Year Plan, about 70 percent of outlays for major repairs were to be self-financed, with 30 percent to be covered by the budget. Similarly, the Plan sets aside for this purpose 4.7 percent of total economic, cultural, and educational outlays for the five year period. On the basis of these relationships, 1952 major repair expenditures would be about Y465 million. Since there is no information on the extent of major repair outlays for 1952 or the size of the retained funds, we were forced to use this method of estimating the size of the repair fund. Actually, Mainland technical articles (quoted below) show that in old plants, major repair expenditures invariably tend to exceed fund reserves by 50 to 200 percent, while in new plants the reverse is the case. Since 1952, in spite of appreciable new investment, was a year still dominated by reconstruction and rehabilitation, one would expect the ratio of self-financed expenditure to be smaller than that during the Five Year Plan Period. The Five Year Plan ratio of 70:30 in effect means that expenditures were expected to exceed payments into the fund by 43 percent. It seems to us more reasonable to assume that in 1952 this percentage was at least 50. Therefore, if we estimate major repair outlays at Y465 million, the self-financed portion, would be Y310 million.

An article in *CCYC,* (April, 1958) written by Hsu I, on "Some Aspects of Economic Accounting" contains the following rather illuminating statement: "In general, the major repair fund set aside for the new plant and new equipment has been more than adequate and the expenditure out of the fund has been from 20 to 50 percent of the payment into the fund; whereas for the old plant and equipment the fund set aside has been inadequate, with the expenditure exceeding the payment by 50 to 200 per cent. For the same factory or mine, there is surplus in the beginning, followed by a period of break-even, and then a last period of deficit."

2. Profits of Cooperative Organizations

(a) FROM TRADE

The total value of sales by cooperative wholesale and retail organizations was Y5,567 million in 1952. (Cf. *HHPYK,* No. 17, [1956], p. 46). An official source (*CYTC,* 3rd series, pp. 556-561) indicated that on a set of transactions engaged in by cooperative trading organs, profits of Y1.58 million were earned on a total turnover of Y47.5 million. Thus a 3.3 percent rate of profit was obtained. The same source points out that, in general, a 3 percent rate of profit may be considered as reasonable for cooperative trade. On this basis, these profits may be estimated as Y167 million in 1952, i.e., Y5,567,000 × 3 percent.

(b) FROM INDUSTRY

The rate of earnings calculated for cooperative trade is much closer to the rates prevailing in private, as compared to public, enterprises. In private industry this rate was about 3.5 percent in 1952, based on gross value of output (given in SSB, *Communiqué for 1955*, p. 22), and on our estimates of private enterprise profits. Assuming that the rate of earnings in cooperatively organized manufacture was the same and given a gross value of output produced by these enterprises of Y1,109 million for 1952 (*SSB, Communiqué for 1955, p.* 22), profits in this sector would be Y39 million. This would yield for cooperative enterprise a total profit of Y206 million. We round these to Y200 million.

3. Income of Social Insurance Funds

For a discussion of the methods used in deriving these figures, see item 8 (d) in Appendix C.

4. Indirect Taxes

According to a preliminary survey, estimated profits of "capitalist industrial enterprises" totaled Y3,107 billion from 1950 to 1955 (Data Office of *TCKT*, "From Dividing Profits into Four Shares to Fixed Interest Policy," *TCKT* [March 29, 1957], p. 31) distributed as follows:

Income tax	35.8 percent
Capitalists' income	19.0 "
Surplus	8.5 "
Employees' welfare	5.1 "
Accumulated surplus & other	31.6 "

As was stated in Chapter III, we assumed that the income tax rate in 1952 was 50 percent not only in industry, but in all business sectors.

Total private sector earnings were estimated by us at Y1,490 million. However, Y540 million of these are earnings in "individual economies," very few of which pay income taxes. Thus, it seems more reasonable to apply the 50 percent only to the commercialized sectors, i.e., to Y950 million.

On this basis, the indirect tax total may be estimated as follows:

Industrial and commercial taxes	Y6,147 million
Less: income taxes	−475 "
Salt tax	405 "
Customs duties	481 "
Total	Y6,560 million

To this must be added the indirect taxes levied in the villages and not included in national budget data. These may be estimated on the basis of the earlier mentioned article by Li Shu-teh (see notes on the agricultural tax in Appendix C) at Y80 million. Li Shu-teh shows a total tax burden of Y3,380 million, while Li Hsien-nien's budget data referring to the principal agricultural tax and the surtax, when converted into value terms, amount to Y3,300 million, Conceivably the discrepancy may be purely statistical, but this is not very likely since Li Shu-teh specifically indicates that his figure includes local slaughter and other similar taxes, while the Finance Minister refers to principal tax and surtax.

Total indirect taxes may, therefore, be placed at around Y6,640 million. This may be an overstatement if income taxes were higher than estimated by us. If we adopt the most extreme assumption that income taxes were levied on all private enterprise earnings, including individual economies, and that all of the earnings total was siphoned off by taxation, this figure would be reduced by Y1,015 million, i.e., by about 15 percent. On the other hand, the income tax figure is most unlikely to be below the industrial average for the period from 1950 to 1955. On the basis of that average of 35 percent, and excluding individual economies, income tax payments would have amounted to about Y330 million, leading to a 2 percent increase in the indirect tax figure.

5. Subsidies

As indicated in Chapter III, subsidies are paid apparently: (a) to cover enterprise losses, (b) for industrial manpower training, and (c) for "promotion of new techniques." In respect to state enterprise losses, one needs to distinguish between planned and unplanned losses. The former were to be financed through budgetary appropriations, while the latter may be covered either by the budget or by bank credit. To the extent that these losses represent a charge on the budget, it is not entirely clear out of which category of expenditures they are paid. On the basis of several accounting handbooks, it is certain that there is a specific subsidy item in the budget within the general category of "economic construction." This subsidy, however, is to cover only those enterprise losses that are a function of government-initiated price reduction policies. This may mean that losses caused by other factors would have to be covered out of some other "economic construction" items, probably either out of so-called "operating expenditure" or out of "working capital."

One of the items in "operating expenditure" is training of personnel. According to a number of eye-witness accounts, workers newly recruited into the industrial labor force are placed in factories as trainees and apprentices. There is a strong possibility or even probability that all or part of the cost of subsistence of these workers is borne by the state. Whether this should be viewed as a subsidy, or as a government service in the field of technical education and training, is really impossible to determine. Both elements are likely to be present.

"Promotion of techniques" is another item ranged under "operating expenditure." This is specified as a category distinct from scientific research. There is very little information concerning the meaning and content of this item, but there are some indications that it refers to subsidies paid to enterprises as a means of encouraging the introduction and adoption of new technology.

II. EXPENDITURES

1. Government Administration

The government budget gives Y1,727.44 million as administrative expenditure. (Feng Chi-hsi "The Growth of the National Economy as Seen Through the State Budget," *TCKT* [June 29, 1957], and "Statistics on State Receipts and Expenditures During the First Five Year Plan Period," *Ts'ai Cheng* [Aug. 5, 1958]). To this must be added locally financed village expenditure of Y380 million (Cf. Agricultural Tax in Appendix C).

2. Defense

The budget gives this figure as Y4,370.99 million. (Same sources as for government administration.)

3. Community Services

As indicated in Chapter III, separation of current and investment outlays is rather difficult. Data on investment expenditures by use are available only for investments which are "comparable from year to year." For health, culture, and education, these are given as Y320 million, i.e., 8.6 percent of the total on this basis. However, this does not include total outlays on fixed capital, as will be shown below. If one were to apply this percentage to total public investment outlays, inclusive of major repairs, the resulting estimate would be Y430 million. On the other hand, of the categories of investment excluded from the comparable series, there are only two which might encompass some community service facilities, i.e., construction of administrative establishments and construction of projects jointly financed by the state budget, the enterprise reward fund, and the workers' welfare fund. Therefore, we might conclude that the Y320 million defines the lower and the Y430 million the upper limit of actual investment outlays in this field, with the real figure probably much closer to the lower limit. For this reason and in the absence of other information, our estimates are based on the Y320 million figure.

The adjustments made in the budgetary figures (in million yuan) may be summarized as follows:

Total expenditure on social, cultural, and educational services		2,280
Less:		
Social welfare transfers	−445	
Student stipends	−320	
Investment	−320	
		−1,085
Current outlays on health, culture, and education		1,195

Feng Chi-hsi gives total outlays on social, cultural and educational services as Y2,279.64 million, distributed as follows:

(a) Culture, education and health	Y1,828.36 million
(b) Social relief and welfare	243.18 "
(c) Pensions	208.10 "

The sum of (b) and (c) is Y451.28 million, which corresponds closely to to the sum of social welfare payments estimated by us with other methods

(Cf. Transfer receipts, Appendix C). However, our breakdowns differ from Feng Chi-hsi's figures as may be seen from the data below:

Rural relief	Y145 million
State unemployment relief	40 "
Veterans' benefits	210 "
Pensions	50 "
	Y445 million

This discrepancy is undoubtedly due to the inclusion of some of the veterans' benefits under relief and the bulk under pensions.

4. Gross Public Investment

(a) THE PROBLEM OF ACCUMULATION

In order to clarify the official estimates of "accumulation," it may be useful to review them briefly.

Niu shows that the "accumulation" rate is 16.1 percent in terms of constant (i.e., 1952 third quarter) prices and 18.2 percent in current prices, but he presents a national income estimate of Y61.1 billion only in constant prices. The same is true for Yang Po and for Lu Kuang's article in the *Peking Review* (April 8, 1958, p. 9). The latter as well as an article in *TCYC* (Jan. 1958, 15), gives certain percentages of capital construction, defense and administrative expenditure in relation to national income. Po I-po, in a speech before the Communist Party Congress, gave such percentages too, but they differ from those in Lu Kuang's and the TCYC articles. The last source seems to exclude both foreign loan receipts and depreciation allowances from budgetary revenue for greater consistency with the national income concept to which the percentages are related. Unfortunately, available data do not permit us to estimate budget revenue net of depreciation allowances. A crude attempt at an estimate would suggest a national income figure about the same as or lower than the constant price figure. Yet this cannot be reconciled with the slowly declining price trend throughout 1952 evident in all of the official wholesale price indices. Under such circumstances, national income, priced in part at third quarter prices is unlikely to be above an estimate based on average annual prices, unless there was a sharp price drop in the last quarter. The supposition of such a drop is contrary to all of the available evidence.

(b) FIXED CAPITAL FORMATION

As indicated in Chapter III, there are several series for fixed capital investment, i.e., "basic construction." The figures in the budget series can be obtained from Feng Chi-hsi's article, "The Growth of Our National Economy as Viewed from the State Budget." The two "within-plan" series are from the statistical tables appended to the SSB, *Communiqué for 1956* and *Communiqué for 1955*. The series on "total investments actually completed" were derived as follows:

For 1954, Li Hsien-nien in his *Report on 1954 Final Accounts and the 1955 Budget* (*HHYP*, [Aug., 1955], 26), states that "total basic construction . . . will be Y9,591,640,000, an increase of 10.43 percent in comparison with last year." A publication on the *1955 State Budget of the People's Republic of China* (Peking, 1955, p. 52) gives the same budget figure for 1955 as Li, and, at the same time, shows Y8,685,730,000 for 1954 as the total investment in basic construction completed. This checks with the percentage given in Li's report.

For 1952 and 1953, the SSB *Communiqués* for these particular years indicate that "investment in basic construction completed" rose by 66 percent between 1952 and 1953 and by 15 percent between 1953 and 1954.

This method of derivation really hinges on the 1954 figure and the 1953-54 and 1952-53 percentage increments obtained from the SSB *Communiqué*. Since, for 1954, the absolute figure is given, in at least one source, we may be justified in using it as a basis for deriving total 1952 investment. The problem, however, is that the SSB *Communiqué* percentages may refer to increments in "within plan" rather than "total" investment. If this actually is the case, then our estimate is inevitably subject to a certain margin of error.

(c) DEFINITION OF COMPARABLE VS. NON-COMPARABLE

What the actual difference in coverage is can not be established with certainty. The original version of the first Five Year Plan excluded the following items from investment "actually completed":

(i) Construction projects of administrative establishments of the central government;

(ii) Housing projects of military organizations;

(iii) Construction projects jointly financed by the state budget, the enterprise reward fund, and the workers' welfare fund;

(iv) Geological survey and drilling for a new project, construction of which is to be started immediately as stipulated in the designing document, and

(v) Designing work financed by non-budget sources. However, according to *CHCC,* (May 31, 1957), 30, all these items are explicitly stated to be included in the 1957 annual plan. Whether the same practice was followed in 1956 and also retroactively for 1955 cannot be ascertained, but it is possible that some of these items may have been included in the revised 1955 investment statistics but omitted from the "comparable" figure.

(d) DEFINITION OF MAJOR REPAIRS

The question may legitimately be raised as to whether major repairs should be considered as replacement or merely as repair and maintenance. The following quote from the *Concise Dictionary of Terms for the First Five Year Plan* may serve to clarify the issue:

> Major repair: refers to a major change of equipment parts and also major change in broken or damaged parts of a building, changing parts of a machine, or of a heating system and roof of a house. It is for the restoration of useful value of the original fixed asset. At the time of big repair, it is generally necessary to stop the operation of some of the equipment... Major repair expenditure is appropriated from the *major repair depreciation fund.*

This certainly sounds like more than ordinary repair or maintenance, and much more like what we normally consider as part of replacement.

(e) INVENTORY CHANGES

Although an estimate of this item is not possible, it may be useful to summarize the available information so as to ascertain within what order of magnitude this kind of investment fell in 1952. Official national income studies show that 60.4 percent of total 1952 "accumulation" was in liquid assets. This, however, is a broader concept than inventory investment, since it also includes changes in cash balances. Moreover, so-called "uncompleted" investment in fixed capital is treated as a liquid asset. Apart from these conceptual problems, even on the basis of the 60.4 percentage, the actual value cannot be reliably estimated. National income is quoted only in so-called comparable prices, the "accumulation" ratios are given both in constant and current (i.e., average 1952) prices, and the ratio of fixed to liquid assets in accumulation is given in terms of current prices. It is possible that accumulation estimated in current prices is related to a constant price net national product. On this assumption, the

1952 increment in liquid assets could be placed at about Y6.7 billion for the whole economy. This undoubtedly is an overstatement and, as such, defines the upper limit of 1952 inventory accumulation.

Another way of approaching the problem is to try to build up inventory change sector by sector. Thus, in agriculture it was estimated at Y1,420 million, Y920 representing growth in livestock numbers and Y500 increment in farm stocks. The increase in trading stocks is estimated below as Y2,580 million. This still leaves as unaccounted inventory changes in manufacturing and mining, transport, construction and central state reserves. Therefore, the actual estimate must be above Y4 billion; how much above cannot be determined from presently available data. However, given the elements left out, it is likely to be closer to the upper rather than the lower limit.

The only segment of the public sector for which an inventory estimate can be made is trade. It was derived as follows:

(i) The rate of turnover in working capital was lowered in state commerce from 2.3 times in 1951 to 1.8 times in 1952 (*JMJP,* May 19, 1953, p. 2).

(ii) The 1952 volume of trade by "purely commercial organizations" was Y15,310 million (Y11,470 million at wholesale and Y3,850 million at retail, [SSB, *Communique for* 1954, 34]). On this basis, the total stock of working capital may be estimated as Y8,505 million.

(iii) This, however, includes not only inventories, but also other assets, which can be isolated since preliminary estimates show a "non-commodity capital" increase of Y455.86 million between 1953 and 1954. With 1952 as a base, such capital rose 10.08 percent by 1953 and 72.37 per cent by 1954. (Article by Chen Shih in *JMJP* of May 6, 1955). Non-commodity capital in 1952 can then be derived as Y731.835 million. Deducting this from the working capital figure estimated above we obtain the trading inventories for 1952.

(iv) The increase in state commerce department inventories is given in published sources as 49.7 per cent between 1951 and 1952 (Jung Tzu-ho "The Problem of Equilibrium between the State Budget, the State Credit Plan, and the Supply and Demand of Commodities," *Ts'ai Cheng,* read in *translation ECMM,* No. 90, [July 15, 1957] 12). Inventory change in state trade may therefore be estimated as (Y8,505,555,000 − 731,834,900) − [(8,505,555,000 − 731,834,900) ÷149.7] = Y2,580,854,400.

(f) NET FOREIGN INVESTMENT

(i) *Foreign Trade Data.* The Chinese Communist statistical authorities have all along published indices of total trade. However, values were given for only a few years with the figures for any one year frequently inconsistent. Although this situation began to change in 1955 when more foreign trade information was published, it was fully clarified only after the release of official total trade, import, and export indices at the China Export Commodity Fair in Canton. These then appeared in *Ajia Keizai Jumpo* (Asia Economic Bulletin, No 316 [March, 1957] 6-13) a publication of the China Research Institute in Tokyo.

The indices thus released are given in Table D-1 below.

Table D-1
Indices of Mainland China's Foreign Trade

YEAR	TOTAL TRADE	EXPORT RATIO IN TRADE TOTAL	IMPORT RATIO IN TRADE TOTAL	TOTAL EXPORT	TOTAL IMPORT
1950	100	49	51	100	100
1951	143	41	59	120	165
1952	156	42	58	135	176
1953	195	43	57	173	216
1954	204	48	52	199	209
1955	265	45	55	242	286

The total trade index series is also confirmed in additional sources, such as, an article by Tsou Szu-yee "A Balanced Foreign Trade" in *China Reconstructs,* (September 1956), 10. These indices can be converted into value terms on the basis of the 1954 total trade figure of Y8,486.73 million given by the Minister of Foreign Trade Yeh Chi-chuang in his "Report on China's Foreign Trade in 1954," (*JMJP,* July 30, 1955). In this conversion small discrepancies arise, depending upon the degree of rounding or upon the particular figure used as a point of departure for the calculation.

(ii) *Soviet Credits.* As was noted in Chapter III, Li Hsien-nien, the Minister of Finance, in his 1957 Budget Report indicated that up to that time, total Soviet credits to China amounted to Y5,294 million, of which Y2,174 million was used before 1953 and Y3,120 million "will have been used in the period of the first Five Year Plan".

For 1953 and the years thereafter, the annual drawings on this credit can be calculated on the basis of annual revenue data, net of Soviet loan receipts, given in Li Hsien-nien's own report, as well as from other sources (for instance, Yang Pei-hsin "The Problem of Accumulation of Funds for the First FYP" *CCYC* [Oct. 1955], 12-35.) Li, in his 1957 budget speech, states that "total revenues excluding foreign loans were Y21,324 million in 1953." The August 5, 1957, issue of *Ts'ai Cheng,* as well as a number of other sources, published from 1956 to

1958, present budget data including foreign loans. For 1953, total revenues inclusive of loans are given as Y21,762 million, so that foreign loan proceeds must have been Y438 million (21,762 − 21,324). In the same source (confirmed by many others) "revenue from loans" is given as Y492 million. This item includes proceeds of both domestic and foreign loans, and, prior to 1955, also insurance incomes. If one compares this "revenue from loans" series with the data for domestic loan flotations for those years for which there were bond issues, as well as with the Soviet loan proceeds calculated from Li's speech and confirmed by other sources, it becomes clear that, in fact, all Soviet loan proceeds (at least all that have been acknowledged by both sides) are contained in the item "revenue from loans." This, of course, does not preclude the possibility of some secret military credits, but if so these would fall outside the scope of Li's figures.

What about 1952? The *Ts'ai Cheng* source quoted above gives budget data for 1952 to 1957 including foreign loans. (The 1957 data must be clearly budget plan rather than final account data.) It also gives the following link indices for yearly revenues exclusive of loan receipts:

1953	122.6
1954	118.9
1955	100.8
1956	112.1
1957	102.6

Thus, given Li's figure of Y21,324 million for 1953 revenues exclusive of foreign loans, we can calculate 1952 revenues. They turn out to be Y17,393 million (21,324 ÷ 122.6). According to the same source, 1952 revenues inclusive of loans are Y17,560 million, so that loan receipts may be derived as Y167 million. The difference between this and the Y193 million (i.e., Y26 million) constitutes insurance income as was indicated in the calculations of government enterprise earnings paid into the budget.

This finding is at variance with C. M. Li's 1952 loan estimate of Y520 million (See his *Economic Development of Communist China*, Table XXXIV, and pp. 147-148), which was arrived at by much more indirect methods. His estimate would have to presuppose that only a small part of this total (i.e., Y167 million) was carried under the "revenue from loans" category of the budget, while the rest would be either accounted for under "other revenues" or would be carried outside the budget. This, however, would be contrary to the explicitly stated budget definitions and practices on which the *Ts'ai Cheng* series are based. The availability of annual Soviet loan data for 1953 to 1957 enables us to establish the fact that the budget data actually follow these practices.

Since the 1952 data appear in the same series, and since the annual link indices given above are in conformity with the yearly loan figures for 1953 to 1957, it would seem most unlikely that different procedures were followed in arranging and defining the 1952 budget categories.

DOMESTIC PRODUCT BY INDUSTRIAL ORIGIN

NOTES TO TABLES 9 AND E-I

I. THE WAGE BILL

Except for agriculture and defense, all figures for the private and public sector are based on Table B-1.

The agricultural wage bill was imputed by deducting from total agricultural product, (1) the Y3,300 million paid by farmers in the form of tax in kind and supplementary payments and (2) Y70 million for interest payments on agricultural loans, as estimated below.

The total of state bank agricultural loans outstanding:

End of 1951	Y205.94 million
June 30, 1952	Y463.63 ''
Dec. 31, 1952	Y437.98 ''

Source: Tseng Ling, "The Rural Market at the Height of Agricultural Collectivization," CCYC [Economic Research] No. 2, [Feb. 1956] 7.

From these data one might be justified in assuming that the average loan outstanding over the year as a whole was about Y400 million.

While some loans were also extended by rural credit cooperatives, all of the available evidence suggests that in 1952 these were still negligible. At the end of 1953, with more than four times the number of credit cooperatives as in 1952, the value of loans outstanding was only Y55.45 million. ("To Develop Credit Cooperation Is An Important Responsibility Of Our Present Agricultural Work," HHYP, [May 1954], 164). Therefore we take the Y400 million as more or less indicative of total farm credit outstanding in 1952.

In June 1952, agricultural loan rates were adjusted downward. The People's Bank charged 1 to 1.5 percent per month for agricultural production loans, and 0.75 to 0.90 percent for irrigation loans (JMJP, June 22, 1952, p. 1). However, rates for short-term credit of an emergency nature were higher, i.e., 1.5 to 2.4 percent per month (Yang Pei-hsin, "On the Interest Rate Problem of Our Country," HHYP, [Nov., 1955], 180). From this we assume that the average monthly rate was 1.5

[175]

Table E-1

1952 Wage Bill and Gross Domestic Product by Industrial Origin in The Private and Public Sector*

	Private Sector (Millions of Yuan)			Public Sector (Millions of Yuan)			Total (Millions of Yuan)		
	WAGE BILL	EARNINGS	VALUE ADDED	WAGE BILL	EARNINGS	VALUE ADDED	WAGE BILL	EARNINGS	VALUE ADDED
1. Agriculture	(27,000)	(3,360)	(30,360)	(60)	(10)	(70)	(27,060)	(3,370)	30,430
2. Mining and Manufacturing	8,993	1,253	10,246	1,804	2,687	4,491	10,797	3,940	14,737
(a) Industry	1,152	383	1,535	1,758	2,687	4,445	2,910	3,070	5,980
(b) Handicraft	7,841	(870)	(8,711)	46	n.a.	46	7,887	(870)	(8,757)
i. Farm	(6,368)	(707)	(7,075)	—	—	—	6,368	(707)	(7,075)
ii. Non-farm	1,473	(163)	(1,636)	46	n.a.	46	1,519	(163)	(1,682)
3. Construction	(415)	(175)	(590)	(885)	(375)	(1,260)	(1,300)	(550)	1,850
4. Transport and Communications	1,240	138	1,378	394	1,248	1,642	1,634	1,386	3,020
(a) Modern Transport & Communications	228	(25)	(253)	394	1,248	1,642	622	1,273	1,895
(b) Native Transport	708	(80)	(788)	n.a.	n.a.	n.a.	708	(80)	(788)
(c) Hauling, Porterage & Warehousing	304	(33)	(337)	n.a.	n.a.	n.a.	304	(33)	(337)
5. Trade	2,675	401	3,076	561	1,747	2,308	3,236	2,148	5,384
6. Modern Banking and Insurance	n.a.	n.a.	n.a.	220	(200)	(420)	220	(200)	(420)
7. Dwelling Services	n.a.	n.a.	2,800	n.a.	n.a.	n.a.	n.a.	n.a.	2,800
8. Government Services	—	—	—	1,675	—	1,675	1,675	—	1,675
9. Defense	—	—	—	1,500	—	1,500	1,500	—	1,500
10. Other	(2,400)	(265)	(2,665)	—	—	—	(2,525)ᵃ	(265)	(2,790)
Total	42,723	5,592	51,115	7,099	6,267	13,366	49,947	11,859	64,606ᵇ

Note:

ᵃ Includes supplementary wage of Y125 million.

ᵇ More than the sum of the two previous columns since it includes dwelling services.

* Figures in parentheses are either imputed or very uncertain estimates.

percent, or 18 percent per year, yielding total interest payments of Y400 million × 18 percent or Y72 million.

The division of the estimated wage and earnings portions of agricultural product between the private and public sector is based on the fact that state farms, encompassing in 1952, 246,900 hectares with 97,000 employees, (SSB *Communiqué for 1955*, p. 35) constituted 0.23 percent of the total cultivated area. On the assumption that average productivity in the state farms would be the same as in all agriculture, we applied this percentage to our farm product estimate.

The military wage bill, representing payments in cash and kind, is based on the estimate derived in Appendix C, Section I, 5.

To the total wage bill were added the supplementary wage payments given in Appendix C, Section I, 2 (b). Since it would have been very difficult to allocate these among the different sectors, we included them under "other."

II. EARNINGS IN THE PRIVATE SECTOR

As already indicated for agriculture, this represents the sum of the agricultural tax in kind, supplementary imposts paid by peasants, and interest on farm loans.

Net business earnings in the other sectors are all based on estimates in Appendix C, Section I, 3. To these were added the private enterprise contributions to social insurance and trade union funds. Since contributions were proportional to wages and salaries, the wage bills in private industry, modern transport and trade were used as a basis for allocating social insurance payments among these sectors.

III. EARNINGS IN THE PUBLIC SECTOR

1. State enterprise earnings paid into the budget

As indicated in Table 5 and Appendix D, these payments (exclusive of operational receipts) were estimated at Y5,450 million in 1952. The inter-industry breakdowns in Table E-1 were derived as follows:

(a) INDUSTRY

Intersectoral distribution of state enterprise receipts is reported for 1955 and later years in the *Final Budget Accounts*. For 1956, "revenues from state industries" are given as Y5,466.8 million. Another source indicates that "profits surrendered by the state industrial enterprises rose to 240 in 1956, taking 1952 as 100." (Wang Cheng-chih, "Dig Up Further the Potential Capacity for Reducing Costs of Industrial Products," *CHCC*, [Dec. 1957.] 15). Accordingly, 1952 profits from state industry may be estimated at Y2,270 million.

There is an element of uncertainty in these calculations inherent in the identification of "enterprise revenues" with "profits surrendered," but since there are likely to be few, if any, industrial enterprises which are not encompassed within the *khozraschet* system, one may perhaps be safe in treating the two terms as synonyms in state industry.

(b) TRADE

Unfortunately, no profits index is given for trade based on 1952, but the 1955 *Final Accounts* show a figure of Y3,319.03 million for "revenues from trade." Moreover, the sources indicate that state enterprise wholesale and retail sales increased by 212.4 percent between 1952 and 1955. Accordingly, 1952 trading profits paid into the budget would be Y1,562.76 million.

One of the difficulties in this procedure is that while the 1955 trading profits figure is stated in terms of current prices, the index of sales is in terms of 1952 constant prices. This would yield valid results only if both the input-output coefficients and the money cost relationships between inputs, wages, and final price remained the same, or if they moved in mutually counteracting directions. The first is almost certainly contrary to reality, while the second is not too likely.

(c) TRANSPORT AND COMMUNICATIONS

For this sector, too, only 1955 or later year profit data were available. The 1955 figure is given as Y1,791.23 to which we applied an index of freight volume (in millions of ton-km.) with 1952=100. (Both freight volume, and retail and wholesale sales figures for 1952 to 1955 are given in SSB, *Communiqué for 1955*, pp. 39-44.) In this case, the margin of error may not be quite as serious as in trade since only the first of the assumptions stated above is implicitly involved.

(d) CONSTRUCTION

See "Private Business Earnings" in Appendix C.

(e) BANKING AND INSURANCE

As is indicated in Appendix D ("Earnings of Government Enterprises" and "Net Foreign Investment"), insurance earnings may be put at Y26 million. The Y5,447 million for state enterprise earnings paid into the budget exclusive of operational receipts, in combination with the profit estimates derived for the other sectors gives a residual of Y167 million. This may be assumed to represent net earnings of the state banking system, although as such it is subject to a considerable margin of error since it incorporates the estimating error for the other sectors.

2. Retained Earnings

The size of the "enterprise reward" and "the major repair" funds was estimated in Appendix D. As noted there, the official regulations provide for the establishment of enterprise reward funds in mining and manufacturing, transport, and communications, with contributions to the fund based on the wage bill. The latter therefore could be used as a basis for an intersectoral breakdown of the fund.

The major repair fund breakdowns were derived from estimates for the value of fixed assets in the public sector of industry and transport. To the extent that valuation of fixed assets is at best difficult and hazardous, these breakdowns must be subject to a considerable margin of error. This is reinforced by the fact that this method in effect assumes that fixed assets in these two sectors will have relatively the same major repair requirements.

The 1952 value of fixed assets in public transport and industry was derived from the following information:

(i) At the end of 1955, industrial fixed assets newly created since 1949 accounted for 51.2 percent of total fixed asset value of industry in the country.

(ii) Newly created industrial fixed assets during 1949-1955 amounted to Y13.46 billion.

(iii) At the end of 1955, industry accounted for about 56 percent of the total fixed assets of the various economic sectors in China (not including individual economy and administrative departments).

(iv) The fixed assets of state industries increased by Y9.52 billion during 1953-55.

(v) Distribution of fixed assets in industry:

	1952	1955
	in percent	
Socialistic—state, coop.	81.1	85.3
Semi-socialistic—joint	4.1	10.7
Capitalistic—private	14.8	4.0
Total	100.0	100.0

(vi) Capital construction investment in railroads, 1953-55:

1953	Y642 million
1954	917 "
1955	1,202 "
	Y2,761 million

On the basis of this information, the value of fixed assets was calculated as follows:

(a) From source information (i) and (ii) above, total industrial fixed assets at the end of 1955 may be calculated ($13.46 \div 51.2$ percent) at Y26.29 billion.

(b) From (iii) and (a) above, total fixed assets in various sectors may be estimated at Y46.95 billion ($26.29 \div 56$ percent).

(c) From (iii) and (b), total 1955 fixed assets in transport may be placed at Y15.49 billion (46.95 x 33 percent).

(d) From (v) and (a), 1955 fixed assets in public industry may be valued as Y22.43 billion (26.29 x 85.3 percent).

(e) From (iv) and (d), 1952 fixed assets in public industry would be Y12.91 billion.

(f) From (vi) and (c), and considering the fact that the state railroad system must occupy a predominant part of modern transport, 1952 fixed assets in public transport may be estimated at Y12.73 billion (15.49 − 2.76).

(g) A comparison of (e) and (f) seems to indicate that in 1952 the value of fixed assets in public industries could not be much larger than that of public transport. On this basis, it is assumed that the total major repair fund is evenly divided between the two.

Sources: For *(i) to (iv):* Data Office of TCKT, "Ch'üan-kuo kung-yeh tzu-chin kai-k'uang" (General Condition of Industrial Capital in China), *TCKT,* No. 1, (1957), pp. 31-32.

For (v), Data Office of TCKT, "Wo-kuo she-hui chu-i kung-yeh-hua ti kai-k'uang" (General Condition of Our Country's Socialistic Industrialization), reproduced in *HHPYK*, No. 2, (1957), p. 61.

For (vi), *SSB, Communiqué 1955, p. 28.*

The results of all of these calculations and derivations are summarized in Table E-2 below.

Table E-2
Interindustry Allocation of Earnings in 1952
(in Millions of New Yuan)

Economic Branch	Private Sector				Public Sector			
	PROFIT	SIF[a]	PROFITS PAID INTO BUDGET	COOP PROFITS	ERF[b]	MRF[c]	SIF[a]	TOTAL
Industry	371	12	2,270	33	180	150	54	2,687
Construction	175	—	375	—	—	—	—	375
Modern Transportation and Communication	138	2	1,046	—	40	150	12	1,248
Trade	380	21	1,563	167	—	—	17	1,747
Banking & Insurance	—	—	193	—	—	—	7	200
Total	1,064	35	5,447	200	220	300	90	6,257

[a] Social Insurance Fund
[b] Enterprise Reward Fund
[c] Major Repair Fund

Appendix F

COMPUTATIONS OF

COMPARATIVE AGRICULTURAL OUTPUT VALUES

IN CHINA, INDIA AND THE UNITED STATES

Following the basic methodology used by Gilbert and Kravis, we divided all of the products into three categories: identical, comparable, and incomparable. Identical products are those for which the outputs and prices are directly comparable, that is, products that are basically homogeneous, and for which the inputs and the end use are more or less the same. Such commodities as wheat and rice, for instance, would be treated

Table F-1

Conversion Into Product Equivalents

PRODUCT LISTED	PRODUCT CONVERTED	PRODUCTION[3]	VALUE[1]	PRICE OF LISTED PRODUCT[2]	PRODUCTION EQUIVALENT OF LISTED PRODUCT[3]
		(1)	(2)	(3)	(4) (2) ÷ (3)
Wheat	Millet (China)	11,474.00	1,835.8	1.66	11,059.0
Jowar	Bajra (India)	2,540.00	810.0	341.00	2,375.5
Jowar	Ragi (India)	1,422.00	350.0	341.00	1,026.6
Flax	Jute & Hemp (China)	305.00	170.8	2.50	683.0
Flax	Ramie (China)	100.00	140.0	2.50	560.0
Poultry	Geese (China)	15.00	7.9	8.51	9.0
Poultry	Ducks (China)	59.00	39.2	8.51	46.0
Poultry	Feathers (China)	12.00	17.0	8.51	20.0
Poultry	Turkey (U.S.)	463.10	343,429.0	569.10	603.4
Wool	Goat Hair (China)	14.94	32.9	22.00	15.0
Wool	Camel Hair (China)	0.81	4.2	22.00	1.9
Wool	Mohair (U.S.)	5.50	11,660.0	1,193.63	9.7
Milk	Ghee (India)	n.a.	2,425.0	341.50	7,101.0
Milk	Dahi (India)	n.a.	675.0	341.50	1,976.6
Milk	Butter (India)	n.a.	320.0	341.50	937.0
Milk	Lassi (India)	n.a.	448.0	341.50	1,312.0
Milk	Other Dairy Products (India)	n.a.	328.0	341.50	960.5

Unit of measure:

[1]Value: For U. S. in thousands of dollars.
For China in millions of new yuan.
For India in millions of rupees.

[2]Price: For U. S. in dollars per metric ton.
For China in new yuan per metric ton.
For India in rupees per metric ton.

[3]Production: In thousands of metric tons.

Table F-2
Comparison of Agricultural Product of China and the United States

Crops:	Production CHINA ('000 MT)	Production U.S.	Price Y/MT	Price $/MT	China's Output Value Y (millions)	China's Output Value $ (millions)	U.S. Output Value Y (millions)	U.S. Output Value $ (millions)
Rice, paddy	68,425.00	2,182.0	108.0	129.44	7,389.9	8,856.9	235.7	282.40
Wheat (inc. Millet)a	29,184.00	35,352.0	166.0	76.78	4,844.5	2,240.7	5,868.4	2,714.30
Corn	16,883.00	83,302.0	110.0	60.25	1,857.1	1,017.2	9,163.2	5,018.90
Grain Sorghum-Kaoliang	11,146.00	2,109.0	83.0	61.63	925.1	686.9	175.0	130.00
Soybean	9,520.00	8,111.0	144.0	99.78	1,370.9	949.9	1,168.0	809.30
Sweet Potatoes	65,300.00	5,783.0	40.0	135.50	2,612.0	8,848.2	231.3	783.60
Cottonseed	2,610.00	5,616.0	100.0	76.74	261.0	200.3	561.6	431.00
Peanuts	2,315.00	619.0	192.0	240.18	444.5	556.0	118.8	148.70
Tungseedb	340.00	120.0	108.0	88.00	36.7	29.9	13.0	10.60
Cotton	1,305.00	3,434.0	1,600.0	762.27	2,088.0	994.8	5,494.4	2,617.60
Flax (inc. Jute, Hemp & Ramie)a	1,343.00	2.2	250.0	52.27	335.8	70.2	.6	.10
Tobacco, cured	220.00	1,022.0	1,170.0	1,100.00	257.4	242.0	1,195.7	1,124.20
Sugar cane	7,115.00	6,899.0	20.0	7.65	142.3	54.4	138.0	52.80
Sugar beet	480.00	9,255.0	30.7	13.18	14.7	6.3	284.1	122.00
Total, Comparable items					22,579.9	24,753.7	24,648.0	14,245.50
Incomparable itemsc					6,030.9	6,611.4	6,707.0	3,890.40
Total Crops					28,610.8	31,365.1	31,355.0	18,135.90
Livestock:								
Porke	4,308.70	5,239.0	833.5	678.76	3,591.3	2,924.6	4,366.7	3,556.00
Muttone	370.70	294.0	1,075.3	986.29	398.6	365.6	316.1	290.00
Beefe	849.00	4,919.0	980.1	1,160.65	832.1	985.4	4,821.1	5,709.20
Wool (inc. Mohair & Camel Hair)	42.72	115.0	2,198.0	1,193.63	93.9	51.0	252.8	137.30
Poultryf	247.60	2,854.0	851.0	569.19	210.7	140.9	2,428.8	1,624.50
Eggs (in mil. dozens)	1,206.00	5,082.0	0.264*	0.415*	318.4	500.5	1,341.6	2,109.00
Total, Comparable items					5,445.0	4,968.0	13,527.1	13,426.00
Incomparable items					1,272.6	1,161.1	5,497.5	5,456.00
Total Livestock					6,717.6	6,129.1	19,024.6	18,882.00
Total Agricultural Product					35,328.4	37,494.2	50,380.1	37,017.90

*Dozen

Table F-3
Comparison of Agricultural Product of India and the United States

	Production ('000 MT)		Price		India's Output Value (in millions)		U. S. Output Value (in millions)	
	INDIA	U. S.	Rs/MT	$/MT	Rs.	$	Rs.	$
Crops:								
Rice, milledᵍ	22,251.50	1,435.6	538.8	241.40	11,990.0	5,371.5	773.5	346.6
Wheat	6,909.10	35,352.0	438.4	76.78	3,030.0	530.5	15,498.3	2,714.3
Corn-maize	1,727.30	83,302.0	347.4	60.25	600.0	104.1	28,939.1	5,018.9
Sorghum-Jowar (inc. Bajra & Ragiᵃ)	9,092.00	2,109.0	341.0	61.63	3,100.0	560.3	719.2	130.0
Cottonseed	1,117.70	5,616.0	340.0	76.74	380.0	85.8	1,909.4	431.0
Peanuts	3,454.60	619.0	625.3	240.18	2,160.0	829.7	387.1	148.7
Sugar caneʰ	61,650.00	6,899.0	37.5	7.65	2,312.0	471.6	258.7	52.8
Cotton	586.80	3,434.0	1,925.8	762.27	1,130.0	447.3	6,613.2	2,617.6
Barley	2,438.50	4,921.0	328.1	61.88	800.0	150.9	1,614.6	304.5
Irish Potatoes	1,625.70	9,499.0	344.5	72.17	560.0	117.3	3,272.4	685.5
Total, Comparable items					26,062.0	8,669.0	59,985.5	12,449.9
Incomparable items					14,150.0	4,651.4	28,430.9	5,748.7
Total Crops					40,212.0	13,320.4	88,416.4	18,198.6
Livestock:								
Milkʲ	19,419.30	52,253.0	341.5	104.26	6,632.0	2,024.6	17,844.4	5,447.9
Porkᵉ	24.30	5,239.0	1,975.3	678.76	48.0	16.5	10,348.6	3,556.0
Muttonᵉ	245.30	294.0	2,278.8	986.29	559.0	241.9	670.0	290.0
Beefᵉ	310.00	4,919.0	1,758.1	1,160.65	545.0	359.8	8,648.1	5,709.2
Wool	20.90	115.1	7,081.3	1,193.63	148.0	249.5	815.1	137.4
Eggs (in million dozens)	87.83	5,082.0	1.195*	0.415†	105.0	36.4	6,073.0	2,109.0
Total, Comparable items					8,037.0	2,928.7	44,399.2	17,249.5
Incomparable items					3,006.0	1,091.8	4,202.2	1,632.5
Total Livestock					11,043.0	4,020.5	48,601.4	18,882.0
Total Agricultural Product					51,255.0	17,340.9	137,017.8	37,080.6

*Rupees per dozen
†Dollars per dozen

Table F-4
Comparison of Agricultural Product of China and India

	Production ('000 MT)		Price		China's Output Value (millions)		India's Output Value (millions)	
	CHINA	INDIA	Y/MT	Rs/MT	Y	Rs	Y	Rs
Crops:								
Rice, milled^k	47,897.5	22,251.50	191.5	538.8	9,172.4	25,807.2	4,261.2	11,990.0
Wheat (inc. Millet)	29,184.0	6,909.10	166.0	483.4	4,844.5	14,107.5	1,146.9	3,340.0
Corn-maize	16,883.0	1,727.30	110.0	347.4	1,857.1	5,865.2	190.0	600.0
Kaoliang-Jowar (inc. Bajra & Ragi)	11,146.0	9,092.00	83.0	341.0	925.1	3,800.8	754.6	3,100.0
Cottonseed	2,610.0	1,117.70	100.0	340.0	261.0	887.4	111.8	380.0
Sesame	525.0	508.00	300.0	905.5	157.5	475.4	152.4	460.0
Peanuts	2,315.0	3,454.60	192.0	625.3	444.5	1,447.6	663.3	2,160.0
Rape & Mustard	930.0	711.20	240.0	970.1	223.2	902.2	170.7	690.0
Sugar cane	7,115.0	61,650.00	20.0	37.5	142.3	266.8	1,233.0	2,312.0
Cotton	1,305.0	586.00	1,600.0	1,925.8	2,088.0	2,513.2	937.6	1,130.0
Jute and Hemp	305.0	598.70	560.0	968.7	170.8	295.5	335.3	580.0
Total, Comparable items					20,286.4	56,368.8	9,956.8	26,742.0
Incomparable items					10,106.8	28,082.8	5,131.3	13,780.0
Total crops					30,393.2	84,451.6	15,088.1	40,522.0
Livestock:								
Pork	4,308.7	24.30	833.4	1,975.3	3,590.9	8,511.0	20.3	48.0
Mutton	370.7	245.30	1,075.3	2,278.8	398.6	844.8	263.8	559.0
Beef	849.0	310.00	980.1	1,758.1	832.1	1,492.6	303.8	545.0
Wool	42.7	20.90	2,198.0	7,081.3	93.9	302.4	45.9	148.0
Eggs (in millions of dozens)	1,206.0	87.83	0.264*	1.195†	318.4	1,441.2	23.2	105.0
Total, Comparable items					5,233.9	12,592.0	657.0	1,405.0
Incomparable items					1,483.3	3,568.2	4,506.9	9,638.0
Total livestock					6,717.2	16,160.2	5,163.9	11,043.0
Total Agricultural Product					37,110.4	100,611.8	20,252.0	51,565.0

*Yuan per dozen
†Rupees per dozen

as identical, regardless of possible quality differences as between China, India and the United States.

On the other hand, commodities which are clearly distinct products, but serve roughly the same end use in the different countries, were treated as comparable products. For instance, millet in China serves as a substitute for wheat. With the output, price, and output value of millet derived from our estimates in Appendix A, for comparative purposes we converted millet into its wheat equivalent. Using the output values of millet and the price of wheat given, we computed the physical output equivalent of millet in terms of wheat. These product conversions and the procedure on which they are based are outlined in Table F-1.

Even after these conversions, many products were left that are really incomparable. They were converted at the purchasing power equivalents derived from the identical and comparable product totals combined.

Basic data for the tables in this appendix were obtained as follows: For the United States from the United States Department of Agriculture, *Agricultural Statistics,* 1954 edition, Government Printing Office, Washington, D. C. For China, from Appendix A. For India, from Government of India, *Final Report of the National Income Committee,* New Delhi, February, 1954. Hereinafter these sources will be referred to as *USAS,* Appendix A and *NIC* respectively.

All United States crop data in terms of quantity and value are from *USAS,* Table 630, pp. 445-447, unless otherwise specified. Livestock production in value terms is given in Table 639, p. 454. Quantities of production for wool, poultry, eggs, and milk are also given in the same

Table F-5
Agricultural Purchasing Power Equivalents
for China, India, and the United States[a]

		Quantity Weights		
		CHINA	INDIA	U. S.
Crop	1 $ = Y	0.9122		1.7289
	1 $ = Rs		3.0188	4.8584
	1 Rupee = Y	1.3599	0.3724	
Livestock	1 $ = Y	1.0960		1.0076
	1 $ = Rs		2.7467	2.5741
	1 Rupee = Y	0.4157	0.4676	
Total	1 $ = Y	0.9422		1.3609
	1 $ = Rs		2.9557	3.6951
	1 Rupee = Y	0.3689	0.3928	
Official Exchange Rates				
	1 $ = U 2.2470			
	1 $ = Rs 4.7619			
	1 Rupee = Y 0.47607			

[a] Derived from Appendix Tables F-2 to F-4

table; meat production of various categories, in Table 503, p. 356. Prices are derived by dividing quantity into value. For China, all data are from Table A-1. For India, crop data in terms of value and production are given in *NIC,* Table 7, p. 36, unless otherwise specified. Livestock production and value from Table 9, p. 51. Prices are based on value/quantity.

FOOTNOTES TO TABLES F-2, F-3, AND F-4

a. See Table F-1 on Product Conversion in this Appendix.

b. United States tung seed production and value from *USAS,* Table 190, p. 131. Price is derived by dividing quantity into value.

c. Value of incomparable items in national currency is simply the difference between total value of crop production and value of comparable items.

d. As the value of China's total crop production does not include that of fodder crops, adjustment is made to exclude the value of hay and various fodder seeds from the total production of 79 United States crops as given in *USAS,* p. 447. A minor adjustment with respect to tung seed is also made for inclusion in the United States total (20,830.7 [USAS total]—2,760.2 [fodder group] + 10.5 [tung seed] = 18,135 [our total]).

e. In the comparison of livestock production for the categories of pork, mutton, and beef, the quantity figures relate to those of meat produced, while the value figures relate to a composite value of meat and such by-products as fat, hog bristle, hides and skins, casings, etc., for each category. This is illustrated by the following production value data:

Item	CHINA (in million Y)			INDIA (in millions Rs.)		
	Pork	Mutton	Beef	Pork	Mutton	Beef
Meat	3,188.4	312.1	628.3	48	439	317
Hides and Skins	—	61.3	203.8	—	120	228
Bristle and fat	367.2	—	—	—	—	—
Casings	35.9	25.2	—	—	—	—
Total	3,591.5	398.6	832.1	48	559	545

f. Includes chicken, geese, ducks and feathers for China, and chicken and turkey for the United States. All items in terms of chicken equivalents. See Table on Product Conversion.

g. In comparison with India, for which data on milled rice only is given, milled rice is used in place of paddy for both China and the United States. United States paddy rice production is converted into milled rice at the ratio of 152:100, this ratio being given in *USAS,* p. x. For the United States price of milled rice, *USAS,* 1955 edition, p. 25 gives average wholesale price per 100 lbs. of milled rice No. 2 at selected markets for 1952, of which the lowest price ($10.95 per 100 lbs. or $241.40 per metric ton at San Francisco) is used on the assumption that this is more nearly the corresponding U. S. price on rice.

h. Production of sugar cane in India was obtained from the Food and Agriculture Organization *Yearbook of Food and Agricultural Statistics,* 1953, Vol VII, Part I, page 44; its price derived on the basis of the 1938 India Tariff Board Report showing cost of cane to be 7% that of gur, this percentage being applied to the 1950/51 gur price obtained by dividing gur's value by quantity, both given in *NIC*, Table 7, page 36.

i. The value of India's total crop production (Rs. 40,522 million) is different from that given in *NIC,* Table 7, p. 36 (Rs. 48,660 million) because of the adjustment made with respect to the exclusion of fodder crops, straw, and rice husk and bran, etc., (see note *f* above), and with respect to the difference in value of gur and sugar cane. The difference in value of total United States crop production between Table F-2 and Table F-3 is accounted for by the difference in value of paddy rice and milled rice.

j. Production of India's milk includes fluid milk and other dairy products in terms of milk equivalents. See Table F-1.

k. China's paddy rice production is converted into milled rice at the ratio of 100:70.

l. The difference in value of China's paddy and milled rice production accounts for the divergence in value of total crop production for China in Tables F-2 and F-4.

NOTES

Chapter I

1. This subsection is based largely upon the author's "Conditions and Prospects for Economic Growth in Communist China," *World Politics,* VII (Oct., 1954), 1-37, where the necessary documentation and source citations may also be found.

2. The "Three-Anti's Movement" was officially launched to eliminate "corruption, waste and bureaucratism" within the state apparatus. It was inaugurated in late 1951 in Manchuria, and spread from there to the rest of China. Gradually it was extended to a Five-Anti's Movement against "bribery, tax evasion, fraud, theft of state assets, and leakage of state economic secrets." At the same time the force of the attack shifted from the state bureaucracy to private industry and trade. It led to the levying of heavy monetary fines upon private enterprise, in effect a capital levy, which resulted in wholesale bankruptcies. Under the impact of this campaign, private industry and trade were brought to a virtual standstill in the first few months of 1952.

3. See Hsueh Mu-ch'iao, Director of the State Statistical Bureau, "Report before the Third National Conference on Statistical Work," *HHYP,* (May, 1954), 103-107.

4. State Statistical Bureau, *Nung-yeh ho-tso-hua ho i-chiu-wu-wu nien nung-yeh sheng-ch'an ho-tso-she shou-i fen-p'ei ti tung-chi tsu-liao* (Statistical Data on Agricultural Cooperation and Income Distribution of Agricultural Producers' Cooperatives in 1955), (Peking, 1957), pp. 11, 13.

5. See Chou En-lai, Report on the Work of the Government *HHPYK,* (July, 1957), 1.

6. Po I-po, "Report on the Implementation of the National Economic Plan for 1956 and the Draft National Economic Plan for 1957," *HHPYK,* (July 25, 1957), 28-39.

7. *Ibid.*

8. See Liao Lu-yen, Minister of Agriculture, "Speech before the National Conference on Agricultural Work," *HHPYK,* (January 25, 1958), 90.

9. For an excellent discussion of the problems encountered in the field of intertemporal comparability see C. M. Li, *Economic Development of Communist China* (Berkeley, 1959).

10. Grain purchased by private traders in 1952 accounted for about 30 per cent of the total grain marketed. (Cf. *JMJP* of November 29, 1952). An article by Tseng Ling on "The Rural Market at the Height of Agricultural Cooperation" in *CCYC* (Economic Research) (Feb., 1956), 1-29 indicates that in 1952 the grain purchased by the state comprised 18.1% of total grain production. On this basis it is possible to estimate the total quantity of grain purchased by the state and by private traders. The quantity delivered as tax grain is officially published, so that the total of 80 per cent can be derived in this way.

11. For the basis of this estimate see Appendix A.

12. See SSB, *Communiqué for 1955,* p. 45; these percentages refer to "purely commercial organizations", thus excluding self-employed small merchants, itinerant peddlers, etc.

13. See "Statistics on State Receipts and Expenditures During the First Five Year Plan Period," *Ts'ai Cheng* (Finance) (August, 1957), 32-33.

14. There are, of course some notable exceptions such as J. L. Buck's *Land Utilization in China* (Shanghai, 1937), and *China's Farm Economy* (Shanghai, 1930).

15. For a brief but excellent summary of this problem see the *Report of the Indian Delegation to China on Agricultural Planning and Techniques* published by the Government of India, Ministry of Food and Agriculture (New Delhi, 1956), pp. 86-87. More specific documentation can be found also in several official Chinese Communist sources; for example, an article in *CHCC* (Planned Economy) (Feb., 1958) 21-24, admits that after collectivization 30 million *mou* of land were found to have been previously unreported and are now included in newly reclaimed land.

16. Li Fu-chun, "Report on the First Five-Year Plan for the Development of National Economy," *HHYP,* (Aug. 1955), 1-22.

17. For instance, data on monetary reserves ceased to be published in 1942. Similarly, the published series on government revenue and expenditure before the war encompassed only a part of government operations.

18. In this respect Chinese Communist statistics do not differ much from Soviet statistics, so that many of the observations made by students of the Soviet economy apply to China as well. See, for instance, "Ap-

praisals of Russian Economic Statistics" by S. E. Harris, Colin Clark, A. Gerschenkron, P. A. Baran, A. Bergson, and A. Yugow in *Review of Economics and Statistics,* XXIV (Nov., 1947), 213-246, also A. Bergson, *Soviet National Income and Product in 1937* (New York, 1953), fn. 10, pp. 7-9.

Chapter II

1. In this chapter the terms "national income accounting," "social accounting," and "national income analysis" are used interchangeably.

2. See Phyllis Deane, *Colonial Social Accounting* (Cambridge, 1953), p. 8.

3. See, for instance, J. R. Hicks, "The Valuation of the Social Income," *Economica,* VII (New Series), (May, 1940), 105-124; Simon Kuznets, "On the Valuation of Social Income," *Economica,* XV, 1-16, XV, 116-131 (February, 1948, and May, 1948); also "Discussion of the New Department of Commerce Income Series" by Simon Kuznets, Milton Gilbert, et. al., and M. Kalecki in *The Review of Economics and Statistics,* XXX (August, 1948), 151-197.

4. Cf. Simon Kuznets, *National Product in Wartime* (New York, 1945), p. 7.

5. For an extremely suggestive analysis of the implications of this approach see a RAND Research Memorandum by Harvey Leibenstein, *Proposal for the Development of a Theory of Economic Growth for a Soviet Type Economy,* RM 1342 (Santa Monica, Calif., 15 September 1954).

6. Strictly speaking, this does not always correspond to Soviet reality. As Hodgman rightly points out, there is "the implicit rationing of empty shelves," and, one might add, the long queues. Cf. "Measuring Soviet Industrial Production: A Reply," *Soviet Studies,* VIII, (July, 1953), 38.

7. Of course, such distortions are not the sole prerogative of Soviet-type economies; however, their incidence is so frequent that in comparison with market-oriented economies one can speak of differences in kind rather than just in degree.

8. See Abram Bergson, *Soviet National Income and Product in 1937* (New York, 1953); A. Bergson and H. Heymann, Jr., *Soviet National Income and Product 1940-48* (New York, 1954); Oleg Hoeffding, *Soviet National Income and Product in 1928* (New York, 1954).

9. Julius Wyler, "The National Income of Soviet Russia," *Social Research,* XIII (December 1946) 501-518; Colin Clark, "Russian In-

come and Production Statistics," *Review of Economic Statistics,* XIX (November, 1947), 215-217.

10. Abram Bergson, *Soviet National Income and Product in 1937,* and A. Bergson, R. Bernaut and L. Turgeon, "Prices of Basic Industrial Products in the U.S.S.R., 1928-1950," *Journal of Political Economy,* LXIV, (August, 1956), 303-328. For the more recent phase of the rational ruble controversy, see P. J. D. Wiles, "Scarcity, Marxism, and Gosplan," *Oxford Economic Papers,* V (October, 1953), 283-316; and by the same author, "Are Adjusted Rubles Rational," *Soviet Studies,* VII (October, 1955), 143-160; "Growth Versus Choice," *Economic Journal* LXVI (June, 1956), 244-255; "A Rejoinder to All and Sundry," *Soviet Studies,* VIII (October, 1956), 134-143. Among those who took issue with Wiles one may cite Joan Robinson, "Mr. Wiles' Rationality: A Comment," *Soviet Studies,* VII (January, 1956), 269-273; D. R. Hodgman, "Measuring Soviet Industrial Expansion: A Reply," *Soviet Studies,* VIII (July, 1956), 134-145; David Granick, "Are Adjusted Rubles Rational: A Comment," *Soviet Studies,* VIII (July, 1956) 46-49; J. M. Montias, "Rational Prices and Marginal Costs in Soviet-Type Economies," *Soviet Studies,* VIII (April, 1957), 369-379.

11. For a most interesting attempt to cope with this problem, see I. B. Kravis, "The Scope of Economic Activity in International Income Comparison," *Studies in Income and Wealth,* XX (Princeton, 1957), 349-377.

12. A. C. Pigou, *Economics of Welfare, 4th ed., (London,* 1932), p. 11. Pigou relates this definition specifically to welfare-yielding activities, but it could be related to other criteria as well.

13. E. E. Hagen in his comments on Kravis' paper points to the production of paper dolls and mud pies by children as instances in which this rule would break down. See *Studies in Income and Wealth,* XX, (Princeton, 1957), 387.

14. See Simon Kuznets, "National Income and Industrial Structure," *Economic Change* (New York, 1953).

15. V. K. R. V. Rao, "Some Reflections on the Comparability of Real National Incomes of Industrialized and Underdeveloped Countries," *Income and Wealth, Series III,* (Cambridge, 1953), pp. 178-210.

16. Kuznets, "National Income and Industrial Structure," p. 158.

Chapter III

1. Abram Bergson, *Soviet National Income and Product in 1937;* Oleg Hoeffding, *Soviet National Income and Product in 1928;* Abram Bergson

and Hans Heymann, Jr., *Soviet National Income and Product, 1940-1948.*

2. For instance, it is interesting to note the British experience in this context, which clearly indicates that in time, as the quality of the data on which national income estimates were based improved, the statistical discrepancy between the income and expenditure accounts became progressively narrower. Cf. J. B. Jefferys and Dorothy Walters, "National Income and Expenditure of the United Kingdom, 1870-1952" in *Income and Wealth, Series V* (London, 1955), Table II, p. 10.

3. For an estimate of Mainland China's product based on the "Sum of Final Sales" see W. W. Hollister, *China's Gross National Product and Social Accounts, 1950-1957,* (Glencoe, 1958). Professor T. C. Liu and his associates are in the process of compiling estimates for the RAND Corporation based on the "value added" approach.

4. See for instance Government of India, Ministry of Finance, Department of Economic Affairs, *Final Report of the National Income Committee,* (New Delhi, 1954).

5. A story brought back from Poland by Professor Brzezinski now of Columbia University's Department of Government, may be illustrative in this connection. In a Polish village where he was staying for several days, he found the peasants lavishly praising the local Communist Party secretary for protecting them against the exactions of higher authorities by certifying that they were meeting their compulsory delivery quotas even when this was not the case.

6. For evidence of underreporting see *Report of Indian Delegation to China on Agricultural Planning and Techniques* (New Delhi, 1956), pp. 86-87 and *CHCC,* (Feb., 1958), pp. 21-42.

7. SSB, *Communiqué for 1955,* p. 30.

8. J. L. Buck, *Land Utilization in China.*

9. Chang Chung-ke and Huang Wei-i, *Tsu-kuo ti hsü-mu yu hsü-ch'an tsu-yüan* (Animal Husbandry and Resources of Animal Products in Our Country), (Shanghai, 1953), p. 214.

10. SSB, *Communiqué for 1955,* p. 34.

11. Data Office of TCKT," Changes in the price gap between industrial and agricultural products since the liberation," *TCKT,* (Sept. 29, 1957), p. 6. For an analysis of the available evidence, see Appendix A.

12. The average 1952 annual wage for all workers and employees is given as Y446 by Chou En-lai in his "Report on the Work of the Government" delivered before the People's Congress in June, 1957; see *HHPYK,* (July, 1957), 8; for a more detailed comparison see Appendix B.

13. This does not deny the fact that forced labor, in Chinese Com-

munist terminology designated as "reform through labor," encompassed a large, though unknown, number of people.

14. Yang Po, "On the Distribution of National Income in China," *CCYC*, (Dec., 1957), 1-11.

15. For definitions of "completed" and "uncompleted" construction and investment, see public investment below.

16. SSB,*Communiqué for 1955,* p. 24.

17. Tsou Tsung-i, " The Problem of Ratio Between the First Type and the Second Type of Social Production during the Transitional Period," *TCYC*, (1957), No. 4, p. 35.

18. Feng Chi-hsi, "The Growth of National Economy as Viewed from the State Budget," *TCKT,* (June 29, 1957), p. 28.

19. For a further discussion of subsidies see Appendix D.

20. Financial and Economic Committee, "Provisional Regulations for the Establishment and Use of Enterprise Reward Funds for State Enterprises," *HWJP,* (Jan. 26, 1952), p. 2.

21. Chen Yün, "The Financial and Economic Work of the CPR during the past year." *CYTC* (June, 1951), pp. 20-28.

22. *TCFK,* p. 54.

23. Hsu Chien et. al., *Ching-chi t'ung-chi-hsüeh chiang-hua* (Lectures on Economic Statistics) (Peking, 1957), pp. 129 and 134.

24. SSB, Communiqués of 1955 and 1956 with statistical appendices.

25. For sources and methods of computation see Appendix D.

26. Li Hsien-nien, "Report on the 1956 Final Account and the 1957 Budget," *HHPYK,* (July, 1957), 16-28.

27. *JMJP,* Feb. 15, 1950.

28. C. M. Li, *Economic Development of Communist China,* p. 181.

29. Paper read before the Seminar on Contemporary China entitled "Influx of Chinese Capital into Hong Kong Since 1937", May 3, 1958 (Mimeo.).

30. See *Far Eastern Economic Review,* XII:20, May 15, 1952, p. 654.

31. M. I. Sladkovskii: "The Indestructible Soviet-Chinese Friendship," (in Russian), *Vneshniaia Torgovliia,* Vol. XXVII, No. 2, Feb. 1957, p. 2.

32. Ke Chih-ta, *Kuo-tou shih-chi ti chung-kuo yü-suan* (China's budget during the transition period), (Peking, 1957), pp. 34-35.

33. Cf. Li Hsien-nien, "Report on the 1954 Final Accounts and the 1955 Budget," *HHYP,* (Aug., 1955), 25, and his "Report on the 1956 Final Accounts and the 1957 Budget."

34. Niu Chung-huang, *Wo-kuo kuo-min shou-ju ti chi-lei ho hsiao-fei*

(Accumulation and Consumption in the National Income of Our Country), (Peking, 1957), p. 21.

35. For estimate of "subsidiary" output, see Table 1.

36. SSB, *Communiqué for 1955,* p. 21.

37. United Nations, *Economic Survey of Asia and the Far East, 1957* (Bangkok, 1958), Table N, pp. 214-215.

Chapter IV

1. Cf. United Nations, *National and Per Capita Incomes, Seventy Countries, 1949* (New York, 1950); Y. L. Wu, *An Economic Survey of Communist China,* (New York, 1956); W. S. and E. S. Woytinski, *World Population and Production* (New York, 1953), Ch. 12.

2. Ou Poa-san, et. al., *Chung-kuo kuo-min so-te* (China's national income) (Shanghai, 1947), 2 vols.

3. Milton Gilbert and I. B. Kravis, *An International Comparison of National Products and the Purchasing Power of Currencies* (Paris 1954).

4. Simon Kuznets, "Quantitative Aspects of the Economic Growth of Nations, II, Industrial Distribution of National Product and Labor Force," *Economic Development and Cultural Change,* V: 2. (July 1957), Part II, Tables 3 and 6.

5. For an excellent and authoritative analysis of turnover taxation in the Soviet Union, see F. D. Holzman, *Soviet Taxation* (Cambridge, Mass., 1955), Part I.

6. See Eckstein, "Conditions and Prospects for Economic Growth in Communist China," in *World Politics, VII.*

7. "Statistics of State Receipts and Expenditures During the First Five Year Plan Period," *Ts'ai Cheng* (Finance), (August, 1957), 32. "Industrial and Commercial Taxes" include a business income tax which is not separable for the years 1953 to 1956. For 1952, this is estimated by us at Y475 million (see Chap. III) and accounts for 2.7% of total government receipts for that year.

8. Rationing of food grains was introduced in November, 1953; see GAC "Directive on the Enforcement of Planned Purchases and Planned Supply of Food Grain," adopted on Nov. 19, 1953, and published in *HHYP,* (April, 1954), 158-159. At the same time, vegetable oils began to be rationed. See "Conditions of the State's Enforcement of Unified Purchase and Unified Supply of Edible Oils and Oil Bearing Crops," *HHYP,* (Oct., 1954), 247. The rationing of cotton cloth was

introduced a year later by a GAC "Directive on the Enforcement of Planned Purchase and Planned Supply of Cotton Cloth," *HHYP* (Oct. 19, 1954) 421.

9. See State Council Directive of Aug. 31, 1955; NCNA news release of Sept. 15, reproduced by *HHYP*, (Oct., 1955), 5.

10. Cf. Tientsin wholesale price index, compiled by the Nankai Institute of Economic Research, *Nan-kai chih-shu tsu-liao hui-pien* (Collections of Nankai Indices) (Peking, 1958).

11. For detailed documentation on these points see Table 16 and Appendix Table 5 in Kuznets' Supplement in *Economic Development and Cultural Change*, V, referred to in note 4 above.

12. For evidence on this point see the author's "Conditions and Prospects . . . " *World Politics, VII,* Table 7, p. 258.

13. This conclusion can be advanced only tentatively since it really depends upon the comparative demand and supply elasticities of farm products and capital goods. Thus, highly inelastic demand for food combined with an elastic demand for capital goods could yield larger increases in food than in capital goods prices even if agricultural production declined much less sharply than capital goods output. Moreover, these relationships may be modified by foreign trade policies. In reality, however, given (a) the planners' scale of preferences, (b) the compelling needs of the Korean war, (c) the limited capital goods producing capacity of Mainland China at the time, and (d) a much more drastic curtailment in capital goods than in farm production, it may be reasonable to assume that scarcity relationships favored a more rapid rise in the price of capital goods than of foodstuffs.

14. For a very interesting discussion of this problem see Fan Jo-i, "More on the Price Policy of Heavy Industry Products," *CCYC,* (June 17, 1957), 54-67.

15. Cf. Bergson, *Soviet National Income and Product in 1937,* Ch. 4, and Hoeffding, *Soviet National Income and Product in 1938*, Ch. III.

16. The situation begins to change in 1953, not only because of price control and rationing of consumer goods, but also because of the introduction of so-called fixed transfer prices for producer goods transactions within the public sector. Thus, in later years, the price situation in Mainland China resembles more that observed earlier in the Soviet Union.

APPENDIX A

1. In recent years, i e., since 1956, soybeans are listed under the oil-bearing crops.

2. Government of·India, Ministry of Finance, Department of Economic Affairs, *Final Report of the National Income Committee* (February, 1954), New Delhi, pp. 36 and 51.

3. Chang Chung-ke and Huang Wei-yi, *Tsu-kuo ti hsü-mu yu hsü-ch'an tsu-yüan* (Animal Husbandry and Resources of Animal Products in Our Country), Shanghai (1953), p. 214.

4. Wang Shou, "Wo-kuo liang-shih sheng-ch'an ti ching-kwang chi ts'un tsai ti wen-ti" (Food Crop Production of Our Country and Its Problems), *Ke-hsüeh T'ung-pao* (Science Bulletin), (1954), 17-20.

5. W. W. Hollister, *China's Gross National Product and Social Accounts, 1950-1957* (1958), pp. 36-38.

6. I am greatly indebted to Prof. Ishikawa for this reconstruction and wish to express my appreciation for his permission to use this material.

7. *JMJP,* Dec. 20, 1958.

APPENDIX B

1. One source (Data Office of TCKT, "Statistical Materials Concerning the Improvement of Standard of Living of Workers and Employees," *TCKT,* [July 29, 1957], 13) specifically states that in 1952 year end employment in industry was 5,260,000. Industrial employment derived from more detailed sources would seem to be 5,196,000. The two figures are sufficiently close to suggest the possibility indicated in the text.

2. Hsu Chien et. al., *Ching-chi t'ung-chi-hsüeh chiang-hua* (Lectures on Economic Statistics) (Peking, 1957), p. 145.

3. Cf. W. W. Hollister, *China's Gross National Product . . . ,* Table 7, p. 75. Unfortunately Hollister does not indicate clearly how, or from where, this figure was obtained.

4. Cheng K'ang-ning and Hsia Wu, "Planning Schedules of Labor and Wages," *CHCC,* (Oct., 1957), 33.

5. Niu Chung-huang, *Accumulation and Consumption in the National Economy of Our Country* (Peking, 1957); and Yang Po, "On the Distribution of National Income in China," *CCYC,* (Dec., 1957) 1-11.

APPENDIX C

1. J. L. Buck, *The Chinese Farm Economy: A Study of Seventeen Localities in Seven Provinces of China* (Shanghai 1930), Table 41, pp. 86-87.

2. Government of India, Ministry of Finance, Department of Economic Affairs, *Final Report of the National Income Committee,* New Delhi, 1954, gives detailed estimates for 1948-49, 1949-50 and 1950-51; p. 101. Ou Pao-san, *China's National Income,* I, 120.

3. 1952 farm population is derived by applying the 1953 ratio of farm to rural population (485.46/506.74) to the 1952 rural population of 499.93 million. Rural population figures for 1952 and 1953 are given in Data Office of TCKT "Population Statistics of Our Country, 1949-1956" *TCKT,* (June 14, 1957), 25; 1953 farm population figure is given by Ma Yin-ch'u in his article on "A New Theory of Population," *HHPYK,* (Aug., 1957), 34-41.

4. Tan Chen-lin: "A Preliminary Study of the Earnings and Living Standards of Farmers in Our Country," *HHPYK,* (June, 1957), 111.

5. Government of India, *Report of the National Income Committee,* pp. 117-120.

6. Based on a non-farm population of 90 million, derived by deducting the estimated 1952 farm population (478.9 million) from the total population (568.9 million) given in "Population Statistics of Our Country, 1949-1956," *TCKT,* (June 14, 1957), 24.

7. International Labour Office, *Yearbook of Labor Statistics, 1956* (Geneva 1956), pp. 379-387.

8. Chien Chia-chu, "Public Finance of New China in the Past Years" in *Hsin Chien She* (New Construction), (1950), No. 12.

9. Ti Ch'ao-pai: "Financial and Economic Prospects for 1950," *CCCP,* (March 9, 1950), 4.

10. *CPJP* and *TTJP.*

11. Data Office of *TCKT:* "Summary Data for Budget Studies of Farm Households in 1954", *TCKT,* (May, 1957), 31.

12. Fang Pin-chu: "My Views on the Improvement of the Sampling Method in the Family Budget Studies of Employees and Workers," *TCKT,* (Feb. 29, 1957), 11-12.

13. Data Office of *TCKT:* "On the problem of the level of living of the farmers and workers," *TCKT,* (July 14, 1957), 4.

BIBLIOGRAPHY

BOOKS

Bergson, A., *Soviet National Income and Product in 1937* (New York, 1953).
156 pp.

Bergson, A. and Heymann, H. Jr., *Soviet National Income and Product 1940-1948* (New York 1954), xii, 249 pp.

Buck, J. L., *China's Farm Economy* (Shanghai, 1930), xii, 476 pp.

Buck, J. L., *Land Utilization in China* (Shanghai, 1937), 3 vols. (text, atlas and statistics).

Chang Chung-ke and Huang Wei-i, *Tsu-kuo ti hsü-mu yü hsü-ch'an tsu-yüan* (Animal Husbandry and Resources of Animal Products in Our Country) (Shanghai, 1953).

Chao I-wen, *Hsin-chung-kuo ti kung-yeh* (Industry in New China), (Peking 1957), 121 pp.

Ch'ien Hua et. al., *Ch'i-nien lai wo-kuo szu-ying kung-shang-yeh ti pien-hua 1949-1956* (Transformation of Private Industry and Trade of Our Country during the Past Seven Years, 1949-1956) (Peking 1957), 184 pp.

China Academy of Sciences, Institute of Economic Research, *I-chiu-wu-szu-nien ch'üan-kuo ko-ti shou-kung-yeh tiao-ch'a pao-kao* (National Survey of Individual Handicrafts in 1954) (Peking 1957), 252 pp.

Ch'ou Ch'i-hua, *Wo-kuo fa-chan yun-shu ho yu-tien ti ti-i-ke wu-nien chi-hua* (Our First Five Year Plan for the Development of Transport, Posts, and Telecommunication) (Peking 1956).

Chung-hua jen-min kung-ho-kuo fa-chan kuo-min ching-chi ti ti-i-ke wu-nien chi-hua 1953-1957 (The First Five-Year Plan for the Development of the National Economy of the People's Republic of China) (Peking, 1955), 238 pp.

Chung-kuo kung-ch'an-tang ch'eng-li san shih chou-nien chi-nien chüan-chi (Special Volume for the Thirty Years' Establishment of the Chinese Communist Party) (Canton, 1951).

Chung I, *Ti-i-ke wu-nien chi-hua ti yun-shu ho yu-tien yeh* (Transportation, Posts and Telecommunications in the First Five Year Plan) (Peking, 1956).

Commission for Promoting China's International Trade, *San-nien lai hsin-chung-kuo ching-chi ti ch'eng-chiu* (New China's Economic Achievements in the Past Three Years) (Peking, 1952).

Deane, Phyllis, *Colonial Social Accounting* (Cambridge, 1953), xv + 360 pp.

Government of India, Ministry of Finance, Department of Economic Affairs, *Final Report of the National Income Committee*, New Delhi, 1954.

Food and Agriculture Organization of the United Nations, *Yearbook of Food and Agricultural Statistics* 1953 (Rome, 1954), 334 pp.

Gilbert, Milton and Kravis, I. B., *An International Comparison of National Products and the Purchasing Power of Currencies* (Paris, 1954), 203 pp.

Government of India, Ministry of Food and Agriculture, *Report of the Indian Delegation to China on Agricultural Planning and Techniques* (New Delhi, 1956), 199 pp.

Hoeffding, Oleg, *Soviet National Income and Product in 1928* (New York, 1954), 156 pp.

Hollister, W. W., *China's Gross National Product and Social Accounts, 1950-1957* (Glencoe, Illinois, 1958), 161 pp.

Holzman, F. D., *Soviet Taxation* (Cambridge, Mass., 1955), xix + 376 pp.

Hsu Chien et al., *Ching-chi t'ung-chi-hsüeh chiang-hua* (Lectures on Economic Statistics) (Peking, 1957), 321 pp.

International Labour Organisation, *Yearbook of Labor Statistics, 1956* (Geneva, 1956).

Ke Chih-ta, *Kuo-tou shih-ch'i ti chung-kuo yü-suan* (China's Budget During the Transitional Period) (Peking, 1957), 170 pp.

Kuznets, Simon, *National Product in Wartime* (New York, 1945), x +156 pp.

Leibenstein, Harvey, *Proposal for the Development of a Theory of Economic Growth for a Soviet Type Economy*, RM1342 (Santa Monica, California, 1954), 56 pp.

Li, C. M., *Economic Deevlopment of Communist China* (Berkeley, Calif, 1959), 284 pp.

Li Tsung-tao, *Huang Ma* (Jute) (Shanghai, 1952).

Liu Ta-chung, *China's National Income, 1931-36: An Exploratory Study* (Washington, 1946), xii + 91 pp.

Nankai University, Institute of Economic Research, *Nan-kai chih-shu tsu-liao hui-pien* (Collections of Nankai Indices) (Peking, 1958), 324 pp.

1955 State Budget of the People's Republic of China (Peking 1955).

Niu Chung-huang, *Wo-kuo kuo-min shou-ju ti chi-lei ho hsiao-fei* (Accumulation and Consumption in the National Income of Our Country) (Peking, 1957), 144 pp.

Ohkawa, Kazushi et al., *The Growth Rate of the Japanese Economy since 1878* (Tokyo, 1957), xvi + 250 pp.

Ou Pao-san, et al., *Chung-kuo kuo-min so-te* (China's National Income (Shanghai, 1947), 2 vols., 174 pp. and 296 pp.

Pan Hsu-lun and Yu Wen-ch'ing, *Kuo-ying ch'i-yeh k'uai-chi kai-yao* (Elements of State Enterprise Accounting) (Shanghai, 1952), 230 pp.

Pigou, A. C., *Economics of Welfare*, 4th ed. (London, 1932), xxxi + 837 pp.

Planning Committee of the Chinese People's Republic, *Chung-hua jen-min kung-ho-kuo fa-chan kuo-min ching-chi ti ti-i-ke wu-nien chi-hua ti min-tz'u chieh-shih* (Concise Dictionary of Terms for the First Five Year Plan) (Peking, 1955), 50 pp.

Rostow, W. W. et al., *Prospects for Communist China* (New York, 1954), 379 pp.

Schultz, T. W., *The Economic Organization of Agriculture* (New York, 1953), xx + 374 pp.

Shen, T. H., *Agricultural Resources of China* (Ithaca, New York, 1951), xviii + 407 pp.

Sladkovskii, M. I., *Ocherki Ekonomicheskih Otnoshenii SSSR s Kitaem,* (Moscow, 1957).

State Statistical Bureau, *Kuan-yü i-chiu-wu-szu nien-tu kuo-min ching-chi fa-chan ho kuo-chia chi-hua chih-hsing chieh-kuo ti kung-pao* (Communiqué on the Development of the National Economy and the Fulfilment of the State Plan in 1954) (Peking 1955), 42 pp.

State Statistical Bureau, *Kuan-yü i-chiu-wu-wu nien-tu kuo-min ching-chi chi-hua chih-hsing chieh-kuo ti kung-pao* (Communiqué on the Fulfilment of the National Economic Plan in 1955) (Peking 1956), 57 pp.

State Statistical Bureau, *Kuan-yü i-chiu-wu-liu nien-tu kuo-min ching-chi chi-hua chih-hsing chieh-kuo ti kung-pao* (Communiqué on the Fulfilment of the National Economic Plan in 1956) (Peking 1957).

State Statistical Bureau, *Nung-yeh ho-tso-hua ho i-chiu-wu-wu nien nung-yeh sheng-ch'an ho-tso-she shou-i fen-p'ei ti t'ung-chi tsu-liao* (Statistical Data on Agricultural Cooperation and Income Distribution of Agricultural Producers' Cooperatives in 1955) (Peking, 1957).

Su Yüan-lai et al., *Kuo-min ching-chi shih-yung ts'u-tien* (The Practical Dictionary of National Economy) (Shanghai, 1953), 9073 pp.

Ta-kung Pao, *Jen-min shou-ts'e 1952* (1952 People's Handbook) (Shanghai, 1952), 582 pp.

Ta-kung Pao,*Jen-min shou-ts'e 1953* (1953 Peoples Handbook) (Tientsin-Peking, 1953), 454 pp.

TCFK: Ministry of Finance of the Chinese People's Republic, *I-chiu-wu-wu chung-yang ts'ai-cheng fa-kuei hui-pien* (Compendium of Central Financial Rules and Regulations for 1955) (Peking, 1957), 572 pp.

Tsen-yang chien-li hsin-min-chu-chu-i ch'ing-nien-t'uan (How to Establish New Democratic League) (Peking, 1950).

United States Department of Agriculture, *Agricultural Statistics,* 1954 and 1955 editions (Washington, D. C.).

United Nations, Economic Commission for Europe, *Economic Survey of Europe in 1954* (Geneva, 1955), 315 pp.

United Nations, Economic Commission for Latin America, *Economic Survey of Latin America, 1956* (New York, 1957), 183 pp.

United Nations, *Economic Survey of Asia and the Far East, 1957* (Bangkok, 1958), 261 pp.

United Nations, *National and Per Capita Incomes, Seventy Countries, 1949* (New York, 1950).

Wei I, *Kuan-yü chien-li she-hui-chu-i kung-yeh-hua ti ch'u-pu chi-ch'u* (On the Establishment of the Preliminary Foundation of Socialist Industrialization) (Peking, 1956).

Woytinski, W. S. & E. S., *World Population and Production,* (New York, 1953), 1268 pp.

Wu Yuan-li, *An Economic Survey of Communist China* (New York, 1956), 566 pp.

Yü Chao-ch'ih, *Kuo-ying ch'i-yeh k'uai-chi* (State Enterprise Accounting) (Shanghai, 1952), 250 pp.

ARTICLES, OFFICIAL REPORTS AND STATEMENTS, LAWS AND REGULATIONS

Ajia Keizai Jumpo (Asia Economic Bulletin), No. 316 (March, 1957), 6-13.

An Tzu-wen, "Chung-hua jen-min kung-ho-kuo san-nien lai ti kan-pu kung-tso" (Report on the Work of the Cadres), *HHYP,* No. 10 (Oct. 1952), 25.

Bergson, A. et al., "Prices of Basic Industrial Products in the U.S.S.R., 1928-1950," *Journal of Political Economy,* LXIV, No. 4 (Aug., 1956), 303-328.

Bjerke, Kjeld, "The National Product of Denmark, 1870-1952," in Simon Kuznets, editor *Income and Wealth, Series V,* (London, 1955).

Chao Ch'ing-hsin, "Lun wo-kuo shih-ch'ang chi-chieh-hsing ti kai-pien" (Seasonal Variations of our National Market), *CCYC,* (February, 1956), 43-54.

Chao Ch'ing-hsin, "Shih-lun nung-yeh ho-tso-hua i-hou wo-kuo shih-ch'ang ti tan wang chi" (Seasonal Variations in our Market after the Agricultural Co-operation), *CCYC,* (Oct. 1956), 19-38.

Chen Yün, "Chung-hua jen-min kung-ho-kuo kuo-ch'ü i-nien ts'ai-cheng ho ching-chi kung-tso ti chuang-k'uang" (The Financial and Economic Work of the CPR during the Past Year), *CYTC,* (1951), No. 11, 20-28.

Cheng K'ang-ning and Hsia Wu, "Lao-tung kung-tzu chi-hua piao-ke" (Planning Schedules of Labor and Wages). *CHCC,* (Oct., 1957), 33.

"Chi-chi k'ai-chan hsing-jung ho-tso shih tang-ch'ien nung-ts'un kung-tso chung i-hsiang chung-yao jen-wu" (To Develop Credit Cooperation Is an Important Responsibility of Our Present Agricultural Work), *HHYP,* No. 5 (May, 1954), 164-165.

Chien Chia-chu, "I-nien lai hsin-chung-kuo ti ts'ai-cheng" (Public Finance of New China During the Past Year), *Hsin Chien She* (New Construction), (1950), No. 12.

Chin Chih "Chi-hua shou-kou shih she-hui-chu-i ti nung-ch'an p'in shou-kou chih-tu" (Planned Purchase in the Socialistic System of Purchasing Agricultural Products), HHYP, No. 11 (November, 1955), 172-176.

"China's Workers in 1955: Their Number, Composition, and Distribution," *TCKTTH* (Dec. 14, 1956), reprinted in *ECMM*, No. 68 (Feb. 4, 1957), 27-34.

Chou En-lai, "Cheng-fu kung-tso pao-kao" (Report on the Work of the Government), *HHPYK*, (1957), No. 14, 1.

Ch'u Ch'ing and Chu Chung-chien, "Wo-kuo nung-ts'un shih-ch'ang shang-p'in liu-ch'uan ti pien-hua" (Variations in the Commodity Turnover in China's Rural Markets), CCYC, (June, 1957), 100-112.

Clark, Colin, "Russian Income and Production Statistics," *Review of Economic Statistics,* XIX, No. 4 (November, 1947), 215-217.

Data Office of TCKT, "Ch'i-nien lai wo-kuo chi-pen chien-she ti chü-ta cheng-chiu" (Great Achievements in Our Capital Construction in the Past Seven Years), TCKT, (Sept. 14, 1957), 1-3.

Data Office of TCKT, "Chieh-fang huo ch'üan-kuo kung-nung-yeh shang-p'in chia-ke chien-tao-ch'a pien-hua ch'ing-k'uang" (Changes in the Price Gap between Industrial and Agricultural Products since the Liberation), *TCKT,* (Sept. 14, 1957), 6.

Data Office of TCKT, "Ch'üan-kuo kung-yeh tzu-chin kai-k'uang" (General Condition of Industrial Capital in China), *TCKT,* (January 14, 1957).

Data Office of TCKT, "I-chiu-wu-ssu nien nung-chia shou-chih tiao-ch'a chien-yao-tzu-liao" (Summary Data of Budget Studies of Farm Households for 1954), *TCKT,* (May 29, 1957), 31.

Data Office of TCKT, "Kuan-yü chih-kung sheng-huo kai-shan ch'ing-kuang ti t'ung-chi tzu-liao" (Statistical Materials Concerning the Improvement of Standard of Living of Workers and Employees), *TCKT,* (July 29, 1957), 13.

Data Office of TCKT, "Kuan-yü kung-nung sheng-huo shui-p'ing wen-t'i" (On the Problem of the Level of Living of the Farmers and Workers), TCKT, (July 14, 1957), 4-5.

Data Office of TCKT, "1949-1956 nien wo-kuo jen k'ou t'ung-chi tzu-liao" (Population Statistics of our Country, 1949-1956), *TCKT,* (June 14, 1957), 25.

Data Office of TCKT, "Tsung szu-ma fen-fei tao ting-hsi ti shu-mai cheng-ts'e" (From "Dividing Profits into Four Shares" to "Fixed Interest" Policy), TCKT, (March 29, 1957), 30-32.

Data Office of TCKTTH, "I-chiu-wu-liu nien ch'üan-kuo sheng-hsü ch'ing-ku'ang" (National Livestock Situation in 1956), *TCKTTH,* (1956), No. 23 reprinted in HHPYK, (1957), No. 1, 88-90.

Data Office of TCKTTH, "Wo-kuo shang-yeh-wang ti fa-chan ho i-chiu-wu-wu nien ti chi-pen ching-k'uang (The Development of our Commercial

Network and Its Basic Condition in 1955), *TCKTTH*, (1956), No. 18 reprinted in *HHPYK*, (1956), No. 24, 80-83.

Data Office of TCKTTH, "Wo-kuo she-hui-chu-i kung-yeh hua-ti kai-k'uang" (General Condition of Our Country's Socialistic Industrialization), reprinted in *HHPYK*, (1957), No. 2.

Eckstein, Alexander, "Conditions and Prospects for Economic Growth in Communist China," *World Politics*, VII, No. 1 (Oct., 1954), 1-37; VII, No. 2 (Feb., 1955), 255-283; and VII, No. 3 (April, 1956), 434-447.

Eckstein, Alexander, "National Income and Capital Formation in Hungary, 1900-1950," Editor Simon Kuznets, *Income and Wealth, Series* V, (London, 1955).

Fan Jo-i, "Tsai-lun chung-kung-yeh ch'an-p'in ti chia-ke cheng-ts'e" (More on the Price Policy of Heavy Industry Products), *CCYC*, (June 17, 1957), 54-67.

Fang Pin-chu, "Tui kai-chin chih-kung chia-t'ing chou-chih tiao-ch'a ch'ou-yang fang-fa ti i-chien" (My Views on the Improvement of the Sampling Method in the Family Budget Studies of Employees and Workers), *TCKT*, (Feb. 29, 1957), 11-14.

Feng Chi-hsi, "Tsung kuo-chia yü-suan k'an wo-kuo kuo-min ching-chi ti kao-chang" (The Growth of Our National Economy as Viewed from the State Budget), *TCKT*, (June 29, 1957), 28-33.

Financial and Economic Committee, "Kuo-ying chi-yeh t'i-yung chiang-li chi-chin chan-hsing pan-fa" (Provisional Regulations for the Establishment and use of Enterprise Reward Funds for State Enterprises), *HWJP* (Jan. 26, 1952), p. 2.

Fu Jung, "Increase Agricultural Production by Means of New and Higher Labor Productivity," *Cheng Chih Hsüeh Hsi*, (March 13, 1956), translated in *ECMM*, No. 36, p. 15.

GAC, "Chung-hua jen-min-kung-ho-kuo lao-tung pao-hsien t'iao-li" (Labor Insurance Regulations of the People's Republic of China), promulgated on February 26, 1951, *CYTC*, III (Peking 1952), 970-982.

GAC, "Huo-wu-sui chan-hsing t'iao-li" (Provisional Regulations Regarding the Commodity Tax,) Dec. 19, 1950, *CYTC*, II, 417-424.

GAC, "Huo-wu-sui chan-hsing t'iao-li shih-hsing hsi-tse" (Rules for Implementing the Provisional Regulation Regarding the Commodity Tax,) Dec. 21, 1950, *CYTC*, II, 424-478.

GAC, "Kuan-yü shih-hsing liang-shih ti chi-hua shou-kou ho chi-hua kung-ying ti ming-ling" (Directive on the Enforcement of Planned Purchases and Planned Supply of Food Grain), adopted on Nov. 19, 1953, *HHYP*, No. 4 (April, 1959), 158-159.

GAC, "Kuan-yü shih-hsing mien-pu chi-hua shou-kou ho chi-hua kung-ying ti ming-ling (Directive on the Enforcement of Planned Purchase and Planned Supply of Cotton Cloth), *HHYP*, No. 10 (Oct., 1954), 241.

GAC, "Kung-shang-yeh-sui chan-hsing t'iao-li" (Provisional Regulations Regarding Industrial and Commercial Taxes), Dec. 19, 1950, *CYTC,* II, 342-351.

Granick, David, "Are Adjusted Rubles Rational? A Comment." *Soviet Studies,* VIII, No. 1 (July, 1956), 46-49.

Hagen, E. E., "Comments on I. B. Kravis Paper," *Studies in Income and Wealth,* XX (Princeton, 1957), 387.

Harris, S. E. et. al., "Appraisals of Russian Economic Statistics," *Review of Economics and Statistics,* XXIX, No. 4 (Nov., 1957), 213-246.

Hicks, J. R., "The Valuation of the Social Income," *Economica,* VII (New Series) No. 26 (May, 1940), 105-124.

Hodgman, D. R., "Measuring Soviet Industrial Production: A Reply," *Soviet Studies,* VIII, No. 1 (July, 1956), 34-45.

Hsiao Yu, "K'ai-k'en huang-ti k'ou-ta keng-ti mien-chi" (Reclaimed Wasteland to Expand Cultivated Areas,) *CHCC,* (Feb., 1957), 21-24.

Hsiung Cheng "Shih-ping shang-yeh t'ung-chi-hsüeh" (Review of Commercial Statistics), *TCYC* (July 23, 1958), 37.

Hsu I, "Kuan-yü ching-chi ho-suan ti chi-ke wen-t'i" (Some Aspects of Economic Accounting), *CCYC,* (April, 1958), 62-74.

Huang K'e, "Ju-ho chieh-chüeh i-chiu-wu-pa nien she-hui kou-mai-li t'ung shang-p'in kung-ying-liang ti pu p'ing-heng" (How to Solve the Problem of Disequilibrium between Social Purchasing Power and the Commodity Supply in 1958), *CHCC,* (November, 1957), 30-32.

Jefferys, J. B. and Walters, Dorothy, "National Income and Expenditure of the United Kingdom, 1870-1952," Simon Kuznets, editor, *Income and Wealth, Series* V (London, 1955).

Jung Tzu-ho, "The Problem of Equilibrium between the State Budget, the State Credit Plan, and the Supply and Demand of Commodities," *Ts'ai Cheng,* translated in *ECMM* No. 9 (July 15, 1957).

Kravis, I. B., "The Scope of Economic Activity in International Income Comparisons," *Studies in Income and Wealth,* XX (Princeton, 1957), 349-377.

Kuznets, Simon, "On the Valuation of Social Income," *Economica,* XV, No. 57 and No. 58 (Feb., and May, 1948), 1-16 and 116-131.

Kuznets, Simon, "National Income and Industrial Structure," *Economic Change* (New York, 1953), pp. 145-191.

Kuznets, Simon et. al., "Discussions of the New Department of Commerce Income Series," *Review of Economics and Statistics,* XXX, No. 3 (Aug., 1948), 151-197.

Kuznets, Simon, "Quantitative Aspects of the Economic Growth of Nations, II, Industrial Distribution of National Product and Labor Force," *Economic Development and Cultural Change,* V, No. 4 (July, 1957), Part II.

Li Fu-chun, "Kuan-yü fa-chan kuo-min ching-chi ti ti-i-ke wu-nien-chi-hua ti pao-kao" (Report on the First Five-Year Plan for the Development of National Economy), *HHYP*, (Aug., 1955), 1-22.

Li Hsien-nien, "Kuan-yü 1954 nien kuo-chia chüeh-suan ho 1955 nien kuo-chia yü-suan ti pao-kao" (Report on the 1954 Final Accounts and the 1955 Budget), *HHPYK*, (1955), No. 8, 23-32.

Li Hsien-nien, "Kuan-yü 1955 nien kuo-chia chüeh-suan ho 1956 nien kuo-chia yü-suan ti pao-kao" (Report on the 1955 Final Accounts and the 1956 Budget), *HHPYK*, No. 14 (July 21, 1956), 1-9.

Li Hsien-nien, "Kuan-yü 1956 nien kuo-chia chüeh-suan ho 1957 nien kuo-chia yü-suan ts'ao-an ti pao-kao" (Report on the 1956 Final Accounts and the 1957 Budget), *HHPYK*, No. 14 (1957), 16-28.

Li Hsien-nien, "Kuan-yü 1957 nien kuo-chia yü-suan chih-hsing ch'ing-k'uang ho 1958 nien kuo-chia yü-suan ts'ao-an ti pao-kao" (Report on the Implementation of the 1957 Budget and on the 1958 Budget), *HHPYK*, No. 5 (March 10, 1958), 3-12.

Li Shu-teh, "I-chiu-wu-liu nien nung-min fu-tan ch'ing-k'uang ho wen-t'i" (Conditions and Problems of Peasants' Burden in 1956), *Ts'ai Cheng* (Public Finance), (Aug., 1957).

Liao Lu-yen, "Speech at the Second Session of the First National People's

Liao Lu-yen, "Tsai ch'üan-kuo nung-yeh kung-tso hui-i shang ti chiang-hua," Congress," *HHYP*, No. 8 (Aug., 1955), 107.
(Speech before the National Conference of Agricultural Work), *HHPYK*, No. 2 (January 25, 1958), 90.

Ma Yin-ch'u, "Hsin jen-k'ou lun" (A New Theory on Population), *HHPYK*, No. 14 (1957), 34-41.

Ministry of Agriculture, "Kuan-yü ssu-nien lai nung-yeh sheng-ch'an kung-tso ti chi-pen ch'ing-huang ho chin hou fang-chen jen-wu" (Basic Conditions of Agricultural Production Work in the Past Four Years and Future Tasks), *HHYP*, No. 11 (November, 1954), 131-135.

Ministry of Finance of the CPR, *I-chiu-wu-wu chung-yang ts'ai-cheng fa-kuei hui-pien*, see TCFK. (Compendium of Central Financial Rules and Regulations for 1955), Peking, 1957.

Montias, J. M., "Rational Prices and Marginal Costs in Soviet-Type Economies," *Soviet Studies*, VIII, No. 4 (April, 1957), 369-379.

NCNA, "Kuo-chia tui shih-yung yu-p'in yu-liao shih-hsing t'ung-kou t'ung-hsiao ching-k'uang" (Conditions of the State's Enforcement of the Unified Purchase and Unified Supply of Edible Oils and Oil Bearing Crops), *HHYP*, No. 10 (Oct., 1954), 247.

NCNA news release, "Chüan-kuo kung-tzu hui-i" (National Wage Conference), *HHPYK*, No. 10 (May 21, 1956), 71-72.

P'eng Jung-ch'üan, "Chi-pen chien-she chi-hua piao-ko" (Planning Schedules for Basic Construction), *CHCC*, (May, 1957), 30-31.

Po I-po, "Cheng-ch'üeh ch'u-li chi-lei ho hsiao- fei ti kuan-hsi" (The Correct Disposition of the Relationship Between Accumulation and Consumption), *HHPYK*, (1956), No. 20, 72-76.

Po I-po, "Kuan-yü i-chiu-wu-liu nien-tu kuo-min ching-chi chi-hua ti chih-hsing chieh-kuo ho i-chiu-wu-ch'i nien-tu kuo-min ching-chi chi-hua ts'ao-an ti pao-kao" (Report on the Implementation of the National Economic Plan for 1956 and on the Draft National Economic Plan for 1957), *HHPYK*, No. 14 (July 25, 1957), 28-29.

Po I-po, "Report to the National People's Congress in 1958" *HHPYK*, (1958), No. 5, 13.

Rao, V. K. R. V., "Some Reflections on the Comparability of Real National Incomes of Industrialized and Underdeveloped Countries," *Income and Wealth, Series III* (Cambridge, 1953), pp. 178-210.

Research Office of the State Statistical Bureau "Wo-kuo kuo-min shou-ju sheng-ch'an ho fen-p'ei ti ch'u-pu yen-chiu" (A Preliminary Study of the Production and Distribution of our National Income),*TCYC*, (Jan., 1958), 11-15.

Robinson, Joan, "Mr. Wiles' Rationality: A Comment," *Soviet Studies,* VII, No. 3 (January, 1956), 269-273.

State Statistical Bureau "Kuan-yü i-chiu-wu-erh nien kuo-min ching-chi ho wen-hua chiao-yü hui-fu yü fa-chan ch'ing-k'uang ti kung-pao" (Communiqué on the Restoration and Development of the National Economy, Culture and Education in 1952), *HHYP*, No. 10 (Oct., 1954), 229-230.

State Statistical Bureau, "Kuan-yü i-chiu-wu-san nien-tu kuo-min ching-chi fa-chan ho kuo-chia chi-hua chih-hsing chieh-kuo ti kung-pao (Communiqué on the Development of the National Economy and the Fulfilment of the State Plan in 1953), *HHYP*, No. 10 (Oct., 1954), 223-232.

Tan Chen-lin "Kuan-yü wo-kuo nung-min shou-ju ch'ing-k'uang ho sheng-huo shui-ping ti ch'u-pu yen-chiu" (A Preliminary Study of the Earnings and Living Standards of Farmers in Our Country), *HHPYK*, (June, 1957), No. 11, 111.

Ti ch'ao-pai, "I-chiu-wu-ling nien ts'ai-cheng ching-chi ti chan-wang (Financial and Economic Prospects for 1950), *CCCP*, (March 9, 1950), 4.

"Ti-i-ke wu-nien-chi-hua shih-ch'i kuo-chia yü-suan shou-chih t'ung-chi piao" (Statistics on State Receipts and Expenditures during the First Five Year Plan Period), *Ts'ai Cheng* (Finance), (Aug., 1957), 32-33.

Tseng Ling, "Nung-yeh-ho-tso-hua kao-ch'ao chung ti nung-ts'un shih-ch'ang (The Rural Market at the Height of Agricultural Cooperation), *CCYC*, (Feb. 1956), 1-29.

Tsou Szu-yee, "A Balanced Foreign Trade," *China Reconstructs,* (September, 1956.)

Tsou Tsung-i, "Kuo-tou shih-chi she-hui sheng-chan ti-i pu-lei yü ti-erh pu-lei chih chien ti pi-li kuan-hsi" (The Problem of Ratio between the First Type and the Second Type of Social Production during the Transitional Period), *TCYC*, (1957), No. 4, 35.

Wang Cheng-chih, "Ch'in-i-pu wa-chüeh chiang-ti kung-yeh ch'an-p'in cheng-pen ti ch'ien-li" (Dig up further the Potential Capacity for Reducing Costs of Industrial Products), *CHCC*, (Dec. 9, 1957), 15-17.

Wang Keng-chin, "Wo tui nung-yeh tsung-ch'an-chih chi suan fang-fa ti chi-tien i-chien" (My Views on the Method of Calculating the Gross Value of Agricultural Output), *TCKT*, (Feb. 29, 1957), 3-4.

Wang Shou, "Wo-kuo liang-shih sheng-ch'an ti ching-kuang chi ts'un tsai ti wen-t'i" (Food Crop Production of Our Country and Its Problems), *Ko-hsüeh T'ung-pao* (Science Bulletin), (1954), No. 5, 17-20.

Wang Shou-tao, "Tso hao chiao-t'ung yün-shu kung-tso chih-yüan nung-yeh ho-tso-hua yun-tung" (Do Well the Task of Communication and Transport, Support the Movement of Agricultural Cooperation), *HHYP*, No. 12 (Dec., 1955), 219-221.

Wang Tieh-sheng, "Chin-i-pu jen-shih ch'ing-kung-yeh t'ung chi-lei ti kuan-hsi" (To Understand Better the Relationship between Light Industry and Capital Accumulation), *Hsüeh Hsi* (Study), (March 18, 1957), 15-16.

Wang Tzu-ying, "Wo-men kuo-chia ti ts'ai-cheng" (Public Finance of Our Country), Tientsin *TKP* (January 27, 1955).

Wang Wei-ts'ai "Chin-i-pu fa-chan jen-min ch'u-hsü shih-yeh" (Develop Further the Work of People's Savings Deposits), *HHYP*, No. 3 (March, 1955), 146-148.

Wiles, P. J. D., "A Rejoinder to All and Sundry," *Soviet Studies*, VIII, No. 2 (Oct., 1956), 134-143.

Wiles, P. J. D., "Are Adjusted Rubles Rational?" *Soviet Studies*, VII, No. 2 (Oct., 1955), 143-160.

Wiles, P. J. D., "Growth versus Choice," *Economic Journal*, LXVI, No. 262 (June, 1956), 244-255.

Wiles, P. J. D., "Scarcity, Marxism, and Gosplan," *Oxford Economic Papers*, V, No. 3 (Oct., 1953), 288-316.

"Wo-kuo ti-i-ke wu-nien chi-hua chien-piao" (Condensed Tables of the First Five Year Plan), *CHCC*, (1955), No. 8, reprinted in *HHYP*, (September, 1955), 132-137.

Wu Chen-ming, "Chung-kuo min-tsu tzu-pen ti t'e-tien," (The Characterstics of the Chinese National Capital), *CCYC*, (1956), No. 6, 111-137.

Wu Ting-cheng, "Kuan-yü she-hui kou-mai li chi-suan fang-an chung chi-ke wen-t'i' ti shou-ming" (Clarification of Certain Problems in the Program for Calculating the Social Purchasing Power), *CHCC*, (Sept., 1957), 27.

Wyler, Julius, "The National Income of Soviet Rusia," *Social Research,* XIII, (Dec., 1946), 501-518.

Yang Pei-hsin, "Ti-i-ke-wu-nien chi-chua ti tzu-chin chi-lei wen-t'i" (The Problem of Accumulation of Funds for the First Five Year Plan), *CCYC,* (Oct., 1955), 12-35.

Yang Pei-hsin, "Kuan-yü wo-kuo ti li-lü wen-t'i" (On the Interest Rate Problem of Our Country), *HHYP,* No. 11 (November, 1955), 178-181.

Yang Pei-hsin, "Wo-kuo ch'ou-chi nung-yeh fa-chan tzu-chin ti tao-lu" (The Way to Finance Agricultural Development in China), *CCYC,* (Jan., 1958), 32.

Yang Po, "Shih-lun wo-kuo kuo-min shou-ju ti fen-p'ei wen-t'i" (On the Distribution of National Income in China), *CCYC,* (Dec., 1957), 1-11.

Yu Tien, "A Preliminary Discussion on Proportion between Consumption and Accumulation in our National Income," *TKP* (Peking), March 24, 1957; translated text in *SCMP,* No. 1510, 18-26.

Yüeh Wei, "Kung-nung-yeh tsung-chan-chih" (Gross Value of Industrial and Agricultural Output), *Hsueh Hsi* (April, 1956), 24-25.

NEWSPAPERS

Ch'ang-chiang jih-pao (Ch'ang-chiang Daily,) Wuhan.

Chieh-fang jih-pao (Chieh-fang Daily,) Shanghai.

Chin-pu jih-pao (Chinpu Daily), Tientsin.

Ch'ün-chung jih-pao (Ch'un-chung Daily), Sian.

Foochow jih-pao (Foochow Daily), Foochow.

Fukien jih-pao (Fukien Daily), Foochow.

Honan jih-pao (Honan Daily), Kaifeng.

Hopei jih-pao (Hopei Daily), Paoting.

Hsin-hua jih-pao (Hsinhua Daily), Chungking.

Hsin-wen jih-pao (Hsin-wen Daily), Shanghai.

Jen-min jih-pao (People's Daily), Peking

Nan-fang jih-pao (Nan-fang Daily), Canton.

Shansi jih-pao (Shansi Daily), Taiyuan.

Su-pei jih-pao (Supei Daily), Yang-chou.

Ta-kung pao (Impartial Daily) Shanghai and Tientsin-Peking.

Tientsin jih-pao (Tientsin Daily), Tientsin.

Tung-pei jih-pao (Northeast Daily), Mukden.

Wan-pei jih-pao (Wanpei Daily), Ho-fei.

INDEX